# Moving images

Concerns about the effects of television on children are a recurrent focus of public controversy. Yet amid all the anxiety, children's voices are rarely heard.

In this book, one of Britain's leading television researchers investigates children's own perspectives on what they find frightening, moving and upsetting. From *Nightmare on Elm Street* to *My Girl*, from *The Color Purple* to *The News at Ten*, what children find upsetting is often difficult to predict.

David Buckingham gives a detailed insight into children's responses to horror films, to 'weepies' and soap operas, to news and to 'reality programmes'. He looks at how they learn to cope with their feelings about such material, and how their parents help or hinder them in doing so.

This fascinating and accessibly written study offers an important new approach to studying the role of television in children's lives, and will be of interest to parents and teachers, as well as policy-makers and educationalists.

*David Buckingham is Lecturer in Media Studies at the Institute of Education, University of London*

David Buckingham

# *Moving images*
## UNDERSTANDING CHILDREN'S EMOTIONAL RESPONSES TO TELEVISION

Manchester University Press

Manchester and New York

Distributed exclusively in the USA and Canada by St. Martin's Press

*Published by* Manchester University Press
Oxford Road, Manchester M13 9NR, UK
*and* Room 400, 175 Fifth Avenue, New York, NY 10010, USA

*Distributed exclusively in the USA and Canada*
*by* St. Martin's Press, Inc., 175 Fifth Avenue, New York, NY 10010, USA

Published in association with the Broadcasting Standards Council. David Bucking-ham's research was funded by the BSC which retains copyright of the findings. The views expressed in this publication are those of its author and not the BSC.

The Broadcasting Standards Council is a statutory organisation. Its role is to monitor the portrayal in programmes and commercials of violence, sexual conduct and matters of taste and decency. The Council does not have power to preview material and does not operate as a censor. The BSC is an advisory body; it considers audience complaints and reports on public opinion, which it tests by means of independent research.

The Broadcasting Standards Council
7 The Sanctuary
London SW1P 3JS
Tel: 0171-233 0544

*British Library Cataloguing-in-Publication Data*
A catalogue record is available from the British Library.

*Library of Congress Cataloging-in-Publication Data*
Buckingham, David, 1954–
    Moving images : understanding children's emotional responses to
television / David Buckingham.
        p.        cm.
    Includes bibliographical references.
    ISBN 0–7190–4595–9. — ISBN 0–7190–4596–7 (pbk. : alk. paper)
    1. Television and children—Psychological aspects.    I. Title.
HQ784.T4B85 1996
791.45′083—dc20                                                                    95–30874
                                                                                            CIP


ISBN 0 7190 4595 9 *hardback*
        0 7190 4596 7 *paperback*

First published in 1996
99 98 97 96 95        10 9 8 7 6 5 4 3 2 1


Typeset in Great Britain
by Northern Phototypesetting Co Ltd, Bolton
Printed in Great Britain
by Biddles Ltd, Guildford and King's Lynn

# Contents

# 1

# *Introduction*

Between the ages of two and four, my older son Nathan was terrified by the character of Big Bird in *Sesame Street*. When Big Bird appeared, he would leave the room or turn off the set; and once he had mastered the remote control, he would rapidly skip past *Sesame Street*, adamant in his refusal to watch it – even if Big Bird was not actually on screen at the time. As other parents will know, Big Bird is a rather bumbling and ineffectual character, with a bright yellow plumage and a ludicrous beak. In no way could he be seen as realistic, let alone threatening. Yet however much we tried to convince Nathan that this was only a person dressed up in an absurd costume, there was absolutely no chance of persuading him to watch the programme.

Both my children have regularly suffered from fears – and sometimes nightmares – as a result of what they have watched and read. For some months after seeing Steven Spielberg's *Hook*, for example, Nathan was frightened to go upstairs to his bedroom, convinced that the Captain would be waiting for him on the landing. My younger son Louis (aged four) often has to be reassured that a particular programme will not 'give me dreams', as he puts it. Likewise, both children have refused to read books we have bought or borrowed on the grounds that they are 'too scary': just recently, Louis was petrified by a children's version of an African folktale called *Bimwili and the Zimwi*, and he steadfastly refuses even to look at *Goldilocks and the Three Bears* or *Where the Wild Things Are*.

Yet if avoidance is one way of coping with the fear evoked by such material, children do learn to develop others. A couple of years ago, when Nathan was about six, I can remember sitting with him and a friend watching the hospital drama *Casualty*. This is a programme that I myself often find upsetting: I am squeamish about watching injections and operations, and I find it particularly hard to cope with stories about children dying, which seem to feature regularly in the programme. Yet Nathan and his friend sat nonchalantly predicting which of the characters was about to be killed off. Someone always dies in this programme, Nathan assured me; but I shouldn't worry, because it was only tomato ketchup.

Academics should beware of generalising on the basis of their own children; yet I suspect that these kinds of responses will be familiar for many readers. My own earliest memories of growing up with television in the late 1950s and early 1960s are of precisely such experiences. Of course, there was the science fiction serial *Doctor Who*, whose electronic theme music still produces a little pang of dread when I hear it now. But I can also recall being terrified by what could only have been a momentary image from a horror movie, of a mummy arising from the grave; and, more strangely, by an episode of *The Charlie Drake Show* that must have been a parody of Agatha Christie's *Ten Little Indians* – although the parody was completely lost on me at the time.

This book is about children's emotional responses to television – and, more specifically, about what might be termed 'negative' responses. It is concerned not only with what frightens children, but also with what they find moving and worrying. It looks at how they make sense of these experiences, and learn to cope with them; and at how parents might help or hinder them in doing so.

As my anecdotes imply, these emotional responses are not always predictable; and as such, they are often difficult to avoid. Indeed, many would argue that such responses are both necessary and useful, perhaps particularly for children. To label them simply 'negative' is to ignore the way in which 'positive' and 'negative' emotions are often bound up together; and the extent to which 'negative' responses may have positive consequences. Many people – including children – actively choose to watch or read things that they know will upset or frighten them; and the sadness or fear is often inseparable from the pleasure. Texts that generate such 'negative' emotions may also enable us to understand and deal with real-life anxieties and concerns. Because <u>children are relatively powerless in our society, childhood is a period that is permeated with insecurity.</u> <u>Children are bound to be drawn to texts that speak to their fear of loss and abandonment, of disgrace and humiliation, and offer them ways of coming to terms with them.</u> It is no surprise that so many of the books, films and television programmes they prefer are those which play on their fear of the large and incomprehensible 'monsters' that surround them. To dramatise such insecurities in fictional form may provide comparatively 'safe' opportunities for children to learn to cope with them. At the same time, of course, children can also be very frightened or worried by reports of *real* events that they watch on the news, or in documentary programmes. Yet here too, many people would argue that such 'negative' emotional responses are a necessary part of learning about the dangers and the suffering they might encounter in real life.

Yet the learning that takes place through these experiences may well go much further. As my anecdotes suggest, coming to terms with such responses involves sorting out the complex and diverse relationships between mediated experiences and real ones. Children's emotional responses are inseparable from their developing knowledge of television as a medium – for example, their understanding of how and why programmes are produced, and of the conventional ways in which they tend to represent the world. Furthermore, in talking about how they feel, and in monitoring and displaying their emotions for the benefit of others, children are also 'learning how to feel': they are discovering what counts as an acceptable or appropriate emotional response, and the ways in which such responses serve to define them as individuals, both for themselves and for others.

For all these reasons, my stance in this book is not simply a protectionist one: I do not think that the responses I describe are uniformly 'negative', nor that they should be prevented at all costs. Yet my position is also far from purely libertarian. Like all parents, I make decisions about what I will and will not allow my children to watch; and like all children, they challenge and negotiate over these decisions. I do not want my children to be upset or traumatised by things they cannot understand or cope with; and I will attempt, as far as possible, to avoid this. I would accept that I sometimes make mistakes in this respect, and that I do not always intervene in the most constructive way. But I would also argue that regulating and intervening in my children's viewing is one of my rights and responsibilities as a parent. On the other hand, of course, I have to accept that I will not be able to shield my children for ever; and that it is not in their best interests for me to do so for too long. The most effective and lasting strategy, in this as in many other areas of parenting, will be one that equips children to cope with the range of experiences they might encounter. Rather than simply restricting children's viewing, or preventing them from watching things that might frighten or disturb them, there is a need to develop a more positive educational approach.

## Effects and responses

This book is based on a research project funded by the Broadcasting Standards Council in Britain. The Council's remit, as defined by the 1990 Broadcasting Act, is 'to monitor the portrayal of violence, sexual conduct and issues of taste and decency in broadcast programmes and advertisements'. As this implies, the Council was founded partly in response to public anxieties about the negative effects of television, and not least to the influential articulation of those anxieties by pressure groups such as the National Viewers and Listeners Association. Significantly, however, the Council has not taken these concerns for granted; as well as responding to specific complaints within its remit, it has conducted extensive surveys of public attitudes on such issues, as well as more qualitative research of the kind represented here.

Like some earlier research funded by the Council,[1] this book sets out to address public concerns about television in a different way. Rather than attempting to assess the 'effects' of particular categories of broadcast material, it seeks to identify how viewers themselves – in this case, children – define and make sense of what they watch. As I have indicated, it is often hard to predict what children will find frightening or upsetting. Yet instead of starting with material that we as adults suspect *might* upset children, this study begins by asking children themselves to identify such material, and to talk about how they respond to it.

'Violence' is an unavoidable issue here. Of course, not all violence generates 'negative' emotional responses; and there are many things that viewers find upsetting that could not reasonably be described as violent. Indeed, research has increasingly suggested that viewers themselves define and perceive 'violence' in very different ways:[2] violence should not be treated as a singular category whose meaning can be taken for granted, as it all too often is. To be sure, violence of various kinds *was* a central concern for many of the children and parents whose responses are recorded here. Yet this book does not attempt to address the question which continues to dominate public debate – that is, whether watching violent television makes children behave in more violent ways in real life. My central concern in this respect is not with the behavioural *effects* of television violence, but with *the ways in which children perceive and make sense of it.*

This is not the place for yet another account of media effects research – a tradition that has perhaps been rather too hastily condemned in some quarters, but whose theoretical and methodological weaknesses are nevertheless well-documented.[3] Perhaps the major limitation of this enormous body of research – and of the public debates that have largely informed it – has been its almost exclusive preoccupation with the question of *imitative violence*. Of course, children do imitate what they see on television, just as they imitate adults and peers and characters they encounter in books. Yet the evidence on whether this causes them to be more antisocial or 'violent' than they would otherwise have been is, to say the least, inadequate. Individuals who are already disposed towards violence may well take cues for their behaviour from television, albeit among many other sources – yet the evidence that such sources do more than provide suggestions for the *form* of their violent behaviour is very limited indeed. Even in such exceptional cases, the crucial question is whether the process can adequately be explained in terms of 'effects' – as if there were a singular stimulus with a given meaning, which would automatically generate a singular response.

This is not to suggest that television has *no* effects – which would clearly be absurd – although it is to argue that we need a much wider conception of the diverse roles that it might play in children's lives. Nor is it to imply that a concern with imitative violence is necessarily false or illegitimate. As we shall see, some of the parents here were worried about their children copying violent behaviour (and particularly martial arts 'moves') from television – although they were equally insistent that their children understood the difference between real fighting and 'play' fighting. However, the parents' main concerns about TV violence were rather different from those that are so regularly rehearsed in public debate. While they occasionally expressed the belief that *other* people's children might be led to copy what they watched, their concerns for their *own* children were primarily to do with them being disturbed or upset. Significantly, *factual* violence – for example, on the news – often seemed to generate more anxiety in this respect than the *fictional* violence that is persistently condemned by politicians and other social commentators.

Yet even if we restrict our attention to such fictional material – such as horror films and violent action movies – it would seem that some of the most significant 'effects' are being ignored. As Martin Barker has pointed out,[4] the principal effect of watching a horror film is to be horrified, not to become horrifying; and for many viewers, it is also to experience pleasure. Many people find violence on television shocking, frightening or disgusting – although they may also find it exciting, enjoyable and even funny. These responses clearly occur as a result of what we watch, and as such they could be called 'effects'. Yet there are important distinctions to be made here between emotional responses, behavioural effects (such as imitation) and longer-term ideological influences. It is largely for this reason that I have used the word 'responses' rather than 'effects', in order to denote the mainly short-term emotional responses that are my primary concern here. While this term also carries a legacy of behaviourism (as in 'stimulus and response'), it does at least potentially imply a more active role for the viewer, and a notion of communication as a kind of dialogue.

This latter emphasis is a crucial one. All too often, psychological research on children's relationship with television has implicitly assumed that they are passive victims of an all-powerful medium. It has paid very little attention to the diverse ways in which they make sense of what they watch; to the kinds of knowledge they bring to television, and the critical skills they develop in relation to it; or to the social contexts in which the medium is used and talked about. Furthermore, despite the evident concerns which surround the issue, there has been comparatively little research on the *emotional* dimensions of children's relationship with television: where it is not simply preoccupied with behavioural effects, the research has tended to manifest a distinct 'cognitive bias', in which emotions appear to be regarded as inherently suspect.

My perspective in this book is drawn not from the tradition of psychological 'effects' research, but from Cultural Studies. While I use some insights from psychology, I also draw at various points on previous work in Film and Media Studies, as well as on theoretical perspectives such as post-structuralism and discourse analysis. One of my central interests here is in the development of children's understanding of television as a medium – or what has been termed their 'television literacy'.[5] As I shall indicate, children respond to and make sense of television in the light of what they know about its formal codes and conventions, about genre and narrative, and about the production process. In these respects, they are much more active and sophisticated users of the medium than they are often assumed to be. Yet in analysing what children say about television, I also focus in some detail on the social dynamics of children's talk, a dimension that is largely neglected by psychological researchers. In describing how they feel about television, and in passing judgment on what they watch, children (like adults) are also making claims about themselves, and thereby constructing relationships with others. For this reason, talk about television cannot be taken at face value, as straightforward evidence of what goes on in people's heads: it is, on the contrary, a profoundly *social* act. In these respects, therefore, emotion cannot be separated from cognition, or from social relationships: what we feel is inseparable from what we think, and from what we say about this to other people.

For the reasons I have outlined, therefore, this book attempts to shift – and indeed, to widen – the agenda of debate about children and television. The narrow concern with imitative behavioural effects which has dominated the debate for so long has proven to be profoundly unproductive. Despite a massive research effort, we are still no nearer to finding conclusive evidence on this issue. Yet the reason for this is not only to do with the many inadequacies of the research methods that have been employed. The central problem, I would argue, is that researchers have been looking for simplistic explanations for extremely complex phenomena. It is time to take a step back from these debates, and to begin to rethink our fundamental questions.

## A brief outline of the research

The research on which this book is based was conducted in the academic year 1993–4. The first phase of the project involved a series of small-group focused interviews with a total of 72 children in four age groups: 6–7, 9–10, 12–13 and 15–16. Equal numbers of girls and boys were recruited; and two suburban and two inner-city schools were used in order to achieve a balance in terms of social class. Broadly speaking, the sample also reflected the ethnic composition of the schools, with a fair proportion of British Asian and British Afro-Caribbean children in the inner-city samples. Children who appeared to watch comparatively little television, or who did not have access to a video recorder, were selected out using an initial questionnaire. The children's teachers were also asked to exclude children who they felt would not be comfortable in a group interview. The children selected were taken out of their regular lessons and interviewed in groups of three for an average of forty-five minutes (less for the youngest age group). Interview groups were both mixed and single-sex (two mixed and four single-sex in each age group). The interviews were conducted either by myself or by another male researcher: both of us are white and middle-class.

Prior to the interviews themselves, we met the children briefly in small groups in order to tell them about the research, and to gain a sense of how they talked about the television programmes they normally liked to watch. Our questions in the first main inter-view, which had been piloted with a range of age groups, were fairly open-ended. We asked the children to tell us about the kinds of things they found upsetting on television: this included things they found frightening, sad, disgusting and worrying. The pro-grammes and films they chose to discuss were therefore nominated by them, rather than by us. The children were asked what in par-ticular had made them feel that way, and were encouraged to describe or retell specific incidents in more detail. They were also asked to recall the context in which they had seen the programme, and what was said at the time. Some rather more closed follow-up questions were also asked, particularly in order to explore chil-dren's coping strategies: 'What did you do when you saw that?' 'Did you do anything to change the way you felt?' 'Why did you do that?' While our questions explicitly asked about 'television', most children automatically included video within this; and unless specified otherwise, the term 'television' is used throughout this book to include material seen on video.

These interviews were followed by a second stage, in which we went back to interview selected groups of children about pro-grammes or genres that we wished to pursue in more detail. These included horror (four interviews), news (four), and the pro-grammes *Ghostwatch* (two), *Casualty* and *Crimewatch* (three each). In our initial interviews, the children's discussions of these pro-grammes had raised interesting questions about the relationships between television and reality, a theme that we hoped to develop through these more specific discussions. The participants in this second stage were selected primarily on the basis that they had dis-played some interest in these topics in their first interview. The interview agendas here were inevitably somewhat more focused, although they revisited many of the areas mentioned above. In each case, we began by asking children general questions about what they liked or disliked about the programme or genre, and about how they first became interested in it, before proceeding to ask more specifically about aspects that they found upsetting. In the case of the news interviews, we also showed the children four video extracts as prompts for discussion: although it is worth emphasising that this was the only point in the interviews where material was screened.[6]

Concurrent with these latter interviews, we conducted a series of twenty interviews with families of children in the sample. The selection here depended largely on parents' willingness to co-operate (a small financial incentive was offered); and in this sense, the sample was self-selected. Nevertheless, we did manage to achieve a balance here in terms of ethnicity and social class,[7] and to include a range of smaller and larger families, as well as six single parent families. These interviews were conducted in people's homes, and lasted between forty-five and sixty minutes: one interviewer spoke with the parents, the other with the children. The parents were asked some general questions about their viewing habits and preferences, followed by a range of more focused questions about the ways in which they attempted to regulate their children's viewing. These questions covered issues such as: how programmes were selected, and by whom; parental 'rules' about TV viewing, including viewing in children's bedrooms, and disagreements about this; differences between siblings; attitudes to the effects of television; concerns about children becoming upset; and perceptions of the 'watershed' for family viewing[8] and of censorship 'ratings' on films and videotapes. The children's interviews here followed similar lines to the first main interview, although questions were also asked about the parents' regulation of viewing similar to those listed above. Parents of all the children in the sample were also asked to complete a questionnaire which included basic demographic information, and some questions on the family's uses of television and video.

In total, these interviews generated around 850 pages of single-spaced transcript.[9] This material was multiply coded using a computer program designed for qualitative analysis.[10] An extensive set of codes was developed through reading and rereading the tran-

scripts: these codes were both descriptive (for example, each programme or film was given a code) and conceptual (for example,
themes like 'coping' or 'regulation' which recurred in the tran-
scripts were broken down into sub-codes and sub-sub-codes in
order to identify particular dimensions of the process). By combin-
ing and recombining codes and categories, the program makes it
possible to move from the fairly mechanical stage of coding
towards the generation of explanatory theories. One important
advantage is that it enables general assertions that might be
arrived at intuitively – for example, about the frequency or distribution of particular phenomena – to be checked with some degree
of reliability. Using the program's capability for cross-referencing,
specific extracts were then identified for more detailed examination,
using discourse analytic methods.[11]

Finally, it is worth emphasising that this is *qualitative* research.
It is not designed to arrive at statistical statements about the distribution or probability of particular phenomena, but to develop a
more powerful set of theories and hypotheses about them. With a
comparatively small sample, such statistical statements are
unlikely to be particularly meaningful anyway. It does not appear
to me to matter whether 30% or 45% of my sample of parents
expressed concerns about violence on television, for example. What
research of this kind is uniquely able to explore is the terms in
which those concerns were raised, and the forms of 'logic' with
which the issues were defined. Similarly, it makes little difference
whether five or eight of my sample of eighteen six-year-olds chose
to discuss how they felt upset about watching animals being killed.
The important questions, I would argue, are not so much to do
with when such responses occur, or indeed how frequently; but
with *why* and *how* they occur, and with what consequences.

### An overview of the book

The book begins with an extended analysis of a debate that effectively overshadowed the whole project. The murder of two-year-
old James Bulger by two ten-year-old boys in February 1993, and
the subsequent furore about the effects of video violence on chil-

dren, was an issue that recurred time and again in our discussions, both with parents and with children. Chapter 2 provides a critical account of these debates and of the film *Child's Play 3* that was at the heart of the controversy. It then goes on to examine children's own responses, both to the film and to the television coverage of the Bulger case. This analysis raises a series of questions – about the 'effects' of television, about children's emotional responses, and specifically about the relationships between fact and fiction – that are pursued in detail in the remaining chapters.

Chapter 3 considers the question of how we make sense of children's and parents' talk about television. It argues that talk must be seen in terms of its social context, not least that of the research interview itself. The analysis here focuses particularly on discussions about the negative 'effects' of television, and on the social positions that speakers take up in addressing this issue. In the process, it outlines a more general perspective on analysing talk that is developed and applied in the remaining chapters.

The central chapters of the book are each devoted to a particular genre. Chapter 4 considers children's responses to horror; Chapter 5 looks at melodrama and soap opera; and Chapter 6 is concerned with news. In each case, the analysis of children's talk is set against relevant critical work in the field. Chapter 7 is organised around a more conceptual issue that recurs throughout these three chapters, and is implicit in the comparison between them: this is the issue of modality, or the 'reality status' of television. This chapter analyses children's responses to three programmes that sit close to (and in some respects cross) the boundary between fact and fiction: the hospital drama *Casualty*, the crime reconstruction programme *Crimewatch* and the spoof documentary *Ghostwatch*.

While the issue of parents' regulation of children's viewing recurs in a number of chapters (particularly Chapter 3), it is considered most directly in Chapter 8. This chapter outlines some general findings in this area, before moving on to a series of six contrasting case studies of specific families. Finally, the concluding chapter provides a brief general summary of the findings of the research; a discussion of some unresolved theoretical issues; and a series of modest recommendations for policy.

While the book does make reference to relevant theoretical and critical work, my aim here has been to produce a readable account that is not unduly burdened by detailed critiques of previous research. For a more extensive account of the general theoretical and methodological perspective, the reader is referred to my previous publications, particularly the book *Children Talking Television*.[12] Those who are interested in a more detailed review of the literature in this area might wish to track down the Broadcasting Standards Council Working Paper which was produced in the early stages of the project.[13]

## Rethinking regulation

Research in such a controversial field as this inevitably has implications for policy. While research is of course only one of the many factors that need to be borne in mind by policy-makers, part of my aim in undertaking this project has been to develop a new approach to questions about the regulation of children's viewing. Such questions are all too often posed in negative terms – as a matter of restricting children's (and by extension, adults') access to material that is presumed to cause them harm. If children's relationship with television is seen as the problem, then the answer is seen to lie in increased censorship.

For various reasons, I would argue that increasing censorship is unlikely to make a significant difference. Compared with most other developed countries, television and video in Britain are already subject to strict regulation. The 'watershed' in broadcasting and the ratings system for video distribution mean that material that is widely available in many other countries is much more restricted here. So-called 'video nasties', for example, that were withdrawn from distribution following the implementation of the Video Recordings Act in 1984, can easily be bought or rented in mainstream shops in North America and in most European countries. Many satellite and cable channels in Europe screen material that would never be seen on terrestrial channels here, and at times of day when children are very likely to be watching.

Like many on the liberal left, I am inclined to regard censorship as an unwarranted intrusion of the state into the private lives of citizens. While it is often justified in terms of apparently laudable aims – such as the protection of children – censorship frequently impacts most directly on groups that are seen to represent the greatest threat to the social order. Many critics have argued that censorship is merely another means of policing 'deviant' behaviour, and of suppressing political or moral dissent: it is informed by a fear of the 'masses', and specifically of the urban working-class – fears that have resurfaced yet again in recent debates surrounding the impact of video violence.[14] To base regulatory policy on the possibility that certain kinds of material might fall into the hands of children inevitably results in restrictions on what is available to adults – and, for many adults, this is not a price they are prepared to pay.

At the same time, as I have indicated, I do 'censor' what my own children watch; and there is material that I think should not be readily available in the public domain. Apart from child pornography (which is, of course, illegal), I would certainly support laws against the incitement to racial hatred, for example, even though such laws appear to contravene the freedom of speech. I would also argue that there should be restrictions on the public display of material that particular groups of people might find offensive – although I would accept that arriving at a reasonable consensus on such issues is not easy. While I am certainly inclined to oppose any general *extension* of censorship, it seems to me to be vital to distinguish between different types of censorship, and between the different groups whom it might be designed to protect. Ultimately, however, I would argue that the censorship or control of material that is made available to *children* is both inevitable and necessary. As a society and as individuals, we have to make clear and well-informed decisions about what children should and should not be allowed to watch.

The major problem here, however, is that censorship is essentially a negative strategy. It prohibits, and yet it largely fails to educate or inform. In Britain at least, the censorship of films and videotapes is far from accountable: the reasons for particular decisions are not made public, let alone subject to any systematic process of external review. Above all, however, censorship is increasingly ineffective. Particularly since the advent of the domestic video recorder in the early 1980s, the ability of the state to control the traffic in moving images has been dramatically reduced; and with the availability of new technologies such as satellite television and digital multi-media, centralised regulation is becoming an ever more difficult struggle. As this research clearly demonstrates, many children in *all* social classes have access to material that they are legally forbidden to obtain; and many of their parents explicitly accept this. Furthermore, while parents acknowledge the need for guidance, they ultimately reserve the right to make their own decisions on behalf of their children. However one may perceive the nature and extent of the 'problem' of children and television, it is hard to see how increasing state regulation will be able to address it.

In this situation, much of the responsibility for regulating children's viewing has inevitably shifted to parents, and indeed to children themselves. Yet the debate about parents' and children's relationship with television has been dominated for much too long by negative arguments. It often seems as though the most responsible thing one can do as a parent is simply to throw out the TV set. Nevertheless, most parents would acknowledge that television can play a very positive role in children's lives, as a source of great pleasure, and of learning. Children may occasionally be upset by what they watch, and this may or may not be a good thing; but the crucial questions for parents are not so much about how to prevent this happening, but about how to intervene in a positive and effective way.

My aim in this book is thus to offer a broader perspective on the question of regulation. Censorship represents a form of centralised regulation, in which decisions about what is and is not appropriate for people to watch are taken by others who claim to act on their behalf. Yet parents also 'regulate' their children's viewing, not only by attempting to prevent them from watching, but also by discussing what they watch, and helping them to make sense of it. Parents often act as 'mediators' of children's viewing: implicitly or explicitly, they *teach* children about television, and about its relationship with the real world – although of course children may also have a great deal to teach their parents. As we shall see, children also attempt to regulate their *own* responses to what they watch: they may actively avoid material that upsets them, but they may also learn to cope with it, in a whole variety of ways. Parents and children inevitably develop their own forms of 'regulation'; and they should be supported in doing so.

My argument, then, is for a more constructive *educational* approach, that empowers children and parents to make informed decisions on their own behalf. This implies the need for much more systematic forms of media education in schools, that go well beyond the limited and uneven provision that currently exists. Teachers can no longer afford to ignore the dominant means of modern communication, or the fact that we live in increasingly media-saturated societies. Yet parents can also play a significant role in discussing television with their children, and in enabling them to become more informed and more thoughtful viewers. Such educational strategies – both 'formal' and 'informal' – will need to be supported by the government, both through providing money and resources, and through developing a more open and informative approach to centralised regulatory policy. Above all, however, these strategies will need to take account of the perspectives of those on whose behalf they are conducted, yet who are all too often ignored. They will need to begin, as I have attempted to do in this book, by listening to the voices of children themselves, and by taking seriously what they have to say.

## Notes

1 Notably the book *Women Viewing Violence* (Schlesinger *et al.*, 1992), which considers women's responses to fictional and factual representations of violence on television.
2 See particularly Gunter (1985).
3 My own views on this are contained in Buckingham (1987, 1993a). Cumberbatch and Howitt (1989) offer a valuable and concise critique of this tradition.
4 Barker (1984).
5 See Buckingham (1993a, b); also Hodge and Tripp (1986).
6 Research in this kind of area obviously raises ethical dilemmas. We took

care to inform the children's parents, and the schools through which they were contacted, of the nature of our discussions, and to obtain their permission. In the case of news, we suspected that children would find it harder to remember particular examples, and therefore decided that we had to screen specific extracts. In this case, we sent a further letter requesting permission, and describing the extracts we were proposing to screen.

7 Social class was determined here in very broad terms (middle-class/ working-class) through a range of indicators included on our questionnaire: education, occupation and ownership of property.

8 In the UK, terrestrial television channels observe the convention of the 'watershed', whereby programmes screened before 9 pm are understood to be suitable for viewing by the whole family.

9 Transcription conventions in this book are minimal, largely in the interests of readability. A single slash (/) denotes a pause; three dots (...) denotes material omitted; a dash (–) denotes an interruption. The ages of the children are mentioned at or near the first reference to them in any passage; where one age is given for a group of children, it applies to all the children in that group.

10 NUD.IST (Non-numerical Unstructured Data Indexing Searching and Theorising), designed by Lyn Richards of La Trobe University, Melbourne, Australia, is widely used in dealing with transcript material. It enables the user to index and subsequently to collate extracts relating to a particular topic or (most significantly) a given combination of topics. For illuminating discussions of the potential and pitfalls of such coding, see Miles and Huberman (1984) and Strauss and Corbin (1992).

11 Buckingham (1993a), Chapter 4, offers a broad framework for such analysis. For a more general account of discourse analysis, see Potter and Wetherell (1987).

12 Buckingham (1993a).

13 Buckingham and Allerton (1995).

14 This issue is taken up in more detail in the first two chapters. For a detailed, but inevitably controversial, critical history of film censorship in Britain, see Matthews (1994).

# 2

# Child's play?

## BEYOND MORAL PANICS

On Friday, 12 February 1993, two-year-old James Bulger was murdered on a railway line in Bootle, near Liverpool, in the north of England. His killers were two ten-year-old boys, Jon Venables and Bobby Thompson. Playing truant that day, the two boys had led James away from the Strand shopping centre in the middle of town and walked over two miles to the railway line where they eventually killed him. Many adults saw the three children, and some stopped to query them; but Jon and Bobby assured them that James was safe with them.

The murder itself must have taken some considerable time. It seems that the boys had thrown bricks in James's face, and then hit him with a heavy metal bar. They also threw paint at him, from a tin they had stolen from a shop earlier that day. They had eventually laid the body across the railway line and covered it with bricks. There was a suggestion that there had been some sexual interference, although the evidence was not conclusive.

Quite why Venables and Thompson killed James Bulger is far from clear, and will probably remain so. In his book on the case, *The Sleep of Reason*, David James Smith[1] recounts the events in painstaking and disturbing detail; but as in many such 'true crime' stories, the tone is resolutely deadpan. Bobby Thompson came from a family with a history of abuse and hardship, and although his older brothers had voluntarily put themselves into local authority care, it is not clear whether he had been abused himself. Jon Venables's brother and sister had learning difficulties, and his parents were separated, and it is likely that he felt neglected as a result. But there are children like these in every class in every inner-city school.

The murder of a two-year-old child is bound to provoke horror and outrage; yet it was the fact that the killers were children them-selves that proved so difficult to understand. Such actions present a direct affront to many of our society's most cherished notions of childhood – and in particular to the Romantic belief in childhood as a period of innocence and natural purity. In fact, while they are obviously very rare, there have been child murderers throughout history. Smith[2] lists many such cases from the past two centuries, some of which have striking parallels with the Bulger killing. Such crimes often seem to involve children who are left in charge of infants, and who appear unable to cope with their demands. Responding to their cries in the only way they know, with vio-lence, only makes them cry harder, and the situation very soon spins out of control. As one thing leads inexorably to another, the children seem to lose the ability to perceive the consequences of their actions, either for themselves or for their victims. At the time of the murder, for example, Bobby Thompson was apparently most concerned that his mother would be angry about the bloodstains on his trousers. It was as if the children had somehow bracketed off the reality of what they had done, and only partially began to recover this in cross-examination. Yet to label them as merely 'psy-chopathic' or 'evil' (as several commentators did) does very little to aid our understanding.

However rare they may be, such events are nevertheless often taken to be representative of much broader underlying problems within society as a whole. They offer a golden opportunity for crit-ics of all moral and political persuasions to weigh in with their analyses of the fundamental malaise of our times. In the weeks fol-lowing the arrest of the killers, for example, the churches and the education system were blamed by some for their failure to provide strong moral leadership; while others pointed to the effects of long-term unemployment and the erosion of leisure provision for young people. 'Permissive' approaches to child-rearing and the 'irrespon-sibility' of single parents – both increasingly familiar targets – were also invoked, as if blaming the parents rather than the children would somehow enable those cherished notions of childhood to survive unscathed.

In the end, however, it is perhaps not too surprising that the debate about the Bulger case came to be dominated by arguments about the effects of the media. Throughout history, assertions about the negative influence of popular cultural forms have served as a focus for much broader anxieties about moral decline and social disorder.[3] Since the Greek philosopher Plato first expressed concern about the influence of the dramatic poets on the 'impressionable minds' of young people, a succession of new media – the novel, music hall, the cinema, comics, television, video and computer games – have each in turn become the focus of recurrent waves of public anxiety. Such arguments hold a particular attraction for social critics of all political persuasions, largely because they provide a convenient explanation for events that are much too complex, or simply too painful, to face. Blaming the media for rising crime, for the decline of the nuclear family, or for falling rates of literacy, has become part of the reliable stock-in-trade of newspaper columnists and politicians. Perhaps the most recent precedent in this respect is the Hungerford massacre, now forever associated in the popular imagination with the image of 'Rambo' – despite the lack of evidence that Michael Ryan, the killer, had even seen the film that was alleged to have provoked his crime.[4]

The spectre of 'media violence' had been raised well before the trial of James Bulger's killers. In the weeks following their arrest, the Prime Minister and the Home Secretary both made high-profile speeches about the need to curb television violence. Television executives were called to account, and new guidelines on TV violence were promised. The British Board of Film Classification (the industry censorship body) hastily commissioned research into the viewing habits of young offenders. TV talk shows featured teenage criminals only too ready to blame their misdemeanours on the media. And the National Viewers and Listeners Association – claiming to speak for Britain's 'moral majority' – also used the Bulger case as fuel for its attacks on television violence, eventually culminating in a 'research report' sensitively entitled 'Did he die in vain?'

However, it was not until the trial itself that this anxiety found a specific focus. In his summing-up, the judge, the Honourable Mr Justice Moreland, suggested that 'exposure to violent video films' may have been part of the explanation for the killing – although in fact the issue had not been discussed at all during the trial itself. Meanwhile, it had emerged that Neil Venables (Jon's father, with whom he was not living at the time) had recently hired the video *Child's Play 3*; and it was argued that there were several similarities between events in the film and the manner of James's murder.

In fact, there was no evidence that either Jon Venables or Bobby Thompson had seen *Child's Play 3*: indeed, it would seem extremely unlikely. In cross-examination, Jon explicitly denied this, claiming that he didn't like horror films – and while it would be wrong to take this at face value, one might well ask what he might have to gain by lying about the matter. It appears that he mainly enjoyed cartoons and soap operas, and that his favourite film was the Spielberg fantasy *Goonies*. In his responses to television violence, he was by no means untypical of the ordinary school children whose discussions are analysed in this book. According to David James Smith:

> He told Dr Bailey [the psychiatrist advising the police on the case] he would make believe it was only acting when he saw 'naughty things', by which he meant blood or fighting. He would turn his face away and put his fingers in his ears if, in the *Rocky* films, someone was punched and blood came out. He watched Kung Fu films which his dad got out on video; when he saw them he thought they were real, and he would cry.[5]

Meanwhile, Albert Kirby, the chief investigating officer, insisted that the police could make no connection between the killing and the viewing of videos – although his comments went largely unheard.

As I shall argue, the similarities between the events of *Child's Play 3* and the murder of James Bulger were effectively non-existent. Yet with powerful support from most of the press, and subsequently from some influential academic researchers, the connection that had been forged between the film and the murder led directly to proposals for new censorship legislation that were supported by MPs of all political persuasions.

In this chapter, I want to examine how the complex feelings of fear and horror provoked by the James Bulger case came to focus on a single film, and why that film might have served as a symbol for the much broader anxieties that were at stake. I begin by considering the intense public debates that took place in the six-month period between the trial and the tabling of an amendment to the Criminal Justice Bill by David Alton MP, which proposed far-reaching new legislation on censorship.[6] I then offer a brief analysis of *Child's Play 3* itself, in an attempt to explain why it might have provoked such outrage. Finally, I offer an account of children's own responses to the film, and to the media coverage of the murder trial. As I shall argue, the controversy which was provoked by the Bulger case serves as a very clear indication of the limitations of much contemporary public debate about young people and the media. By contrast, examining the children's own perspectives provides at least the starting point for a more constructive and well-informed discussion of the issues.

## The anatomy of nastiness

It is appropriate to begin, as all the best Cultural Studies analysis does, with Britain's most notorious tabloid, the *Sun*. Its front page on the day after the trial (26 November 1993) is largely taken up with a colour photograph of a dustbin containing burning copies of *Child's Play 3*. 'For the sake of ALL our kids ...' it screams, 'BURN YOUR VIDEO NASTY.' The report below describes how 'a video chain boss yesterday torched his entire £10,000 stock of tapes linked to the Jamie Bulger murder'. Launching its 'nationwide campaign to get all other copies of *Child's Play 3* burned', the *Sun* quotes David Alton's condemnation of the 'gratuitous nastiness' of the film, and the video shop owner's estimation of it as 'spine-chilling, really nasty'.

The *Sun*'s resurrection of the term 'video nasty' is one that was echoed by many of the papers. It refers back, of course, to the earlier controversy about video violence that led to the Video Recordings Act in 1984, which remains one of the strictest pieces of censorship legislation in the Western world. As Martin Barker's analysis of that campaign suggested, the 'nasty' was a category that remained strategically undefined.[7] Yet one consequence of the Video Recordings Act has been that uncertificated films such as *Driller Killer* and *I Spit on Your Grave*, which were the main focus of anxiety at that time, can no longer be obtained legally in the UK – although they are easily available in North America and in other European countries.

In fact, *Child's Play 3* was passed by the British Board of Film Classification with an '18' certificate on video, although (with two small cuts) the film was given a '15' certificate for cinema exhibition. The two preceding films in the series were both passed at '15', both for video and cinema exhibition. This 'borderline' status would suggest that, even in the eyes of the censors themselves, the violence in the film would have to be seen as comparatively mild.[8] To refer to the film as a 'video nasty' merely demonstrates the extraordinary elasticity of the term.

Perhaps the ultimate irony here, however, is that the film had recently been screened (once during the Bulger trial itself) by BSkyB, the satellite channel owned by the *Sun*'s proprietor Rupert Murdoch – and was likely to have been seen there by tens of thousands of children. For some reason, the *Sun* did not see fit to mention the fact that BSkyB had abandoned plans to screen the film again later that night. Significantly, in the legislation that was eventually proposed, satellite broadcasting appeared to be exempt from the restrictions that were to be placed on video rental companies. In broadcasting, as in many other areas of social policy, the government's commitment to 'free market' policies often seems to contradict its tendency to resort to authoritarian solutions on questions of morality.

The question of *evidence* – which was later to become a significant issue in the debate – was also addressed in the *Sun*'s coverage. The front page story notes that Jon Venables 'may' have seen the film, displaying a degree of caution that was later thrown to the winds. On an inside page, under the heading 'Terror of Sun girl', there is a graph purporting to represent the fluctuating heart rate of its reporter Mary Keenan as she watched *Child's Play 3*. 'During the scariest parts,' the story notes, 'her heart rate jumped from a normal 90 beats per minute to as high as 200.' The graph accordingly peaks at particular moments: 'barber has throat cut' rates 170, while 'doll is sliced to pieces' climaxes at 200. This veneer of scientific credibility might temporarily delude the reader into believing that this experiment supports the paper's argument about the links between violent videos and violent behaviour – although of course all it does prove is that the film is exciting. Yet as I shall indicate, even where apparently more authoritative academic sources were adduced, the status of the evidence was equally lacking.

The *Sun's* emphasis on *Child's Play 3* was shared by most of the other papers, and the leering face of Chucky, the film's demonic living doll, was featured prominently on a number of front pages. The *Daily Mirror*, subsequently to vie with the *Sun* for the praise of the pro-censorship campaigners, led with a report on the film's producer, David Kirschner, the 'tycoon' who had apparently made £40 million from the 'Bulger horror'. In many of the papers, further evidence of Chucky's mesmeric power was found in the ongoing trial of the murderers of Susanne Capper, currently being held at Manchester Crown Court. In that case, the victim had apparently been tormented by one of the killers playing a tape of music which included the film's repeated catch phrase 'I'm Chucky, wanna play?' Here again, the video connection seemed to be considered more newsworthy than the fact that the killers had been out of their brains on drugs.

Looking across the press coverage of the case, a very familiar rhetoric emerges. Violence is being 'pumped out into our living rooms'. Young people are 'saturated', 'hooked' and 'corrupted': their 'impressionable minds' are 'bombarded' and 'warped'. The videos themselves are described as 'an addictive pollutant': they are 'evil', 'sick', 'brutalising', 'poisonous', 'insidious', 'abhorrent', 'vile muck'. The scale of the problem is enormous – and it must be contained by firm and decisive action. This 'stuff' must be stopped.

But what is 'this stuff'? As in the earlier 'video nasties' affair, the films that are referred to in these reports are very diverse. The term 'horror' is often substituted for 'video nasty', particularly in the broadsheet papers. But the examples named or pictured include comedy horror and 'art' horror, as well as films as diverse as *Reservoir Dogs*, *Conan the Barbarian*, *Falling Down* and *Man Bites Dog*. What appears to define the offensiveness of the films, however, is not so much their content as their presumed effects on the viewer. Thus, we are told that the victims in these films are 'subhuman' and 'cannot be pitied'; and that viewers identify with the perpetrator rather than the victim – assertions that, as we shall see, are highly questionable. This is, it is argued, simply 'violent pornography' – a notion that rhetorically unites two taboo areas, yet whose meaning is nowhere defined.

If the outrage of the tabloids was apparent from the start, the position of the upmarket broadsheets was more complex. *The Times*, for example, acknowledged that Jon Venables may not in fact have seen *Child's Play 3*, and that the connection between depictions of violence and violent crime could not be proven. Nevertheless, it shared the view that 'members of a whole generation of children are growing up in a culture saturated by images of gratuitous cruelty and bestial violence'. Yet these were clearly *other people's* children:

> Today's festering culture of video nastiness thrives in corners of Britain remote from the experience of liberal drawing rooms where 'freedom of expression' is so uncritically defended ... There is now a widespread addiction to viewing monstrous horror – often misogynistic and sexually degrading – which is presented so naturalistically that, to the impressionable, it has become part of the furniture of reality. (Editorial, 26 November 1993)

Initially, however, the broadsheets seemed to favour a liberal approach, rather than the legislation that was already being called for. *The Times*'s editorial concluded by noting the cancellation of BSkyB's screening of *Child's Play 3*, suggesting that it showed the value of 'moral censure' as opposed to 'legal constraint'.[9] But it was the traditionally right-wing *Daily Telegraph* that most directly challenged the call for legislation:

> If anything can be done, it is to encourage parents and teachers to

take greater pains to exert control over what children watch and do. As individuals, we need to stigmatise such vile films rather than to pass yet another buck to the police and courts. (Editorial, 26 November 1993)

Nevertheless, all this had changed by the time David Alton's amendment was tabled in the Commons in April 1994. Among other things, the amendment proposed that any video recording should be banned for private use 'either because it presents an inappropriate model for children, or because it is likely to cause psychological harm to a child'. While it rejected these prescriptions as 'worryingly imprecise and subjective', the *Telegraph* now joined the call for tighter legislation, seemingly convinced that parents could no longer be trusted:

> It is always best in a free society to let individuals and parents make up their own minds on such matters, but it has increasingly become clear that some parents are so feckless and irresponsible that the law has to intervene for the sake of others. (Editorial, 12 April 1994)

So what had caused this change of view? We need to beware of the idea (which seemed to be accepted even by many of his opponents) that Alton's amendment represented a consensual view among the population at large. Nevertheless, there were very few indications of opposition to the legislation reported in the press. The film director Michael Winner, a perennial opponent of censorship, was easily discounted – along with the various official representatives of the video industry itself – as cynically self-interested. More crucially, Alton's amendment had gained support from many Labour politicians – and while this may partly have resulted from a sense of political expediency, the call for a tough line on violence was clearly compatible with a similar position on pornography, adopted for example by Clare Short MP.[10] It was perhaps predictable that one would encounter right-wing Labour frontbenchers such as Gerald Kaufman attacking irresponsible parents (*Telegraph*, 12 April 1994) or Roy Hattersley fulminating about children being 'brainwashed' by the 'pornography of violence'

(*Daily Mail*, 2 April 1994). Meanwhile, broadsheet columnists such as Edward Pearce (*Guardian*) and Melanie Phillips (*Observer*) also weighed in on the side of increased censorship.

Ultimately, it was only the *Guardian* that was prepared to stand out against this position, condemning the legislation as a 'quick fix' that would have no impact on juvenile crime. While the *Telegraph* seemed to have abandoned its faith in parental control, the *Guardian* stood firm in the argument that 'family values are defended in the family' (editorial, 13 April 1994) – although it was very much the lone voice. In general, the liberal opposition to increasing censorship had effectively been routed.


## A body of evidence

The most decisive reason for this change, and perhaps for David Alton's apparent victory (his amendment was withdrawn, follow-ing a promise from the Home Secretary to introduce new legisla-tion),[11] relates to the question of *evidence*. In the case of the murder of James Bulger, as in that of the Hungerford massacre, dubious anecdotal evidence became progressively firmer as time went by. Five months after the trial, the *Daily Mirror* (13 April 1994) was claiming that 'police were shocked by similarities between the killing of James Bulger and *Child's Play 3*' – although in fact, as I have noted, they had dismissed any such connection. Reporters would typically claim that *Child's Play 3* 'had been linked' to the murder of James Bulger, neglecting to identify who had done the linking, and simultaneously avoiding the requirement to commit themselves.

However, it was a group of academic 'experts' who played a decisive role here. In the past, advocates of stricter controls on tele-vision violence have often displayed considerable frustration with the equivocations of academic research on these matters. Researchers who argue that the connection between screen vio-lence and real-life violence remains unproven are often condemned as 'ivory tower' academics who have little understanding of the everyday world.[12] It is, to use the word that was repeatedly invoked in these debates, simply 'commonsense' that watching violence causes people to go out and commit violent acts; and anybody who disagrees with this is simply talking nonsense.

In the immediate aftermath of the Bulger verdict, it was possible to locate academics who would support the call for greater censorship. Thus, Professor Brian Clifford of the University of East London 'analysed' *Child's Play 3* at the request of the *Daily Mirror* (26 November 1993). Like many 'experts' quoted, he seems to accept that there is a causal connection between the film and the murder of James Bulger. Paradoxically, he argues *both* that the film is 'extremely powerful' in terms of arousal *and* that it could 'desensitise children to pain and suffering'.[13] Children, he argues, 'wouldn't really know how to take [the] almost jokey attitude to death' that the film allegedly promotes, and could be seriously damaged by images of violence that are 'detached from human relationships' – statements that might interest the makers of such popular children's films as *The Addams Family* and *Home Alone*.

As in the case of the 'video nasties' scare of the early 1980s, research was hastily commissioned to support the proposed legislation.[14] David Alton invited Professor Elizabeth Newson, a child development specialist at Nottingham University, to produce a report for MPs which would summarise existing research on the issue. Newson's report, endorsed by twenty-five eminent doctors and academics, was released to the press ten days before Alton's amendment was due to be debated. The report was widely hailed as a victory for 'commonsense', and as an indication that academic opinion in general had undergone a significant about-face. 'The scientific tide has turned', argued the *Telegraph* (2 April 1994), suggesting that 'Professor Newson's paper studied the conclusions of several hundred reports on screen violence'. The front pages of the *Mirror* and the *Express* were both again adorned with images of Chucky, the former claiming 'At last, experts admit: movie nasties DO kill' – imputing a power to the medium that appeared to bypass human agency.

To turn to Newson's paper after reading this coverage was, I suspect for many, a considerable shock. The paper is very far from the sober review of the research one had been led to expect. While it does refer to a couple of secondary reviews of the field – one of them a paper written by two of the contributors to the notorious 'video nasties' research of the early 1980s – its primary source is in fact Michael Medved's populist tract on screen violence *Hollywood versus America*.[15] Despite press claims to the contrary, neither Newson herself nor any of the 'experts' who endorsed the paper in fact have any record of research in this field,[16] nor did the paper contain any 'new evidence'. The growing methodological and theoretical criticisms of 'effects' research (not least among psychologists), and the inconsistencies and equivocations of the research itself, are simply ignored.

Perhaps most significantly, however, almost half of the paper is given over to a highly emotive account of the murder of James Bulger, which goes into considerable detail about the precise methods of the killing. Like most of the 'experts' quoted by the press, Newson gives an extraordinary degree of credibility and status to what was little more than unsubstantiated rumour. The connection between video violence and violent behaviour – both of which are seen to be increasing, although on the basis of no hard evidence – is seen to be self-evident:

> What, then, can be seen as the 'different' factor that has entered the lives of countless children and adolescents in recent years? This has to be recognised as the easy availability to children of gross images of violence on video.[17]

As Richard Boston, the *Guardian* video critic, observed, correlations of this kind can be established between any such social phenomena. By this logic, he argued, the 'increase' in violence could just as easily be explained by the growth in popularity of Velcro.

Meanwhile, genuinely new research undertaken in the wake of the Bulger killing had been published. In a study undertaken by the Policy Studies Institute, Ann Hagell and Tim Newburn[18] had found that young offenders' viewing habits were very similar to those of ordinary school children: their preferences were not for 'video nasties' but for soaps and police series like *The Bill*. Yet for some reason, this research was given much less prominent coverage by the press.

A full account of Newson's paper, and of the debates that surrounded the ensuing legislation, is beyond the scope of this book. What is striking, however, is the way in which *Child's Play 3* consistently remained the central focus of the controversy. On the day after the Alton amendment had been debated, Chucky was again on the front pages of the *Daily Mirror*, the *Star* and *The Times*. The *Mirror* was not alone to claim the credit: above the obligatory colour shot of the video cover, it screamed 'BANNED – Thanks to your Daily Mirror' (13 April 1994).

## Another panic attack?

Critics have often referred to such waves of public anxiety as 'moral panics'. As Geoffrey Pearson[19] and others have shown, concerns about the impending collapse of the social order have recurred throughout history; and as potent symbols of modernity, the media are often seen to play a major role here. Yet it would be wrong to imply that such concerns are therefore somehow timeless – or indeed that they are necessarily 'irrational' or without foundation. On the contrary, moral panics often reflect fundamental tensions in society, and have to be seen in terms of their historical context.[20] This latest 'panic' around video violence – if indeed the notion of 'panic' can be seen as an apt description of what took place[21] – was a specific response to the genuine emergence both of new cultural forms and of new technologies of distribution. The irony, of course, is that it was such a belated panic; and that the legislation that was eventually proposed was so patently incapable of dealing with the real nature of the 'problem' – if indeed it is to be perceived as such.

Thus, the attempt to introduce even stricter controls over the use of video arose at a time when a whole series of new and less controllable technologies was becoming much more widely available. Significantly, both satellite broadcasting and the so-called information super-highway, that were left untouched by the legislation, transcend national boundaries. The advent of modems and satellite dishes, combined with the government's ideological commitment to 'free market' policies, has effectively put an end to the centralised control of moving images. Meanwhile, the pirate video trade in Britain has a turnover that is between one-third and one-half of the legal video business – a trade that is of course made possible by the technological potential for duplication. Particularly in Britain's inner cities, it is easy to obtain illegal copies of films well before they are distributed in the cinema, and many months before they are officially available on video. Stricter censorship legislation could only encourage these developments, thus effectively undermining its intentions.

In the case of the cultural form itself, it is clear that 'violence' in contemporary horror films *is* more 'extreme' and more graphic than in the classic horror movies of the 1950s and before – although here again, this development could be traced back at least as far as *The Exorcist*, first screened in 1971 (and still banned on video in the UK). Yet it could also be argued that the meaning of 'violence' in these films has changed, as audiences themselves have become more sophisticated. As critics have noted, contemporary horror is becoming ever more self-reflexive as a genre: it is, to use Philip Brophy's words, 'a genre about genre'.[22] *Child's Play 3*, for example, is suffused with the kind of sardonic irony that has become typical of a great deal of horror movies. The 'violence' in the film is, I would argue, explicitly intended as a joke, not to be taken literally: and while this might be disturbing for those who are unfamiliar with the genre, the suggestion that it therefore cultivates a dismissive attitude to pain and suffering *in real life* is to deny the high degree of self-consciousness of horror fans themselves. Even in the case of children, as I shall indicate, very clear distinctions are being made between reality and fantasy, and between different examples of the genre.

At the same time, of course, this debate is only partially about video violence in the first place. As in earlier waves of concern, much more fundamental anxieties are at stake, that cannot simply be dismissed as 'panic'. Thus, what is typically invoked in these debates is a highly contradictory notion of childhood. On the one hand, there is a broadly Romantic view, in which children are defined as innocent and vulnerable, and thus in need of adult protection. Yet on the other, there is an even older Christian view which sees them as potential monsters, whose anti-social tendencies are liable to be triggered at any moment – in effect, as guilty of original sin. These tensions are, if not timeless, at least of long standing, and they infuse many other areas of social policy relating to children.

Yet the concern over young people and video should also be seen as a manifestation of more specific contemporary anxieties about the relation between the public and the private, particularly in the context of historical changes in family structure. In 'rolling back the nanny state', Thatcherism appeared to hand over much of the responsibility for social control to the family – although of course this move was based on a particular definition of the family that was simultaneously becoming an anachronism. These almost neurotic contradictions are readily apparent, for example in the widely-publicised cases of child murders and 'home alone kids' over the past decade, the recent attacks on single parent families, and perhaps particularly the confused position of the state in relation to child abuse (in cases such as Cleveland, Rochdale and the Orkneys). And of course video violence is frequently described as a form of child abuse in its own right – albeit one perpetrated by a cynical and manipulative industry with the permission of parents who can only be described as feckless and irresponsible.

Finally, this debate also raises significant questions about the role of academic evidence and its place in the political process. There are issues of academic ethics that are raised by Newson's paper, and particularly by the way in which it was commissioned and released to the press. Yet there are also questions that need to be asked about the lack of effective opposition to Alton's amendment. On one level, it is clear that the popular press was Alton's most significant ally – although one should beware of assuming that it therefore represents a consensus among the population at large. The problem, I would suggest, is that the arguments that are traditionally used in opposition to such moves are themselves so weak and so inconsistent – or alternatively so academic and obscure – that they represent little challenge to the power of 'commonsense'. This is an issue to which I return in my concluding chapter.

## Child's Play 3: look who's stalking

What can be said of the film that was at the centre of this controversy? The *Child's Play* films are probably the most widely-known
examples of what might be termed the demonic doll movie, a popular sub-genre in contemporary horror. Stories of toys that come
to life can of course be found throughout the history of children's
literature, from the Brothers Grimm and *Winnie the Pooh* to contemporary examples such as *Paddington Bear*. Angela Carter's *The
Magic Toyshop* provides a recent fictional reflection on this theme,
refracted through the concerns of contemporary horror films. In
the cinema, there are countless children's films with this theme,
from *Pinocchio* onwards; while Richard Attenborough's *Magic* may
represent the inspiration for a whole series of adult horror films on
a similar theme, such as *Dolly Dearest*, *Dolls*, *Death Doll* and *The
Manic Toys*, as well as the *Child's Play* series.

The *Child's Play* series has undoubtedly been extremely popular
– and of course the current controversy has only fuelled this (my
local video shop had to put the film on overnight loan only, instead
of the usual three days, in order to cope with demand[23]). Press estimates of the money that has been made from the series vary
between twenty and forty million pounds – although these stories
merely serve to confirm the image of the film's producer David
Kirschner as another child abuser exploiting innocent kids, not a
million miles from the evil capitalists in the film itself.

*Child's Play 3* is a further instalment in the adventures of
Chucky, a doll who is possessed by the demonic spirit of a child
murderer. Like earlier films in the series, it follows Chucky's
attempts to find a child's body to inhabit, and thus be released from
his entrapment in the doll. The 'hero' of the film is Andy, who as
a child had been pursued by Chucky in earlier films, and whom we
now meet as he enters a military academy, attempting to put his
past troubles behind him. Meanwhile, the cynical manufacturers of
'Good Guy' dolls have chosen to re-launch the product, despite
what they know of Chucky's earlier evil deeds. Chucky is reborn,
and after killing the boss of the company, contrives to get himself
sent in the post to the military academy. There he meets Tyler, a

young black boy who is effectively the mascot of the academy, and whom Chucky immediately perceives as a more appropriate target than Andy, who is no longer of interest because of his age. The bulk of the film concerns Andy's attempts to prevent Chucky from possessing the body of Tyler. These attempts frequently result in Andy falling foul of various authority figures, many of whom are subsequently dispatched by Chucky. The film climaxes in a children's amusement park, as Andy and his newly acquired soldier girlfriend save Tyler and send Chucky falling to his death.

Ultimately, the fact that *Child's Play 3* became the focus of this controversy may be merely a matter of coincidence: it happened to be the last tape Jon Venables's father had hired, and there happened to be (at least in the eyes of some people) similarities between the film and the murder. In fact, the relationship between the events in the film and the murder of James Bulger is extremely tenuous, if not non-existent. Yet for the press, it was as if the murder was little more than an acting out of Chucky's story. Noting that 'Child's Play 3 was rented by boy killer Jon Venables' (which of course is untrue), the *Daily Star* goes on: 'Like James, Chucky has paint spattered on its face, its head is battered and it is butchered beside railway tracks' (26 November 1994). In fact, Chucky does not have paint 'spattered' on his face: the paint is in pellets fired from the guns of military cadets during their training exercise, not thrown from a tin as was the case in the Bulger murder, and it is fired at a door in the training ground. The doll's head is crushed rather than battered; and this takes place in a ghost train at a funfair rather than beside railway tracks. Chucky is finally killed by falling into the rotor blades of a large fan. These scenes are very far from being, in the words of the *Telegraph*, 'sickeningly reminiscent' of the Bulger murder.

This kind of copycat theory implicitly relies on the notion that such crimes are premeditated and planned. In this case, for example, we are being asked to believe that Jon Venables and Bobby Thompson stole the can of enamel paint from the shop in the Strand in Bootle with the explicit intention of then finding a child to play the part of Chucky on whom they could throw it (although of course this is not actually what happens in the film). Likewise, it is implied that the distorted imagination of the criminals prevents them from recognising the differences between fiction and reality. In their minds, it is assumed, the branch line from Bootle to Edge Hill stands in for the ghost train at the funfair; and so on. Yet from the existing evidence, it is hard to believe that the crime was pre-meditated or planned. On the contrary, it seems as though a great deal of what happened was quite fortuitous, and that what may well have begun as a joke or a momentary whim gradually turned into a situation from which the two boys were struggling to escape. Finally, such arguments also depend upon popular assumptions about 'identification': it is because the boys 'identified' with the fictional killer that they were led to take his part in real life. Yet for much of the film, Chucky is of course the killer and not the victim: he is chasing the children, rather than being abducted by them, and he is eventually killed in self-defence. If Jon Venables and Bobby Thompson were indeed acting out the events of *Child's Play 3*, whose part did they think they were playing – that of the evil killer or that of his victims?

Nevertheless, for the pro-censorship campaigners who happened to see it, *Child's Play 3* clearly was regarded as offensive and dis-turbing. On one level, of course, this could be seen merely to reflect their lack of experience and understanding of the contemporary horror genre. Nevertheless, there are some significant aspects of the film that may shed light on these reactions, and on the com-ments of the children I go on to consider.

The first of these concerns the degree of realism – or what I go on to call the *modality* – of the film. 'Modality' is a term derived from linguistics that refers to the relationship between a given statement (or a text) and reality.[24] Texts clearly make different claims about their relationship with the real world, not least by their use of particular codes and conventions: cartoons, we would generally agree, are less realistic than the news, or than realist drama. Yet even these judgments are dependent upon our cultural knowledge: for example, we might perceive the use of a wobbly, hand-held camera in a programme like *NYPD Blue* as a guarantee of realism, largely because of our experience of watching docu-mentaries – yet this perception may not be shared by children, and it may well change over time, as it comes to be seen as yet another stylistic device. However, our judgments about what is and is not realistic also depend upon what we know or believe about the real world. Thus, even very young children know that the families in *The Cosby Show* or *Roseanne* are not 'real', in the sense that they are played by actors, and that the programmes are scripted and filmed in a studio. They learn to recognise that the programmes obey certain rules or conventions, whereby things are played for laughs, or conflicts are easily resolved. Yet they may also regard the programmes as more or less 'realistic', depending upon how they compare with their own family lives, or with what they believe about families in general. The modality of television is thus not simply a property of the medium itself: on the contrary, it depends upon our perceptions and judgments as viewers.

As we shall see, this question of modality is a crucial aspect of children's relationship with television – and it was raised in a number of discussions of *Child's Play 3*. Yet if we confine ourselves for the moment to an account of the text, it is clear that the *lack* of realism of the fictional world is consistently and self-consciously emphasised. On one level, this is evident in the very implausibility of the events: the doll coming to life, sending itself to the military academy and so on. Yet it is also marked on a formal level. Unusual camera angles, stylised and dramatic lighting, frequent point-of-view shots and the use of generic suspense music all contrive to undermine the claim to realism. The concluding scene in the ghost train at the children's funfair consistently locates Chucky among artificial horror monsters, such as animated skeletons and mummies – images which, it could be noted, are all common in humorous books aimed at young children. In all these ways, the film appears to discourage the viewer from 'taking it too seriously': it is, as its title suggests, 'playing' with the idea of evil, not only to shock but also to amuse. As we shall see, the extent to which viewers recognise this is bound to depend partly on their familiarity with the genre.

This leads on to the second aspect here, which is the film's ironic and self-conscious treatment of notions of childhood, also signalled by its title. Andy's induction into the military academy, for exam-

ple, is described by the colonel as a matter of 'putting away childish things'. This is particularly apparent in an early scene, in
which his hair is cut by a sadistic barber (who significantly is later
killed by Chucky), in what amounts to a familiar form of initiation
rite. During this scene, an advertisement for 'Good Guy' dolls plays
on the TV, and the dolls are admired by the child Tyler; and it is
the body of this child, rather than the 'adult' body of Andy, that
Chucky now wants to occupy. Chucky himself, of course, is a direct
affront to these cherished notions of childhood: he is an adult killer
in the body of a self-consciously 'cute', Cabbage Patch-style doll,
complete with dungarees and freckles. In this context, the fact that
he is so foul-mouthed is a vitally important part of his character.
As he murders the company boss at the start of the film, for example, he yells 'don't fuck with the Chuck!'; while as the Colonel has
a heart attack before Chucky is able to finish him off, he says
incredulously 'you've gotta be fucking kidding me!' Not least in
view of his appalling decayed teeth, Chucky is very consciously the
opposite of the Hollywood child – as the legend that appears on the
video cover, 'Look who's stalking!', makes very clear.

Thirdly, the film could be seen to play on the child's desire to
take revenge on the adult world. In common with films like *Nightmare on Elm Street*, *Child's Play 3* represents the adult world in
highly unsympathetic terms. The evil capitalists who are responsible for the production of the doll describe children as 'consumer
trainees'; and while they know its history, they reject the argument that the doll should not be produced just in case 'one child
is affected by it' – a more or less explicit reference to popular arguments about media 'effects'. While Chucky does attempt to dispose
of Andy (the nominal hero) in his attempts to take on his new
body, many of the victims he dispatches along the way are authoritarian adult characters who have done wrong to Andy, and whose
deaths could (at least in most cases) be seen as 'deserved', such as
the sadistic barber or the evil company boss. In this sense, despite
the opposition between them, Chucky could be seen to be acting out Andy's (and perhaps by extension the viewer's) hidden
desires for revenge against authority. Yet, like a great deal of contemporary horror, *Child's Play 3* could also be seen to address

fundamental anxieties about the child's transition to adulthood. Andy's acquisition of adult masculinity is seen in decidedly ambivalent terms, while Chucky represents the return of repressed dimensions of childhood, not least Andy's own. As the slogan on the video box has it: 'There comes a time to put away childish things – but some things won't stay put!'

It is not my intention here to engage in a detailed textual analysis, still less to make a claim for the film as a misunderstood masterpiece. *Child's Play 3* is not a 'rich text' (in the classic Film Studies mode), and subtlety is not one of its strengths – although of course that is precisely the point. To condemn the film for lacking a clear moral viewpoint – as some of its critics have done – is equivalent to condemning heavy metal music because it doesn't have very nice melodies. In fact, while the film may allow us to take pleasure in Chucky's revenge on the unacceptable face of the adult world, it constantly exposes the delusion that he is one of the 'Good Guys'. There is undoubtedly an ironic relishing of evil here, but the moral universe of the film is extremely clearly delineated, and Chucky receives his come-uppance in a very spectacular form. What makes the film much more problematic for its critics, I would argue, is that it could be seen as a 'children's film', in the sense that it seems to take a child's point of view – a phenomenon that is comparatively rare, even in films that many adults would categorise as 'children's films'.[25] The problem, of course, is that the child's point of view it takes is not one that David Alton or his followers would like to acknowledge, much less promote.

**Horror talk**

The kinds of debates I have described in this chapter are typically carried on without reference to children's own perspectives. As in many other areas, it is adults who claim to act in the best interests of children – yet children themselves are often simply ignored. In attempting to move beyond the limitations of these debates, therefore, I want to begin by exploring children's responses, both to *Child's Play 3* and to the television coverage of the James Bulger case. In the process, I introduce a number of themes that are pursued in much more detail in subsequent chapters.

Well before the film was linked to the murder of James Bulger, many of the children we interviewed talked at some length about the *Child's Play* series. Indeed, with the possible exception of the *Nightmare on Elm Street* films, these were probably the most popular horror films among the children in our sample. While a few nine- and ten-year-olds had seen them, a majority of the teenagers had seen at least one film from either series, in a number of cases in the company of their parents.

Of course, what children say about such material should not be taken at face value. On the one hand, horror films clearly do have a considerable social status among many young people. Viewing horror is often perceived as a test of one's maturity, and perhaps also of one's masculinity; and in certain situations, there may be a great deal to be gained from claiming that you are old enough, or indeed 'man enough', to handle it. One might reasonably expect children (and particularly boys) to play down feelings of fear or disgust, and to profess indifference to the effects of such material. On the other hand, many children will have heard adults express anxieties about the effects of television on young people: they may wish to use such arguments as a way of demonstrating that they share such 'adult' concerns – or alternatively they may attempt to displace those concerns onto children younger than themselves. To argue that 'young children' really shouldn't be watching such things is to imply that you yourself have moved beyond this stage, and are much too mature to be seriously affected. In fact, most of the children here appeared surprisingly willing to admit to potentially embarrassing emotional responses – albeit often with a degree of self-deprecating irony. Yet any adult inviting children to talk about their emotions in the company of their peers – and in particular to discuss their responses to such 'forbidden' material – is clearly not asking neutral questions. The children's observations need to be read, therefore, not as some form of intimate 'confession', but in terms of the social context in which they are produced.

Despite these qualifications, it is clear that the *Child's Play* films were not taken seriously by the large majority of these children, and were often contrasted with films that were genuinely frightening. While *Child's Play 3* was occasionally described as 'scary' and 'sick', it was more frequently described as 'unrealistic' and 'funny' – and in one case as 'hilarious'. The humour here was largely perceived to be intentional, although this was not exclusively the case. Steven and Adrian (15), for example, both agreed that earlier films in the series had been rather 'gory' in places, but that *Child's Play 3* was much less so:

*Steven:* I actually thought it was funny. It made me laugh ... The doll just makes me laugh 'cause it's just –

*Adrian:* It walks down the toy shop aisle and it's got a great big silhouette of it on the wall [*laughing*] and it's just, it's just –

*Interviewer:* It's funny?

*Steven:* } Yeah.
*Adrian:*

*Interviewer:* What's funny about it?

*Adrian:* I mean it's so small –

*Steven:* The doll, yeah, the way he walks and everything, it just makes me laugh.

*Interviewer:* Yeah.

*Steven:* It's like a little, like, cartoon thing / it makes me laugh.

For these boys, it was the weak modality of the film (it is compared with a cartoon) and its self-conscious emphasis on the absurdity of the killer doll motif that seemed to have provoked the laughter. This is particularly apparent in Adrian's reference to the silhouette of the doll, which is both a stereotypically 'expressionist' generic convention and a comic means of drawing attention to the doll's diminutive stature.[26]

There were frequent references to the constructed nature of the film throughout these discussions. Many of the children commented on the use of 'camera tricks', while others praised it for the quality of the special effects, particularly the doll itself – as Sonia (12) argued, 'the way it moves, it's like it's an actual person'. At the same time, there were aspects of the film that were condemned as implausible, for instance the way in which Chucky exchanges the paint pellets for real bullets. Above all, however, the film's basic premise of the killer doll possessed by a human spirit was clearly seen as implausible – and here it was distinguished from more 'serious' horror films, particularly those dealing with the supernatural, which many of the children said they found much more plausible, and hence more frightening.

On the other hand, the film's self-conscious play with notions of childhood innocence was recognised by some of the older children as a characteristic strategy of the genre, as in this group of fifteen-year-old girls:

*Lisa:* It is quite ironic though, Chucky being so sweet and that with his little legs ...

*Martha:* 'Cause he wears these little sort of denim dungarees and these little trainers and, you know, little stripy jumper on underneath, you know, running about / and he's quite cute-looking really but then he gets a bit evil.

*Lisa:* He does, and he has sort of a laugh.

*Martha:* Yeah, his laugh is awful and whenever he laughs the camera always goes right on him and he looks really evil ...

*Interviewer:* What is it you like about Chucky films?

*Martha:* I don't know, there's just – I suppose it's similar to clowns really, the way you think they're so cute and lovable and they'd do nothing wrong and little dolls do, you know what I mean, and then they can be so evil. Whereas with something like Freddie [*Nightmare on Elm Street*] or that Jason or whatever in *Friday the Thirteenth*, you know they're so evil right from the start. But with something like a clown or a little doll –

*Lisa:* Yeah, it's different when it's like a little child's / friend.

*Martha:* And it's like in those *Poltergeist* films, the little girl, she's pretty evil really, isn't she?

As a fairly experienced horror viewer, Martha is able to locate the film within a broader knowledge of the genre, and to evaluate the ways in which it plays with the viewer's expectations. Like the boys, the girls here acknowledge the constructed nature of the film, most explicitly in their references to the camerawork; and the description of Chucky as 'evil' suggests that they too have an almost ironic perception of the manichean moral universe of horror. Later in the discussion, as they try to recall how the film ends, Martha confidently asserts that Tyler does not die, "cause that's the way they always work, isn't it? It's always the good defeats the evil.' In both groups here, it is as if the very self-consciousness of the film (its lack of realism, and its play with notions of innocence and evil) is enabling the children to learn the 'rules' of the genre – and hence, perhaps, to cope with the emotional responses it evokes.

Yet the relationship between this recognition of the constructed, conventional nature of the film and the children's emotional responses to it remains a complex one. At least on the basis of the parts of the film they chose to recount, it was clear that these girls particularly enjoyed the film's 'black' humour, and its sardonic attitude towards violence. Yet on the other hand, they also found the killer doll motif quite frightening:

*Martha:* I definitely wouldn't buy [a Chucky doll] for anyone. I wouldn't suggest getting one either. I'd be scared if I had one in my room.

*Lisa:* So would I / I wouldn't have a clown in my room though.

*Martha:* No, that's another thing, I'm really scared of clowns.

*Lisa:* Yeah, I think they're evil.

*Interviewer:* Have you seen *It*? [film based on a Stephen King novel about a demonic clown]

*Martha:* Oh my god, that is one of the worst. That is terrible!

As the discussion proceeds, the girls shift between the position of the distanced expert, who is able to note the conventional and constructed nature of the text, and that of the scared child, who is frightened of the dark and hides under the covers at night. While Martha is more inclined towards the position of expert, it is Lisa who 'confesses' early on in the discussion 'I can't even watch *Crimewatch UK* on my own', and who tends to pull in the opposite direction – albeit with some irony. As I indicate in more detail in subsequent chapters, this process of sharing responses seems to involve the more or less self-conscious adoption of particular emotional 'roles'. Arguments about 'effects', which I consider briefly below, also play a part in this process. In this case, for example, both girls argued that they would not let a child of theirs watch the film, on the grounds that it is too 'gruesome' – although it was clear that they themselves had seen it several years previously.

These shifts between emotional responses and distanced critique were also typical of the younger children's comments. Carol (12), for example, was generally very concerned to present herself as a seasoned horror fan, but sometimes seemed to be caught between the role of expert viewer and that of scared child:

*Carol*: It was a bit, when I was like, I used to play with dolls and stuff, and it was about a doll coming to life and he was really evil, so I used to have, it did scare me a bit I suppose 'cause I used to have bad dreams, that my dolls came to life and they were really evil and they were trying to kill me. But I suppose any young girl that watched it, and they played with dolls, they'd probably have the same nightmares. But it didn't really scare me. It wouldn't scare me now. I've seen the other two, they don't scare me.

Carol attempts to disclaim her fears, both by locating them well in the past, and by generalising them, most notably in the formulation 'any *young* girl'. Nevertheless, this involves her in some contradiction: having said that the film scared her, and acknowledged the more general potency of the killer doll motif, she then asserts that 'it didn't really scare me', and returns (in her final two sentences) from the past tense to the apparent security of the present.

These comments reveal a dynamic but ambiguous relationship between 'distress and delight',[27] which may be characteristic of responses to the genre. This was perhaps most aptly expressed in Alison's depiction of her own viewing behaviour:

*Alison (12)*: Yeah, I hide my eyes at everything though. I sit there with my hands over my eyes just peeking out, which is really, I know it's really stupid because you can still see, but I just feel safe. 'Cause you know how some people, they hug a pillow or something, well I have to hide my eyes, but I still watch it all with my eyes covered, and I can still remember the bit at the end of *Child's Play 3*, just when the doll's trying to kill everyone.

This characteristic pose of the horror viewer, peeking through the gaps in her fingers, reflects a desire to see but not to look – a desire on which the fundamental tensions and pleasures of the genre are based. Here too, there is a recognition that there is a choice of roles to be assumed – which is most apparent in Alison's comment about 'some people ...' – and a sense of distance from the role that she does actually assume – as in 'I know it's stupid, but ...'.

A number of related issues emerge from this brief reading of the children's accounts of *Child's Play 3*. Most obviously, there are questions about their emotional responses – for example, about the relationships between 'positive' and 'negative' emotions, and about their potential 'identification' with the characters. Yet these responses are clearly related to their understanding and interpretation of the film, and to their knowledge of the genre and of the production process. The children's judgments about modality, and the extent to which these might enable them to cope with their own emotional responses, are clearly central here. Finally, there are questions about the social context of the discussion, and about the ways in which children claim or define their identities through talk. All these issues are addressed in more detail in subsequent chapters.

## Talking facts

As I have noted, much of the pleasure of *Child's Play 3* for these children seemed to consist in its sardonic humour – in fact, in precisely the 'jokey attitude to death' that some psychologists have deemed so dangerous. Alan (9), for example, gave a detailed and almost deadpan account of the most violent incidents in the film, noting that he 'nearly died laughing' when Chucky was finally crushed to death. It might be easy to take this as evidence of the 'festering culture of video nastiness' that so exercised *The Times*'s editorial writer. In fact, of course, Alan was taking particular pleasure in his attempts to outrage the interviewer, as well as his less experienced friends. Yet even if we were to read such comments at face value, as evidence of some kind of 'desensitisation' to violence, it would clearly be unjustified to extend the argument from *fictional* violence to *real* violence. Alan may perhaps be as indifferent to violence in films and television as he claims, but this in itself tells us nothing about his attitude to violence in real life.

This distinction between real and fictional violence is particularly apparent when one contrasts the children's accounts of *Child's Play 3* with their observations on the media coverage of the Bulger case itself. Many children said that the press and television reports of the case had upset them a great deal: a number said they had cried, and one boy said that he had been unable to sleep after watching a documentary on the case. In contrast to their discussions of *Child's Play*, the children repeatedly related the events to their own experience. It was the fact that the killers were so close to them in age, or that they themselves had brothers or sisters of a similar age to James Bulger, that was so disturbing. For many, the media's concentration on the details of the murder had been particularly distressing: David (9), for example, described how he had been 'disgusted' by the image of the boy's shoe 'smothered with blood', while his friend Owen recalled how he had felt 'sick' when he saw the chalk mark the police had drawn around the body. A number of children recalled seeing the footage of the boys abducting James from the shopping centre, which had been captured by video surveillance cameras. Particularly for some of the younger children, these feelings of sorrow and disgust fed into an angry desire for revenge: like many of the newspapers, they argued that the sentence imposed on the killers was unduly lenient, and some even suggested capital punishment.

Nevertheless, there was some debate about whether such material should be shown at all. In a later series of interviews, we screened extracts from news coverage of the case, and from a reconstruction featured on ITV's *World In Action*. While the children acknowledged that they had been upset by this material, they also argued that it was important for it to be shown, not least as a warning to parents and to children: as Richard (9) put it, 'it could be like a message to the adults, like, don't leave your baby wandering around'. At the same time, this material provoked considerable fascination: despite their disgust, David and Owen wanted to see more of the reconstruction programme, while their classmates Emma and Miranda were disappointed that the court case had not been shown 'live'. On the other hand, most of them argued that it was inappropriate for *younger* children to see the full details of the case, on the grounds that it might provoke unnecessary fears, and that it should be screened at a time when they were less likely to be watching. Maintaining a balance here was seen to be a difficult but necessary task: as Emma (9) put it, children should be 'aware' of such threats, but not unduly 'scared'.

Jenny (12), however, argued that there had been too much coverage of the case, and objected to the use of detailed reconstructions. She described one programme which she said had made her feel particularly 'sick':

*Jenny:* They didn't have to say 'well, this is where they took them and this is the brick they used' ... and like the route. They could have shown a couple of pictures of the railway line, but they didn't have to show – I don't know what programme it was, but they had it, like the camera was like the eyes of one of the boys, or it was like the eyes of James, and they were doing like the camera looking up at these boys and then him walking along the road and then people like looking at him. They didn't have to do that.

Some of the fifteen-year-olds went further, criticising the media coverage of the case as manipulative and exploitative: Martha, for example, complained that the stories about the killers' families were an 'invasion of privacy' that had 'blown it out of proportion'. Others were highly cynical about the motives of television producers and newspaper editors: Lisa, in the same discussion group, argued that 'a lot of the programmes, and in the newspaper, just used it to get more people to watch their programmes and more people to buy their papers'. In some cases, the broader commentary on the case was condemned as misleading and unfair. Caroline (also 15), for example, recalled having seen a programme about two girls who had committed a murder over twenty years ago, and used this to challenge the assertions that had been made about the Bulger case: 'everyone was going, you know, it's the children of today, it's the parents of today, it's the teachers of today, but it had happened when all these adults that were saying it were our age ... it was like they were trying to blame us, you know, the society today'.

While the older children were often able to take this kind of dis-tanced, critical view, some of the younger children inevitably found it much harder to cope with what they had seen and heard. One mother talked about how she had attempted to deal with the questions of her younger son, aged six:

*Helen:* The Jamie Bulger thing, it's very hard. Jack actually came out with, a few weeks ago he said 'if I killed Owen, would you be cross?' ... he said 'would you be really really angry?' And I said 'but you wouldn't, it wouldn't happen'. 'But if I did?' And I said 'if you did I'm afraid it wouldn't be up to me, the police would come and take you away and lock you away for ever'. And this was obviously a follow-on from that [case]. I actually thought, that really took me back, and I was trying to think, well, is this just picking up some-thing that he's heard, or is this expressing the way he feels towards his brother? [*laughs*] ... They asked an awful lot of questions about that: 'when will those boys come out of prison?' 'Never.' 'Won't they ever see their mummies and daddies?' 'Yes, they'll see their mummies and daddies, but they'll never be able to go back in their bedrooms again.' And 'well, they didn't really kill that little boy, did they, because the train ran him over'. And, you know, then you say 'well, do I let that go, or do I say, well, they did actually, they're nasty evil little children' ... 'They didn't mean to do it' is another one. 'Did they mean to do it? Was it an accident?'

This contrast between these responses and those which arose in relation to *Child's Play 3* is obviously very striking. It may be that in the case of fictional material, the children's developing expertise with generic conventions and their knowledge of production processes offers a kind of defence against potential distress. Of course, this is not to suggest that such material merely loses its ability to provoke fear or shock the more it is seen: if it did so, there might be little pleasure to be gained from continuing to watch it. Nevertheless, there is very little one can actively *do* to change many of the things that provoke sorrow or worry or fear in real life, perhaps particularly in instances where there are no easy explanations. As Helen's partner argued:

*Peter:* With Rwanda or with famines, they can feel that they can do something about that, because they can save their milk bottle tops or they can run a stall at school and make money to give to people ... they can actually do something that for them is resolving the problem. But they can't actually do anything about the Jamie Bulger incident. They can't actually lock it away in a little compartment that makes it OK. It's very difficult to deal with things like that sometimes.

Yet for some of the older children, there was a sense in which sharing conventionalised expressions of emotion was itself seen as pointless. As Martha (15) suggested, the coverage of the case was upsetting, but it left her feeling powerless: 'it always makes you stop and think, you know, what is the world coming to and all that, but we can't do anything about it'.

Here again, these responses throw up a series of broader questions, which are addressed in more detail in later chapters. The central chapters of the book trace the contrasting ways in which children respond to factual and to fictional material, and how they learn to cope with them. The relationships between 'negative' emotional responses – such as the fear of crime – and the more positive desire for information are considered specifically in relation to news and crime reconstruction programmes. Finally, the question of how parents help children to cope with such responses, and their role as mediators of children's viewing, are considered in the penultimate chapter. As I shall argue, the emphasis on *fictional* material that typically characterises public debates about children and television may have led to a neglect of the more problematic aspects of *factual* programmes.

## Talking 'effects'

How did the children themselves perceive the arguments about media 'effects' which had surrounded the murder of James Bulger? Most were aware of the connections that had been drawn between *Child's Play 3* and the Bulger case, and few expressed any doubt that the killers had seen the film. Indeed, in some cases, they appeared to exaggerate or invent elements in their accounts of the film in order to reinforce those connections, and make it seem more violent or horrifying than it actually is. Martha (15), for example, described a scene in which Chucky kills a dustcart driver, suggesting that 'all his guts [were] hanging out' – which is certainly not the case. Most significantly, Jenny (15) asserted that Chucky 'throws bricks at him on the railway', which happened in the Bulger case but not in *Child's Play 3*.

Nevertheless, almost all the children were keen to refute the suggestion that the film alone had caused the boys to commit the crime. While some suggested that they might have 'got their ideas' from the film, most agreed that 'it must have been something else as well'. Most argued that the boys must have been 'a bit disturbed' or 'mental' to start with, perhaps because of their upbringing. As is typically the case in such discussions, 'effects' are readily displaced on to other people, thereby absolving the speaker from blame. In some instances, this is expressed in terms of differences of personality:

*Martin (12):* If someone's a bit weird [and] they watch programmes
   like that, they'll get ideas, and they'll do it. People who are normal
   just have a laugh at it. They might have a laugh at it, find it scary,
   then have a laugh at it, knowing it's not real.

In other cases, potential effects were displaced onto younger children: Elaine (12), for example, accepted that the film might 'give kids ideas', but was quick to claim 'it don't give *me* no ideas though'. Nevertheless, most children doubted that a single film, particularly a 'comedy' like *Child's Play 3*, would be able to exert such influence. Even Alan (9), who expressed such amusement at the scene in which Chucky got crushed, doubted that the film could 'send off special powers to go and kill someone'. Lisa (12) mocked the idea that the killers would have identified with a 'toy' – 'so they're thinking like if a toy can do it, they can do it, it's all right if they do it?'

Some of the older children explicitly challenged the hypocrisies of popular discourses about media 'effects'. Gavin (15) noted that newspaper reviews of the film published before the trial had described it as 'funny', and had recommended that readers only watch the 'gory stuff' at the end; while after the trial, they had described it as 'disgusting and sadistic'. Anthony (15) rejected the idea that there were similarities between the murder and the film, and argued, in common with a number of others, that 'it was just something to blame it on'.

If there was a concern here, it was not with the possibility that children would become violent as a result of watching such material, but rather that they might be distressed or 'messed up' by the more 'gruesome' aspects. Jane (15) argued strongly that the responsibility for control of such films should lie with parents, not with the censors. 'Why', she argued, 'should people who want to watch them have to suffer because people can't control their kids?'

The most powerful arguments here, however, came when the film was compared with other texts. Jane, for example, developed an interesting comparison with the popular children's comedy *Home Alone*:

*Jane:* They was wrong in banning it though, they was totally wrong. Because like that was the evil way, and if a kid was to watch that and watch *Home Alone*, he'd think in *Home Alone* it was OK to do that, but in *Child's Play* he knows it's wrong ... They make a joke of it as well [in *Home Alone*]. So like if a kid watched that, they'd say 'yeah, I can do that, it's a laugh'.

While the possibility that viewing might lead to violent behaviour is not refuted here, Jane's use of a film that most would regard as wholesome entertainment effectively reverses the terms of public debate.

Likewise, Caroline (15) implied that notions of cultural value may have been a factor here:

*Caroline:* The thing is, it's a bit hypocritical because there'll be people working for the BBC who in one programme before 9 o'clock will go 'oh no, violence is so bad on telly'. After 9 o'clock they'll go 'and here's a film about violence' ... And the other thing is, it's kind of, it seems that it's all right for them to have murder and stuff and child abuse in kind of quality books and plays or like you know kind of arty films, but as soon as it's even after 9 o'clock, as soon as it's on telly, it's bad. It's like there's murder in *Macbeth*, there's murder

in, and there's like child abuse in *Jane Eyre* and there's like all these
like books which we have to study. As soon as it's on telly they start
complaining about it, which is a bit bad.

Caroline went on to discuss the ways in which violence was often
seen to be acceptable in what she called 'arty films' on BBC2 –
'they think that that's art 'cause it's French and it's subtitled, but
really it's just like *Terminator* in French'.

These kinds of arguments about the negative effects of television
are addressed more specifically in the next chapter, although they
inevitably underlie a great deal of those that follow. As I shall indicate, such arguments are often used in ambivalent and contradictory ways, both by parents and by children. Yet the fact that so
many of these young people were prepared to reject a position that
is often presented as simply 'commonsense' – and to use such effective and powerful arguments in their support – surely points to the
need for a much more sophisticated and informed public debate on
these issues.

## Conclusion

As this chapter is written, the future implications of the new legislation on video classification contained within the Criminal Justice
Act remain far from certain.[28] Nevertheless, I have two predictions
to make. The first is that any such legislation will not make any
difference to either of the phenomena with which this controversy
has apparently been concerned. Attempting to restrict people's
access to video will not lead to a decrease in violent crime, since
the causes of crime are complex and largely endemic to contemporary societies. Neither will such legislation be capable of limiting
the viewing and distribution of violent films, which are likely to be
even more widely available through illegal sources. Neither 'problem' is likely to be resolved by such authoritarian solutions, much
less by a 'quick fix' of the kind that emerged in the wake of the
Bulger case.

My second prediction, on the other hand, is that the Bulger case
and *Child's Play 3* will enter the popular mythology of media

effects, alongside *Rambo* and the Hungerford massacre. It will continue to be cited as evidence of the pernicious influence of violent images upon the young, and as a justification for greater centralised control. In future debates, it will be taken as read that the killing of James Bulger was simply an enactment of the events of the film, and that the film itself is merely depraved and brutalising trash.

The notion that the media exert a powerful, damaging influence on young people often serves as a convenient – and in some ways reassuring – explanation of events that we may be unwilling to face. To argue that it was video that killed James Bulger is precisely to avoid the uncomfortable questions that such cases are bound to raise, and to sanction a dangerous form of complacency. Ultimately, 'video violence' is merely a cipher for much more fundamental anxieties about changes in the social order, perhaps particularly in the relationships between adults and children. This is not to suggest that there is no cause for concern – although it is to argue that many of the concerns are misplaced and confused, and that the solutions which are offered are unlikely to work. Looking directly at children's responses to such material, and attempting to understand them in their own terms, might perhaps provide the basis for a more constructive and effective approach.

## Notes

1 Smith (1994).
2 Smith (1994), pp. 2–7.
3 See, for example, Barker (1984), Drotner (1992).
4 See Webster (1989). In 1987, Michael Ryan shot sixteen people in the small town of Hungerford in southern England: his actions were widely explained as a result of his viewing of the film *Rambo*.
5 Webster (1989), p. 176.
6 David Alton is a Liberal Democrat MP, although his fundamentalist Catholic views (notably his opposition to abortion) have been controversial in his own party.
7 Barker (1984).
8 Margaret Ford, Deputy Director of the BBFC, suggested to me that the video distributors simply could not be bothered to make the cuts that would have enabled the video to be classified at a lower rating.
9 *The Times* is of course also owned by Rupert Murdoch.

10  See Segal and McIntosh (1992) for a critique of the feminist Labour Party
    line on these issues.
11  A somewhat more carefully-worded clause was eventually inserted in
    what became the Criminal Justice Act (1994).
12  Melanie Phillips's vicious attack on Guy Cumberbatch, who is probably
    the leading British researcher on the effects of television violence, was a
    particularly unpleasant example (*Observer*, 17 April 1994).
13  It is perhaps worth noting that of all the popular hypotheses about the
    effects of television violence, the notion that viewers are 'desensitised' to
    *real-life* violence is the one that is least adequately supported by research
    evidence: see Buckingham and Allerton (1995).
14  The 1980s research was published as Barlow and Hill (1984). This noto-
    rious study in fact fails to prove the connection between violent videos and
    aggressive behaviour: it merely proves that selected experts will say there
    is a connection if researchers ask them. See Brown (1984) for an account
    of the extraordinary circumstances under which this work was produced.
15  Medved (1992).
16  Except possibly Professors Sims and Melville Thomas, who both con-
    tributed to the earlier 'video nasties' study (Barlow and Hill, 1984).
17  Newson 'Video violence and the protection of children' (unpublished),
    page 3. (Subsequently published as Newson, 1994.)
18  Hagell and Newburn (1994). This study was commissioned by the British
    Board of Film Classification, in conjunction with the Broadcasting Stan-
    dards Council, the Independent Television Commission and the British
    Broadcasting Corporation
19  Pearson (1984); see also Drotner (1992).
20  For a discussion of the problems with this notion, see Sparks (1992), pages
    65–6; Cohen (1985).
21  As Martin Barker (1992) has noted, it is the *opponents* of censorship who
    seem more prone to panic in such situations.
22  Brophy (1986).
23  The film was eventually withdrawn, on request of the distributors, for
    some months after the trial – although I found no difficulty whatsoever in
    obtaining it. After the victorious claims that the film had been 'banned'
    following the passing of the Criminal Justice Act, it now appears to be back
    on general release.
24  For a detailed discussion of research on this issue, see Hodge and Tripp
    (1986) and Buckingham (1993a), Chapter 9.
25  See Bazalgette and Staples (1995). Interestingly, Kirschner is now chair-
    man of Hanna-Barbera, a fact which caused the *Daily Mirror* (26 Novem-
    ber 1994) to suggest that he now 'wields enormous power on the minds
    of millions of children around the world'.
26  This scene in fact occurs in the second film in the series.
27  This phrase derives from the work of Zillmann (e.g. 1980, Zillmann *et al.*
    1986), one of the very few psychologists to have begun to acknowledge

the dynamics of horror viewing.

28 The Act does appear to increase the power and discretion of the British Board of Film Classification, specifically in relation to material that might be seen by children; although BBFC head James Ferman has argued that it merely confirms its existing powers in statute.

# 3

# Emotions and 'effects'

## READING CHILDREN'S AND
## PARENTS' TALK

Talking about television is not a neutral activity. In discussing what we watch, and in making judgments about what we like and dislike, we are inevitably making claims about ourselves – about who we are, or indeed who we would like to be. What we say is inextricably bound up with the context in which we say it: consciously or unconsciously, we adjust what we say in the light of how we perceive our listeners, what we think they expect and what we would like them to believe about us. Talk is, in this sense, an unavoidably *social* act. It cannot be taken as straightforward evidence of what people 'really' think or feel or do.[1]

Researchers are, of course, traditionally suspicious of the reliability of 'self-reporting'. In the field of television research, for example, measures of the *amount* of viewing gained in this way are often seen to be invalid. People may tend to underestimate how much they watch, not only because they find it hard to recall or work out, but also because of the social stigma that is attached to viewing 'too much' television. Likewise, when it comes to identifying the actual programmes they have seen, people may well forget or deliberately attempt to deceive. Here again, we might expect people to overestimate their viewing of 'socially acceptable' programmes such as news and documentaries, and to play down others. Yet while viewing itself may be measured more accurately by other means, it is much harder to gain access to the ways in which people make meaning from what they watch. Measuring people's brain waves or perspiration, for example – which are the traditional psychological methods in this field – may give us a very accurate indication of *when* they get excited, but it ultimately tells us very little about *why*.

Talk should not therefore be dismissed as merely unreliable or inaccurate. On the contrary, it is largely through dialogue with others that the meanings and pleasures of viewing are established and defined. Yet in studying talk about television, we are inevitably studying a *social* process: we are looking at how people construct their relationships with others, and thereby attempt to define their own identities. This is equally true when it comes to discussing our emotional responses to what we watch. Talking about how we feel cannot be seen simply as a means of access to people's 'internal' psychological experiences. In describing their responses, speakers inevitably take on emotional 'roles', which in turn serve particular social or interpersonal functions. This is particularly apparent in the explicit statements that speakers make about themselves or about each other. 'I'm the kind of person who doesn't get scared.' 'I like to have a good cry.' 'You always work yourself up into a state about things.' 'My mum says I have a really vivid imagination.' These are everyday observations of the kind that were frequently made in our discussions, yet they are far from neutral descriptions – although there is a sense in which, if they are repeated often enough, they may come to produce the behaviour they purport merely to describe. Identity, then, is not something that is simply fixed or given: on the contrary, it is largely constructed through dialogue.

Research with young children has shown that the rules and conventions which govern the display of emotions, and the linguistic terms which are used to identify them, are learnt rather than innate. Children actively have to *learn* the appropriate ways of displaying emotion in different contexts; and they do this, for example, in response to other people's expectations, as a result of imitation, and in line with adult teaching. Even very young babies appear to take the cues for their emotional displays – such as crying – from their mothers' facial expressions. Yet as they are gradually 'socialised' into these forms of behaviour, this may in turn come to influence or determine the emotions they actually experience in the first place. Children are not, in this sense, simply learning how to express their feelings; they are also learning how to feel.[2]

Likewise, anthropological and historical studies have indicated that emotions vary across times and cultures – not just in terms of how they are expressed or communicated, but also how they are experienced.[3] These differences are not simply to do with the rules that govern emotional displays: they are also to do with what 'feeling' is seen to mean in the first place. Talking about one's emotions is thus not simply a matter of bringing private experiences into the public sphere, or a kind of neutral accounting of personal feelings. On the contrary, it is subject to cultural conventions, that serve in turn to construct the experience of emotion itself. Emotions are not simply 'expressed', but constituted by the social relationships in which they are enacted.

Nevertheless, as I have begun to indicate, this is far from being an inexorable process. Talking about our emotional responses should be seen as a social performance, a form of social conduct, which may involve the trying on of emotional 'roles'.[4] Displays of emotion involve the construction of what might be called 'narratives of the self' – that is, versions of one's identity that are formed in dialogue with others. The meaning of emotion, then, is established in the public realm of dialogue: it is bound to be provisional and inconsistent, and will often be contested. In a sense, therefore, we need to look at what emotions *do* in the context of social interactions, and at the ways in which the *rhetoric* of emotion serves to persuade others that one's claims to a particular identity are valid and legitimate.

In this chapter, I want to trace two particular dimensions of this process. The first concerns the ways in which children and parents talk about the 'effects' of television. As I shall argue, the concerns that are typically raised in these discussions are rather different from those which so frequently recur in public debates on the issue. Yet at the same time, this process almost invariably involves a kind of displacement onto 'other people' who are seen to be much more vulnerable to the influence of what they watch. It is this process of defining one's own identity – not least through distinguishing oneself from others – that forms the second aspect to be considered here. As I shall indicate, talking about 'effects', and about one's emotional responses to television, inevitably invokes broader assumptions about what is appropriate for children, and about how they develop – and, ultimately, about what it means to be a child.

## Media 'effects': the making of popular mythology

The controversy surrounding the James Bulger case was merely one instance of an ongoing debate about the effects of the media – a debate that is of course conducted not only in the press and on television, but also in everyday discussion. As we have seen, the evidence in such instances is often highly inadequate. Yet cases such as the murder of James Bulger almost invariably come to form part of what I have called the 'popular mythology' of media effects. It is this mythology, perhaps to a greater extent than the more equivocal evidence provided by academic research, that informs the dominant discourses about media effects, and hence the dominant arguments for regulating and intervening in children's viewing.

Almost inevitably, these discourses about media effects played a significant part in many of our discussions. Indeed, they often seemed to determine the expectations that parents and children brought with them. This was perhaps most apparent in an incident that occurred at the beginning of one of our interviews. Having initially met the children a couple of weeks previously, I began by asking them if they could remember what the research was about. Jane (15) confidently asserted, 'it's about that boy and that video' – making explicit an assumption that I suspect many of the older children and the parents would have shared. Of course, to ask children about what upsets them – what makes them frightened, disgusted, sad or worried – is likely to invite such arguments, even if (as I have indicated) our concerns were actually rather different. In fact, we rarely asked either parents or children directly about the 'effects' of television, nor did we introduce terms like 'violence'. Yet the topic often seemed to be inescapable.

At the same time, these arguments were often characterised by a considerable amount of ambivalence, qualification and inconsistency. Individuals did not simply take on the terms provided by public debates on the issue, but inflected and sometimes challenged them in the light of their own concerns and social purposes at the time. Yet the question of whether we ourselves are vulnerable to the effects of the media – and if not, then who is – formed a powerful hidden agenda in many of these discussions.

If the Bulger case emerged as a major preoccupation here, there were many further instances of this popular mythology of media effects. Nabeel (12), for example, himself an experienced viewer of horror films, reported how 'some people in Scotland' had seen *Nightmare on Elm Street*, and then stolen some 'doctor's knives' and proceeded to 'chase people round, trying to scratch them'. Michael and his friends (9) described an incident that had apparently also been blamed on the *Child's Play* films:

*Michael:* This little boy, he started driving a car, you remember on the news, where he started driving his car and then he burnt his house ... and then he went 'no more house for me, mummy, daddy' ... He was watching *Child's Play* ... this little baby, and then he started putting his house on fire.

*Peter:* Oh yeah ... He was on his own, he was watching *Child's Play* and his mum was out shopping and what happened is, when she came back the house was all on fire and he was inside ... You should have seen all the wreckage, it was all on the floor.

Adrian (15) related a similar incident, apparently incited by the MTV cartoon *Beavis and Butthead*, and his friend Anthony (also 15) went on to link this with the effects of a much earlier series, *Roots*:

*Adrian:* In America, like, after watching *Beavis and Butthead*, lots of houses got set on fire, and lots of little children died, so it influences them a lot ... it influences them in America.

*Interviewer:* But ... do you think that happens here too?

*Anthony:* It could happen. Because for instance, if you remember when *Roots* first came out, there was a lot of people going around beating up on different races afterwards ... And my mum was there one time and she saw a bunch of black people beating up on about five white people, and she said it was really wrong, you know what I mean? It was a movie of what happened a long, long time ago, and people took it and said 'right, I'm going to get my own back'... So I reckon probably films do influence people, or give people a bad attitude about certain things sometimes, you know what I'm saying?

*Interviewer:* Yeah / but not you?

*Anthony:* No, not me, 'cause I know it's a movie.

*Ghostwatch*, a spoof documentary that is discussed in more detail in Chapter 7, seemed to have generated a number of such stories:

*Angela (12):* They said in the news how they were suing the company who made it, or the director, because the woman had gone into labour because she got so scared, did you hear about that? But I think it was in the *Sun*, so I'm not sure ...

*Caroline (15):* Some boy committed suicide because he believed it ... It was this boy, I think he was about sixteen or seventeen, and he was in and out of homes and everything 'cause he was mad, and he used to, you know, see things like schizophrenics do. And he watched *Ghostwatch* and he reckoned the ghost had come out of the TV and into him, and he went mad, and he got worse and worse, and in the end, like because of that and other things, he committed suicide.

Finally, a number of children discussed concerns about the potential effects of computer games, which had emerged in the wake of the Bulger case, and in recent months had led to the introduction of a ratings system:

*Kevin (12):* I was watching a documentary about computer games and how they influence, um. And the kids, like they were playing *Streetfighter* and they started beating each other up, and they were filming it. But them kids, when they were being interviewed and everything, they, you know, looked quite normal, they were just hyperactive ... Coke used to do that to my friend. He drank it and then he'd go like that and be crazy.

Such stories could be seen as 'urban legends' – a form of contemporary folklore which may derive initially from the media, yet which rapidly enters into everyday oral culture.[5] In the process, what may have begun as an allegation or rumour rapidly gains the status of fact. In the act of retelling, the stories may become confused and amalgamated – as is probably the case with Michael and Peter's version of the *Child's Play* story. They may also be exaggerated, not least in order to confirm that the story is representative of a wider phenomenon: in Adrian's case, for example, 'lots' of houses have been set on fire and 'lots' of children have died, rather than the single instance reported in the press at the time.

However, these anecdotes are also related with a mix of authority and scepticism. On the one hand, many of the incidents are reported as though their truth were incontrovertible; and the fact that they were 'on the news' is frequently seen to guarantee this. Furthermore, particularly in the case of the *Beavis and Butthead* and *Child's Play* stories, the events appear to reinforce a wider set of concerns about inadequate parenting that (as I have noted) have become a recurrent preoccupation in these debates. The blame here implicitly lies as much with the parents who leave their children 'home alone', or who are irresponsible enough to let them watch such material, as it does with the media themselves.

On the other hand, as in their comments about the James Bulger case, the children often demonstrate considerable scepticism about some of the arguments, and indeed about the sources from which they are drawn. For example, Angela's scepticism about the *Sun* – a scepticism that is widely shared, not least by young people[6] – appears to qualify any faith in the facts; while Kevin directly challenges the evidence of an apparently objective scientific experiment reported in a documentary. Even where the children are not overtly sceptical, many of their stories seem to involve a degree of distance. They happen in another country (Scotland or America), or at another time (twenty years ago), or – most significantly – to people who are in various ways different from oneself. Thus, both Kevin and Caroline clearly suggest that the people concerned had other problems. Anthony (who is black himself) seems to imply that the black people who were influenced by *Roots* were somehow politically mistaken in attempting to take revenge for the past (and, indeed, a fictional version of the past) in the present; while in his final comment, he also explicitly distances himself from such effects. And in the case of Adrian and Michael, it is 'little kids' – indeed, a 'little baby' – who are seen to be most at risk.

Effects, it would appear, are things from which *other people* suffer. We ourselves – not least by virtue of our ability to talk rationally about such matters – are somehow immune. Most explicitly in the case of Anthony and Caroline's anecdotes, these other people are seen to be unable to distinguish between fiction and reality. They are somehow too immature or mentally inadequate to know any better. Yet for all Nabeel's concern about the influence of horror films, he watches them regularly himself; and while Angela acknowledged that she had been scared by *Ghostwatch*, she also expressed the wish to see it again. In defining effects – and perhaps particularly in displacing them onto 'other people' – we are also inevitably defining ourselves.

## Debating effects: parents' perspectives

In researching children's and parents' relationship with television, this popular mythology of media effects is bound to be influential, albeit often in contradictory ways. Certainly, when it came to the parents' discussions, there was much more speculation about negative effects than positive ones. While some parents were willing to acknowledge that television might provide opportunities for relaxation, only one suggested that it might have positive educational value – in this case, an African woman who argued that watching *Neighbours* had helped her daughter to improve her English. More common was the assertion that 'too much' television would have a negative effect on children's academic achievement. Thus, for example, it was argued that television took time away from homework and from family interaction. In some cases, there appeared to be a constant struggle to tear children away from the set, for fear that they would become 'hooked'. Yet significantly, this 'television zombies' argument was one that was employed almost exclusively by middle-class parents.

As I have argued in relation to earlier research, there is a sense in which such arguments are produced partly because it is assumed that this is what researchers want to hear. There is a 'social desirability bias' built in to the situation, particularly where the researchers themselves are middle-class academics – although one might expect much less deference in this respect from children than from adults.[7] As we have seen, discourses about the effects of television are often interwoven with discourses about the responsibilities of parents: unsupervised viewing is widely regarded as an indication of inadequate parenting, while letting your children watch horror movies is seen as tantamount to electronic child abuse. Parents may thus have a great deal to gain in this situation from being seen to criticise the powerful influence of the medium.

At the same time, some of the stronger claims about the effects of television were challenged by many parents. The arguments about the role of video in the Bulger case were cited by many, although most rejected them as exaggerated. In this case, and more broadly, the central issue was seen to be that of the children's 'background', and specifically the role of the parents. In some cases, parents who did express concern about the negative influence of television felt obliged to excuse themselves. 'Call me old-fashioned ...' said one mother, complaining about the influence of 'bad language' on 'impressionable people'. Another admitted to a 'bit of a phase' in which she had banned *Grange Hill* on the grounds that it showed children 'treating older people disrespectfully'; but she then retreated, saying 'that's very idealistic of me really'.

Such statements were often quite generalised, however. When it came to providing concrete *evidence* about the effects of television, the situation was rather less clear. A number of parents, for example, expressed concern about their children imitating anti-social or violent behaviour that they had seen on television – and, as we shall see later, a number of children admitted to having done so, at least when younger. In some instances, the parents had responded by banning particular programmes, such as violent cartoons and American wrestling shows. Yet parents' accounts of these incidents were often somewhat qualified.

Colin and Wendy, for example, expressed a number of such concerns in the case of their five-year-old son Gareth, both in relation to violence and, initially, in relation to the influence of Chris Evans, the manic host of Channel Four's *Big Breakfast*:

*Wendy*: I think when you're a bit older, you can look at the / lunatic behaviour from another angle, and see that this person is actually supposed to be mature. However, Chris Evans, he wanders around and he pulls stupid faces, and if a child walked into a room and behaved like Chris Evans behaves, everyone would think he was totally precocious and absolutely wouldn't want them in the room. And I don't particularly want my kids copying his behaviour. Um / whereas on the television in front of millions of people, maybe he can be amusing.

*Interviewer*: Have they done that, then?

*Wendy*: Um / Louise [7] wouldn't, but Gareth could be encouraged to / copy that kind of / He hasn't actually, but apart from that ...

*Wendy*: But violence and aggression, there are, with Louise, she's never shown any inclination to be influenced by television particularly, but Gareth, there was a time with the *Turtles* –

*Colin*: And *Karate Kid*, things like that, I mean –

*Wendy*: They send him crazy.

*Colin*: He's bouncing around for days afterwards, karate kicking and, all of these karate things, it really does influence ...

*Interviewer*: What did you do about that?

*Wendy*: Well, while he was doing it, 'cause he's actually quite good at it, and I have told him when he's a bit older, he can do karate, because I think it's a good idea, and they're both going to do it. And while he's not injuring himself or anyone else, then it's OK. He did seem to be slightly more in control. But he does copy it, doesn't he? ... He doesn't ever make contact with anything or anybody, he just stands in the room and kicks his legs up and all this, you know.

*Colin*: He does make contact, he beats the hell out of his imaginary assailants.

*Wendy*: Well, that's right, but he doesn't try to kick me or you or Louise ...

*Interviewer*: So if *Karate Kid* was on again, or there was a sequel on, would that worry you?

*Colin*: No.

*Wendy*: No, he could watch it, but then / you know, we do talk to him
and say 'if you don't calm down, that's it, you're just going to have
to sit down, or you go to bed' or whatever. And we say that if
you're going to do this, explain the ethics a bit behind the karate,
and / it doesn't, that sort of thing doesn't particularly worry me.

As middle-class parents, Colin and Wendy are fluent in what might
be termed the 'elaborated' discourse about the effects of television,
for example in their use of terms like 'influence' and 'aggression'.
Yet as the discussion proceeds, the evidence they adduce in support of these arguments begins to falter. Gareth 'could be encouraged' to imitate Chris Evans, but actually he hasn't been. He has
indeed copied the moves from *Teenage Mutant Ninja Turtles* and
*Karate Kid*, but it is acknowledged that he himself understands the
distinction between real violence and fantasy play. Thus, he has
'*imaginary* assailants' rather than real ones (such as members of
the family), and is careful not to 'make contact'. In a section omitted, Wendy talks about Gareth's allergies to certain foods, which
might have contributed to his state of 'excitement': 'he's obviously
got that within him, and certain things trigger it off'. Particularly
by contrast with Louise, Gareth's reactions to television are implicitly traced to a prior 'inclination'. While Wendy repeatedly
expresses concern about the problems of 'influence' and 'copying',
by the very end of the extract she has retracted these claims somewhat: it is as though the more generalised arguments cannot be
sustained, at least in relation to one's own children.

At the same time, there is a recurrent concern here with defining what constitutes 'appropriate' behaviour for children, and
simultaneously with identifying the characteristics of a 'mature'
approach to television viewing. Chris Evans is a problem precisely
for this reason: his behaviour is implicitly defined as immature, and
yet as leading to 'precocious' (in other words, prematurely adult)
behaviour. While viewers who are 'a bit older' might be able to see
through this performance, children are by implication assumed to
take it literally. As a result, they may be inclined to transgress the
boundaries between television and reality – to take something that

might be 'amusing' at a safe distance, 'on the television in front of millions of people', into the more intimate context of everyday life, and the gaze of other adults (hence the concern about what '*everyone* would think ...'). Likewise, the mature viewer of *Karate Kid* is the one who appreciates the 'ethics' behind the practice of martial arts, and the parents try to reinforce this – although elsewhere in the discussion, Colin is somewhat sceptical about whether any of this teaching 'gets in'. And while untutored karate on the living room carpet is unacceptable, institutionalised classes are certainly 'a good thing' – not least, perhaps, because they provide a means of 'controlling' and channelling these potentially anti-social energies.

Of course, there is a kind of stigma attached to acknowledging your children's problems, which might lead parents to underestimate their difficulties – at least in the context of a research interview. Colin and Wendy were possibly somewhat embarrassed that Gareth had behaved a little wildly as we had arrived, and commented upon the fact. Yet Gareth's problematic behaviour is largely situated in the past. *Turtles* had in fact been banned in this household eighteen months previously, Wendy said, 'because *then* he couldn't control himself'. By contrast, in copying the moves from *Karate Kid*, Gareth is now seen to be 'slightly more in control' – and karate itself has meanwhile been redefined in educational terms.

Interestingly, towards the very end of this discussion, it was Colin who introduced yet another instance of the 'popular mythology' identified above – in this case, a news story about two boys who had wrecked a neighbour's house, allegedly because they had seen a similar event on the game show *Finders Keepers*. Colin argued that, in this case, the boys' father had been 'trying to blame somebody else other than himself', and that the arguments about media effects had been 'blown up out of all proportion': why, he asked, hadn't the other two million children who had seen that programme wrecked their neighbour's houses? 'What you've got', Colin argued, 'is two naughty children, who need to be dealt with by their parents.' Wendy was somewhat more cautious, arguing that the boys had been 'given the idea' by the programme, although she eventually came to the same conclusion:

*Wendy:* I think that some children are / more susceptible, more influenced by what they see than others, and maybe some children can't easily distinguish between fact and fiction. But I have to agree with Colin that really um / responsibility has to come back to the children and the parents and the family.

While Wendy is concerned to sustain her broader position about the effects of television, she ultimately deflects the 'problem' elsewhere. As this indicates, discourses about media effects are often intimately connected with discourses about parenting – which, in this context, are used by parents to define their own position. Thus, there is little doubt that Colin regards himself as a parent who would 'deal with' naughty children; or that Wendy would see herself as taking 'responsibility' for controlling such behaviour. The parents and children who represent the primary cause for concern here are, almost by definition, 'other people'.

Similar anecdotes featured in other interviews with parents. Yet while a number expressed such concerns about imitative violence, there was never any doubt that this was regarded by all concerned as 'play fighting'. Jill, for example, a working-class single parent, described very similar scenes of her two daughters (aged five and seven) imitating *Teenage Mutant Ninja Turtles*, which she said drove her 'up the wall' – although she also said that she would not have attempted to ban the programme, for fear of the 'murders' and 'uproar' that would have resulted. Ultimately, she too concluded that this was not an issue she took particularly seriously:

*Jill:* If it's violence / I don't know why, I just don't seem to, it doesn't seem to bother me. It's like I said to you, with *Teenage Mutant*, it annoys me that they copy it, because they don't have to copy it, they know they don't have to copy it / and if it's violent it doesn't really bother me, because they should know / better than to copy, they should know better than to copy it, 'cause they should know reality from what's on the telly. They should know it.

The repeated use of the word 'should' here is interesting: it implies, not so much a moral injunction, as a normative statement of what children at this age are expected to know. Jill does voice concern elsewhere in the discussion over this distinction between fiction and reality. For example, she expresses her irritation at the way in which Colette (5) kicks Donna (7) when they are watching *Turtles*: 'she thinks it's funny, and it isn't funny'. Likewise, she describes Donna talking to her Little Mermaid doll in an accent that is 'totally American' – which, she argues, is clear evidence that children 'copy' what they have seen, albeit of course in the context of fantasy play. Yet here she seems to imply a trust in her children's ability to sort out this distinction, and hence to 'know better'.

Yet if Jill did not appear particularly concerned about violence, she was extremely concerned about the possibility of her children viewing horror films. Donna had in fact seen such films at a friend's house, and Jill had now taken steps to prevent this happening again. We revisit this family in a later chapter; but what is important to note here is the way in which the parents' concerns about the potential dangers of television and video seemed to focus much more on the possibility of their children being upset or frightened than on the likelihood of imitation. While *other people's* children might become disrespectful or violent as a result of watching television, the primary concern in relation to your *own* children was much more to do with such emotional distress. Indeed, even where we referred directly to such arguments, the question was often turned around, as it was by these working-class parents:

*Interviewer:* There's a lot of stuff about all this in the newspapers and on TV at the moment, about video, so-called video nasties. What do you think of all that?

*Liz:* Well, some videos are nasty. I don't think children should be allowed, I don't think *adults* should be allowed to see them, let alone children.

*Interviewer:* I mean, you talked about *Nightmare on Elm Street*, you wouldn't let them watch that. Why wouldn't you let them watch that particular film?

*Liz:* 'Cause it frightened me, so I would expect it to frighten them.

*Mark:* Frighten them not to go to sleep.

*Liz:* Yeah, they wouldn't go to sleep.

*Interviewer:* So it's because it would frighten them, rather than because it might make them go out and ...

*Liz:* I don't think they would do that.

*Mark:* They'd be awake all night, that's all. [*laughter*]

Significantly, the term 'video nasty' was defined here not as a film that will incite children to commit imitative crimes, but as one that might frighten them – and, indeed, adults too. Mark and Liz also referred to their children's tendency to copy the fighting in the *Turtles* and in *Karate Kid*, but rejected the idea that this would be translated into real violence. Like the other parents, they saw it as mildly annoying, but ultimately of little consequence. As Liz concluded, using the classic rationalisation:

*Liz:* It's not just the telly, I don't think. It must be the way they've been brought up. And, you know, I can't see that just watching a programme is going to make you want to go out and do horrible things. It never happened to me.

Almost inevitably, then, the issue of media effects was a recurrent theme in these interviews. Many parents were familiar with the received wisdom of politicians and media commentators, and a number referred to specific incidents drawn from the 'popular mythology' of media effects. Yet the role such discourses played was a complex and ambiguous one. In some ways, the interview forced parents to set these generalised discourses about media effects against their experiences with their own children, which often told a rather different story. Many parents directly refuted the more extreme arguments about the power of the media, particularly in relation to imitative violence, on the grounds that they were exaggerated and simplistic. This is not to suggest that they felt the media had little effect on children – although it is to say that their concerns were rather different from those that are so regularly rehearsed in public debate.

Yet as frequently happens in such discussions, negative effects tended to be displaced onto 'other people', in such a way as to define the self. Inadequate or irresponsible parents, who failed to control their children's viewing (and indeed their behaviour as a whole), were implicitly seen to be the *real* cause of the problem. In the act of identifying and distinguishing themselves from such people, the parents effectively sought to demonstrate their own adequacy and responsibility. If 'they' are the bad parents, then we must be the good ones. Such arguments clearly move beyond the limited view of television as a kind of free-floating effects machine. They explicitly locate the effects of the medium within the broader context of the family and of other social relationships. Yet in doing so, they often seem to end up simply replacing one form of demonology with another: 'bad media' come to be replaced by 'bad parents'.

## Debating effects: children's perspectives

These expressions of concern about the damaging effects of the media were not, however, confined to parents. Perhaps unsurprisingly, few of the children raised questions about the impact of television on educational achievement or on levels of social interaction. Where the 'television zombies' argument did arise, it was largely mocked and rejected. Yet there were similar discussions of the possibility that television might encourage violence and other forms of anti-social behaviour.[8]

While some children did express generalised concerns about the dangers of imitative behaviour, much of the evidence that was provided here was distinctly bizarre. Emma (12), for example, reported that her brother had seen a television programme featuring a baby pouring milk on his head, and had gone on to do the same to her neighbour. Barry (6) described how he had bitten his sister with a 'fake *Jaws* head' after watching the film, although he reassured us that 'it's only a play'. Thomas (9) gave an elaborate account of 'war play' partly copied from a war film:

*Thomas*: I saw this war film and it was 'PG' and there was lots of
  ·fighting but you didn't see the people getting killed, so I thought it   ·
   was a bit boring. But there's lots of wars, so I sort of did that, and
   I pretended after the film … to do the same sort of thing. Then I pretended I was the only one left, I was crawling back from this huge

war and I was the only one left so I went [*gestures*] sort of like playing but I do it myself ... and I pretend to talk to the captain and he
goes 'well done, mission complete!'

On one level, Thomas could be said to have a taste for violence –
and despite the fact that the film is a 'PG' (which for him implies
higher status), it is clearly not sufficiently gory to satisfy this. Yet
his account is nevertheless humorous and almost self-mocking. It
is clear that this is 'pretend' play (the word is used three times), in
which Thomas is able to step out of role and switch characters in
order to congratulate himself on the successful completion of his
mission.

This tone is characteristic of most of the children's accounts of
this kind of imitative behaviour. Here, a group of twelve-year-old
boys moves on from discussing the Bulger case to consider the distinction between 'play' violence and real violence:

*Interviewer:* Mike, you were saying about the videos, you said people
were saying it was all to do with the videos. What do you think of
that? ...

*Kevin:* I don't think you get influenced by them. If you're really stupid
– you must be to get influenced by violent videos.

*Mike:* Like you said, they might have been disturbed or something and
they saw him [Chucky] running around and [said] 'oh, this looks
easy'.

*Interviewer:* Do you think there might be some truth in it?

*Mike:* Yeah.

*Kevin:* But if you watch *Superman* you're not going to try and fly or
anything ...

*Mike:* Yeah, but it's not possible for you to fly, but it is possible for you
to kill. 'Cause when my brothers watch a martial arts film, they,
after it's finished they get up and start fighting.

*Kevin:* [*laughing*] Yeah, I do that as well, do it to my big brother. But
I don't want to kill him or anything, just break his back.

*Mike:* They start fighting.

*Kevin:* Just having a bit of fun.

*Interviewer: [to Mike]* What, seriously fighting, hurting each other?

*Mike:* It's funny [*laughing*]. I just sit there and watch it, it's like another film to me.

*Kevin:* This is a real person, though, I know it was a real person they were fighting against. But they wouldn't do it to a little kid, would they?

As in many similar accounts, the distinction between fiction and reality is maintained consistently here, and there is a good deal of laughter at the absurdity of 'play fighting'. Like their peers, the boys are clear that this kind of fighting is just 'a bit of fun' (and with some exceptions, as we have seen, it is largely boys who are seen to behave in this way). While Mike is more prepared to consider the possibility that violent videos might influence people, he clearly distinguishes between the 'funny' behaviour of his brothers and that of the killers of James Bulger. As in the other observations on the Bulger case discussed in the previous chapter, it is agreed that television is only likely to influence people who are 'stupid' or 'disturbed' in the first place. Nevertheless, Mike implies that he himself is not involved in these fights – although this would seem implausible, since he is one of four brothers who are very close in age. Interestingly, Mike's parents had encouraged their children to attend martial arts classes, and were distinct enthusiasts for such films: and as a result, they were able to make clear distinctions between the inauthentic fighting in films like *Karate Kid* and what they described as the more authentic and technically correct approach of stars like Steven Seagal. (This family is considered in more detail in Chapter 8.) By contrast, Kevin admits to such 'play fighting' himself, and displays the kind of sardonic humour I have argued is common in films like *Child's Play*: he doesn't want to kill his brother, 'just break his back'.

These children were not alone in questioning received notions about the effects of television. Indeed, such arguments were often mocked or directly challenged. For example, Martha (15) and her friends satirised the people who had written to women's magazines and to the BBC's *Points of View* complaining about the spoof documentary *Ghostwatch*, even though they admitted that they themselves had found it very frightening at the time: 'those people are just really gone in the head. It's like that woman who claims she got abducted and raped by aliens. I mean, come on, you know, get a life!'

In one middle-class family, clear lines of battle appeared to have been drawn on this issue. The parents, who were both teachers, were the most consistent critics of television among all those we interviewed. While there was some concern here about 'bad language', their main arguments were to do with the ways in which television viewing might detract from more worthwhile activities, and from their daughters' school work – although both parents were bound to admit that this did not actually seem to have occurred. The father in particular argued that watching soap operas would become 'habit-forming', a 'Pavlovian behaviour pattern', that would not 'lead the children on'. While he was prepared to concede that *EastEnders* was occasionally 'quite well-written', he condemned *Neighbours* as 'trashy' and sometimes 'absolute rubbish'- although he acknowledged that his criticisms had been ignored, and the programme remained 'sacrosanct in the house'.

Meanwhile, their children parodied and rejected these arguments:

*Caroline (15):* They're teachers, and when they've been taught at teacher training college all about [how] the psychology of kids is, you know, related to TV, and they take it all so much to heart that they think we're going to go mad if we watch five seconds of violent TV ...

*Elise (16):* They probably think, when they see things that criticise TV, they tend to believe it more than – You know, they wouldn't go and look for the opposing view to it, like they would for everything else. They're more prepared to accept that TV's bad.

*Caroline:* They trust, like there's one TV critic they trust as if he's God or something ...

*Elise:* They listen to what their friends say as well.

*Caroline:* Their friends are all like teachers, 'cause they work in a school, all these teachers have been going to their training days and heard about how bad, how they should discourage kids from TV ...

*Elise:* But if they go out and like talk about something and like 80% of them think TV's bad for kids, then they'll all come home with the view suddenly that TV's bad.

In criticising their parents' views, Elise and Caroline also seek to challenge the reliability of their sources. Far from deferring to the academic evidence they suspect their parents have acquired from their professional training, they suggest that it may be biased in itself, and that their parents may have read it uncritically and selectively. Likewise, their inclination to trust a single TV critic is seen to be somehow inconsistent with the balanced approach they display elsewhere. Of course, this account serves to present these young women as more discriminating and less prejudiced than their parents: by implication, they would not see themselves as being so easily swayed by peer pressure as they suggest their parents are. In the tone of the discussion, there is a reversal of conventional notions of maturity, in which the parents almost become infantilised: they seem to suffer from a naive and credulous 'trust' in authority, and take all these ideas 'so much to heart'.

At the same time, these young women did not wholly reject their parents' attempts to protect them from the negative influence of television. In discussing *Ghostwatch*, for instance, Elise argued that their father might have been right to turn the programme off: 'I think they're honestly worried that it would disturb us.' Significantly, however, the form of protection that is seen to be justified here relates not to the dangers of imitative behaviour nor to questions of cultural value, but again to the possibility that children might be upset or frightened by what they watch.

This distinction was apparent in a number of discussions, particularly with the older children. While these children frequently refuted arguments about imitative behaviour, for example in the case of the Bulger murder, they also argued that they would prevent their own children from watching material that was too horrific. Even Trevor (15), who ridiculed the idea that children would copy violent behaviour from the screen, and declared that he would impose no restrictions on his own children, admitted that he would not relish the prospect of having a child who was unable to sleep because of what he had seen: 'if I think, yeah, he's going to be up at like 12 o'clock, "I can't sleep", getting in bed with me, sort of thing, [I'd say] "no, man, you ain't watching it"'. In this instance, as in a number of others, the children effectively turned the issue around, as we saw the parents Mark and Liz do earlier in their discussion of 'video nasties'. They were indeed concerned about 'effects', but effects of a different kind from those that have tended to monopolise public debate.

## In search of the 'other'

As I have argued, dominant discourses about media effects are primarily concerned with 'other people'. Imitative violence, which is the central focus of anxiety, is largely seen to arise from the inability to distinguish between fiction and reality. People who copy what they see are regarded as somehow too immature, or simply too stupid, to know any better. In expressing our concern about these matters, we implicitly position ourselves as somehow immune from such afflictions. Using the discourse thus in itself appears to guarantee our ability to 'see through' television, and thereby distinguishes us from the dupes who cannot.

In discussing the question of media effects, both parents and children tended to distance themselves from this concern about imitative violence – and, as I have indicated, found some difficulty in accepting the evidence that was adduced to support it. Even where parents described how their children had copied violent programmes, or children themselves admitted this, the crucial distinction between fact and fiction, or between 'real' violence and play, was consistently maintained. In practice, the concern about 'effects' was much more to do with the dangers of children being frightened, upset or disturbed by what they watched – in other words, with what I have suggested might more usefully be termed 'responses' rather than 'effects'. As we shall see in subsequent chapters, children were often very willing to talk about their own experience of such responses. Being scared or worried or moved to.

tears by a television programme was by no means an uncommon event – although it was also one that was often seen as pleasurable, or at least necessary. Yet even here, there was often a sense in which the *real* problem lay elsewhere, with other people who, for whatever reason, were seen to be less able to cope with such experiences.

Nevertheless, the attempt to identify these 'other people' is often problematic. Elite discourses about popular culture have of course traditionally been infused with patronising assumptions about the audience, based largely on a contempt for women and other members of the 'lower orders'.[9] Criticisms of 'women's genres' such as soap opera, for example, have often defined the typical viewer as intellectually and emotionally inadequate – a view that is in fact prefigured by much earlier concerns about the dangerous habit of novel-reading.[10] Likewise, anxieties about popular theatre and literature in Victorian times, and more recently about the reading of comics, were partly motivated by a fear of the urban working-classes, who were seen to be irrational and inadequately socialised.[11] As we shall see in the following chapter, the horror film is another genre that has attracted similar assumptions about the pathological weaknesses of its audience.

Throughout such debates, therefore, it is particular groups of people who are seen to be at risk, rather than the population at large; as in the trial of D. H. Lawrence's *Lady Chatterley's Lover*, where the primary concern was not that one might be depraved or offended by such material oneself, but that it might fall into the hands of one's wife or one's servants. When challenged, the upstanding citizens who take it upon themselves to police violence and obscenity will invariably assert that *they* are not affected by what they have seen – although the irony, of course, is that they are far from alone in making such claims. 'Other people' are, by definition, always elsewhere.

In fact, there is very little evidence from these interviews that these 'other people' were conceived in terms of social differences such as class or gender, even where one might have expected this to be the case. Thomas (9), an upper-middle-class boy, assumed a working-class accent in imitating his next door neighbour's son, who he said regularly watched films like *Terminator 2*, and would fast-forward past the Video Standards Council warning at the beginning of the tape. (Meanwhile, Thomas himself had seen *Nightmare on Elm Street* several years previously, and was able to recall a good deal of it.) Yet this was an isolated example. While some of the middle-class parents were quite ready to criticise other parents who they felt were much too lax, this was primarily seen to be a matter of differing attitudes rather than social class. When we eventually met *those* parents – or at least the ones who we suspected had been the target of some criticism on these grounds – they turned out to be just as middle-class as their critics.

Gender occasionally surfaced as an issue here, albeit with problematic consequences. As I have indicated, it was almost exclusively boys who were seen to be more likely to copy violent behaviour from the screen, although this fact was rarely explicitly discussed. As some feminist critics have argued, the 'problem' of violence is of course largely the problem of *male* violence, although this generally goes unspoken.[12] In a couple of instances, we asked directly whether boys were more likely to be interested in horror films. Carol (12) strongly refuted the suggestion, saying 'I *hate* sexism!' – although her friend Sonia disagreed, arguing that while girls might watch horror for the characters and the storyline (as she claimed to do herself), boys were more interested in the blood and violence. Martha and Lisa (15) suggested that men liked to *think* they could cope more easily with horror – it was a 'big macho sort of thing' – although they disputed whether this was actually the case. In a few instances, parents noted similar differences between male and female children, both in terms of their tastes and their ability to 'handle' distressing material; but these were generally put down to differences in 'personality' rather than gender. These broader social differences are considered in more detail in later chapters; although it is important to note here that they were rarely made explicit by parents or by children themselves.

In fact, the arguments that were most frequently used in this context were those that invoked essentially *psychological* discourses of individual personality or (as we shall see in a moment) of child development. As I have already noted, many of the children disputed popular arguments about the 'power' of moving images on the grounds that this would only apply to people who were already 'disturbed' or 'weird'. Only people who were 'sick in the head' – or otherwise 'totally thick' – were likely to confuse fiction and reality, and hence to copy what they had seen. When it came to emotional responses such as fright, a number of parents noted that some children were more 'sensitive' or 'easily upset' than others – and some children defined themselves in this way. Yet this was predominantly explained in terms of the inexorable logic of personality, as a matter of 'what kind of person' you are. Some people, one mother argued, enjoy horror films, just as some people enjoy roller coaster rides, while others avoid them: 'all kids are different', she argued, 'it's the way the person is, how they cope with things'.

Yet in attempting to explain the powerful effects of television on 'other people' – and, in the process, to explain one's own apparent immunity from such effects – it was the notion of 'maturity' that was the most recurrent preoccupation here. In many respects, of course, this reflects the ways in which children are typically constructed within the dominant discourses on such issues. Both in academic research and in popular debate, it is children who are defined as quintessentially 'other', and who have historically been seen to be most at risk from the negative effects of the media. This in turn reflects dominant constructions of childhood itself, whereby children are largely defined in terms of what they lack – that is, in terms of their inability (or unwillingness) to conform to adult norms. Vulnerability, ignorance, and irrationality are seen as part of the inherent condition of childhood.[13]

Yet if adults often attempt to displace such concerns onto children, children themselves will frequently engage in the same kind of displacement.[14] Of course, ten-year-olds will say, we aren't influenced by what we watch: it's only little kids who copy what they see. We might have done this when we were much younger, but we certainly don't do it now. And yet, when you talk to these little kids, the story is the same. There is a kind of infinite regression here, as children in each age group claim to have already attained the age of reason some years previously.

Thus, even the older children who most strongly challenged

such arguments about media effects were inclined to make exceptions for 'little kids' – both in general terms, and specifically in relation to their younger siblings. It was generally accepted that younger children would be much more likely to imitate what they saw, and also to be scared or upset. The hospital drama *Casualty*, for example, was a programme that was frequently seen to be inappropriate for younger viewers on both grounds. Mehtap (12) suggested that it might encourage children to 'cut themselves with knives' on the grounds that 'they might think it's fun'; while Andrea (9) argued that 'it might scare some of the younger ones'. In this case, however, the arguments also seemed to be informed by a sense of the 'adult' status of the programme. Emma (9), for example, suspected that younger children might not understand the complicated plots, since 'it's quite a grown-up programme'. Significantly, all these girls appeared to have struggled with their parents in order to be allowed to watch the programme. Yet while Mehtap felt that such arguments did not apply to her, she nevertheless agreed that an age limit was necessary:

*Mehtap:* I thought it was stupid, what she was saying ... I watched it all the time when she was not around. And my big sister, she used to leave her to look after me, like I just begged her to let me watch it. I don't really, I wasn't that stupid when I was little. I wouldn't [copy] it, but my mum thought I would do it.

*Interviewer:* Do you think people will go out, do you think little kids will go out and do that?

*Mehtap:* Yeah, if they're less than four, I think.

Mehtap is not alone in her ability to evade her parents' regulation, although this does not mean that she sees it as unjustified in general. As this example shows, some very fine distinctions were often made here in the attempt to exclude oneself from the category of children at risk.

Nevertheless, there was occasionally some difficulty here among the younger children, for whom the competition for 'adult' status seemed to conflict with the concern about effects – and whose viewing was likely to be more strictly regulated in the first place. Here, a group of six- and seven-year-old boys have been discussing the difference between the film and the cartoon version of *Ghost-busters*: while the former is agreed to be 'scary' in places, the latter is not.

*Alan:* Well, [the cartoon] is something like for threes, fours and fives.

*Sam:* I watch it, I watch it.

*Alan:* And six, but not for sevens.

*Sam:* And you're seven.

*Alan:* Yeah, I'm seven.

*Sam:* And I'm six.

*Interviewer:* So when you get to seven, you think the film is probably better then?

*Alan:* Yeah, it's better.

*Sam:* I like both of them, and I like the film better, but my mum never lets us see it ... I'm allowed to watch some 'PG's.

*Alan:* 'PG's, I'm allowed to watch every single 'PG'.

*Interviewer:* Well, you've seen *Terminator*. Isn't *Terminator* a '15'?

*Alan:* Yeah.

*Sam:* And it's an '18', Alan, and you watch it and you're only about seven / it's an '18', and so is *Beetlejuice* and so is ... Well, *Doctor Who* isn't. [*Alan laughs*]

This is, of course, a familiar game, and Alan is clearly on the winning side. He goes on to boast, for example, about how he is allowed to watch *Gremlins* and *Batman Returns* and 'all these scary things' – although he claims to do so in the company of his father, without his mother's knowledge. At the same time, there is more than a hint of disapproval in Sam's comment 'you watch it and you're only about seven', which is reinforced by the way in which he inflates and then repeats the censorship ratings of these films (which Alan had mentioned earlier). As this example shows, the children were highly aware of such categories, and frequently used them as a means of calibrating their maturity as viewers – although, as in this case, the system often appeared to have precisely the opposite effect of that intended, by investing status in the forbidden texts.[15]

The way in which Alan situates the boundary here – just below his own age – is also typical of the younger children. As one rises through the age groups, these distinctions seemed to shift, yet they also became less problematic. For the nine-year-olds, the boundary often appeared to be set at around seven or eight, while for the twelve-year-olds, it was more like nine or ten – although there were distinctions between different kinds of material here. Some of the older children argued that these decisions should not be based simply on age, although boundaries were drawn in these terms here too. Martha (15), for example, claimed to have watched horror films since she was 'about ten', and argued that whether this was appropriate for a child should depend on 'what kind of person they are'. Nevertheless, she ultimately accepted the need for some distinctions on the grounds of age: 'I don't think, unless they're exceptionally mature, I don't think under ten it's suitable, I really don't' – although in situating the boundary at exactly the point at which she claims to have started watching such material herself, Martha continues to define 'other people' as the ones who are most at risk.

Thus, while they were subject to considerable amounts of negotiation, most children clearly subscribed to what might be termed 'lay theories' of development,[16] which defined what was seen as 'appropriate' for different age groups, and indeed for their own. Owen (9), for example, expressed this directly, arguing that his parents were right to prevent him from watching horror films on the grounds that 'they don't want my mind to get filled with stuff that isn't *for my age*' (my emphasis). As in the case of the girls' discussion of *Casualty*, the definition of what it means to be an 'adult' or a 'child', or a child of a certain age, is established partly in response to their parents' regulation of their viewing. The discourse and the knowledge that it claims to embody are thus intimately connected with the operation of power.[17]

The issue of modality (or perceived reality) – which may be partly what is at stake in Alan's distinction between the cartoon and the more graphic film of *Ghostbusters* – was a central dimension in this process. Younger children were seen to be more at risk of confusing television and reality because of their lack of experience, both of television and of life itself. Thus, Martha (15) argued that 'five- or six-year-olds' would be scared of *Terminator 2*: 'when you're that young, you don't know that it's all in the movies, and you don't sit there and think that there's about six or seven cameras around some stupid robot prancing about'. Likewise, Alan and Martha argued that younger children would be misled by scenes in *Casualty*, because they had little experience of such events in real life:

*Alan:* It's probably because they're thinking ... it's not real. Even though it does look real to older people, they're probably thinking that's not a real accident happening.

*Martha:* 'Cause they haven't seen, at such a young age they wouldn't have been open to um – They would probably have had a graze on my knee or something like that, so they wouldn't think that things like that really existed. Like if someone walked into some / they probably think the toxic stuff was water, and thinking if you walked into water, that could never happen, it's just made up, 'cause they don't know what happens in the world.

As this implies, however, the problem is not simply that younger children will believe that television is real when it is not: in this case, it is precisely the opposite. Older people, according to Alan, know that television is not real, even though it might *look* real; and yet, as Martha points out, they have enough experience of the world to know what *might* possibly happen. While younger children understand that such programmes are 'made up', it is argued, and hence not *real*, they are not yet able to make reliable judgments about how accurately they represent the real world – or, in other words, how *realistic* they are. As this implies, judgments about modality depend not only upon a knowledge of the medium (for example, about the fact that programmes are 'made up', or that they use special effects), but also upon knowledge of the world in general. Indeed, as Alan and Martha suggest, there may be a sense in which knowledge of the medium *alone* may be actively misleading.

Yet the consequences of this in terms of imitation, or indeed in terms of children becoming scared or upset, were seen to be ambiguous. Jessica (12), for example, argued that younger children were in fact *less* likely to be scared by crime reconstruction programmes such as *Crimewatch* for this reason: 'they don't really know what it's about, so they're just watching and they just shrug it off, but *now* we know what it's about'. A couple of parents made similar arguments about their children's responses to distressing material on the news: Sarah, for example, argued that the reports of the James Bulger case had been less upsetting to her seven-year-old than to her nine-year-old because they were 'less realistic to younger ones'. On the other hand, Laura and Lisa (15) argued that, at least in relation to sex, children were not as 'stupid' as adults sometimes assumed: as Lisa argued, 'I watched films when I was young and I can remember my mum thinking that I can't be really watching it and I don't know what's going on, but I knew *exactly* what was going on.'

Nevertheless, while many children rejected the idea that *they* should be prevented from watching such material, this was seen to be justified for younger ones. Anthony (15), for example, was a self-declared fan of what he himself termed 'violent' films, and provided several enthusiastic and detailed descriptions of gory killings and dismemberings. Yet while he claimed that this material had not caused *him* to become more violent, when it came to his little sister, he argued that a degree of protection was required:

*Anthony:* My mum don't want no violent blood spurting in front of [my] baby sister ... She might, for instance a film I saw where some guy stabs a knife in his hand, I wouldn't want me to be sitting at the table doing my homework or something, and my sister see it on TV and stab me in the hand or something, thinking it's all right because she seen it on the TV.

The slightly comical tone of Anthony's anecdote recurred in other accounts of younger siblings. Nabeel (12), for example, described how his younger sister would hide behind a pillow while watching horror films, while Carol (12) laughed at how her sister had screamed her way through *The Lost Boys*. Such anecdotes clearly served to position the speakers themselves on the side of the mature adults. On the other hand, Andrea (9) reported how her mother had 'kept on clutching at me' during *Jurassic Park*; and more than one parent reported how their children would discourage them from viewing a particular programme on the grounds that *they* might be upset.

Yet even where it was regarded as inappropriate to ban programmes, other forms of parental intervention were sometimes seen to be necessary. Alison and Jenny (12) had an extended debate about the screening of violent scenes from the Los Angeles riots, and in particular whether they should be shown in the early evening news or held over until the *News at Ten*. Jenny argued that it could be useful for parents to see such material first, and then to mediate it to their children: 'if adults understand it ... if they hear it and they say "oh, they're all over-reacting", the adult can like explain what happened'.

Like a number of others, these girls argued that scheduling should be used to restrict children's access to such material – although, as in the case of censorship categories, the situation was often more ambiguous in practice. In the case of *Ghostwatch*, for example, it was generally agreed that the programme should not have been trailed in order to attract younger viewers, and that it was wise to schedule it later in the evening. Martha (15) expressed concern that younger children had seen it none the less – although Lisa pointed out that Martha herself had been frightened, and she could hardly have been expected to be in bed. One group of fifteen-year-old girls commented on the way in which *Casualty* had 'gone off' since it had been rescheduled at an earlier time, and toned down in response to complaints: they argued that it had been much better as a 'grown-up programme', rather than the 'family programme' it had become. Nevertheless, these forms of regulation and parental intervention were generally seen to be justified by children themselves – although significantly in relation to *younger* children, rather than to themselves. As we shall see in Chapters 6 and 7, there was often a further tension in relation to factual programmes and realist dramas such as *Casualty*: while it was agreed that children should be protected, it was also asserted that they would have to learn to 'face the facts' and indeed to make their own choices about what they should watch.

As I have indicated, then, anxieties about the effects of television are typically displaced onto 'other people'. By expressing our concerns about such matters, we are effectively claiming that the real focus of concern is elsewhere, and that we ourselves are somehow immune. The discourse enables its users to distinguish themselves from 'others' who are seen to be less intellectually capable or emotionally stable – in effect, less 'mature' – than they are, and hence more vulnerable to influence. Not only for adults, but also for children, these 'others' are predominantly defined as those younger than oneself. The discourse thus constructs an *object* of concern – 'children and television' – and embodies a system of *knowledge* about that object – a set of assertions, for example, about what is 'appropriate' for children of different ages – that is used to regulate behaviour. And since age differences are such a highly significant dimension of power relationships within contemporary societies – and, of course, such a contested one – there is likely to be a great deal invested in such debates.

Thus, while many children acknowledged the need for parents to regulate their children's viewing, and for centralised controls over what children should be allowed to watch, they were often reluctant to extend this argument to themselves. Adult power was seen as necessary and acceptable, as long as it wasn't applied to *them*. In developing such arguments, they were in a sense adopting an 'adult' position, and hence a position of power. Yet in the context of a research interview, in response to questions from a 'concerned' adult academic, such statements should of course be regarded with scepticism. As we shall see (particularly in Chapter 8), while adult regulation may sometimes be accepted in principle, it is often contested in practice.

**Narratives of the self**

This process of defining and distancing oneself from the 'other' was not only manifested in relation to younger children. It was also achieved by telling stories about one's younger self. Yet while such stories are often used to explain the roots of one's current state, the children here seemed to be very concerned to draw a line between past and present, as though they were describing somebody fundamentally different from themselves. Thus, these anecdotes were often related in tones of mockery or wry amusement – as instances of how silly or illogical or cute little kids can often be. And of course, in distinguishing ourselves from the person we used to be, we are inevitably identifying who we are now.

Thus, a number of children described how they had been frightened or upset by television programmes they had seen when very young. No less than three children at different ages described how they had been scared by *The Wizard of Oz*; and hiding behind the sofa during *Doctor Who* was a tradition that appeared to have been carried through into another generation. Yet there were also descriptions of being frightened by Fairy Liquid commercials, by the cartoon rabbit Hartley Hare and by the educational series *Look and Read*. Even some of the 'tough' fifteen-year-old boys had stories about how they had been frightened by the child catcher in *Chitty Chitty Bang Bang*, or had cried over the ending of *Mary Poppins*. While they are sometimes hard to evaluate, these anecdotes do illustrate the highly *unpredictable* nature of what can upset children – and were sometimes seen in this way by children themselves. As Jessica (12) said, in relation to *Doctor Who*, 'now you see they're selling off all the [models] and you think "why was I scared of *that*?!"'

As this implies, these anecdotes were frequently infused with a considerable degree of irony and self-deprecating humour. Jenny (15), for example, described how she had cried over a number of Disney cartoons, and had recently refused to watch *Bambi* again for this reason:

*Jenny: The Fox and the Hound*, I stood up in the cinema, started shouting, it was really sad ... I was only little, but I stood up and I goes *'Don't leave him!'* Everyone was looking at me, and I was crying.

Yet Jenny and her friends were also quite self-conscious about this process. For example, they described how they had been frightened and disgusted when viewing the anti-nuclear drama *Threads* in a Humanities lesson; yet they argued that the boys in their class would be unlikely to admit to such responses, even though they may have felt them. In fact, the boys whom I interviewed later seemed to have responded in a very similar way. Yet for the girls, being 'emotional' was seen as part of the condition of being female: as Sarah put it, girls were more likely to 'open up', and Jane agreed, 'girls cry more at things like that'. Yet if gender was part of their explanation, age also played a significant part, particularly in relation to horror films:

*Sarah:* I always used to get scared if I saw a horror film, I'd be scared to go in my bedroom and my brother would grab me from under the bed, start jumping into the bed. But you still feel that, even if you're not as scared as when you was little ...

*Interviewer:* So why is it that you're not so scared now?

*Jenny:* It's because you're brought up, and you can tell it's not true, this isn't real, so you don't have to think about it, it's just in someone's mind, it can't happen, none of this will ever happen, so ...

*Jane:* Specially when you're little, you believe everything / Santa Claus.

*Sarah:* When I was little I believed in Snow White and the Seven Dwarves. You believe in anything, even if it isn't true.

*Jenny:* You say, 'oh yeah, there's Santa Claus', and you think 'yeah! Santa Claus!' So if somebody says 'oh look, there's Freddy', you think 'oh my God, there's Freddy!' and you wet yourself. [*laughter*]

*Interviewer:* So you think when you're younger, you're just more kind of disposed to believe in those sorts of things?

*Jenny:* Yeah, 'cause you look up to adults. And if an adult, there's someone bigger than you, not necessarily a parent, says 'yeah, there's a Freddy', you're going to believe them, because they say like, 'yes, there's a Santa Claus'.

The logic of the analogy here is certainly questionable. Despite the popularity of *Nightmare on Elm Street* masks and gloves, you would be unlikely to encounter somebody claiming to be Freddy Kruger in your local shopping centre; and most children will have outgrown a belief in Santa Claus well before they stand a chance of encountering Freddy on film. Yet what is interesting, and symptomatic of a number of such accounts, is the way in which the girls

construct a narrative of development, in which their past confusions are now left well behind. Earlier on, Jenny in particular had
been keen to reject any suggestion that she was scared by horror
films – while she admitted that she used to be scared of the *Nightmare on Elm Street* films, 'now', she said, 'you sit there watching it
and you think "oh my God, this is hilarious!"' The girls agreed
that, while Freddy might still be what Jenny called 'a threatening
figure' – and, in this extract, that they still felt somewhat scared of
him – they had fundamentally 'grown up' and moved beyond such
things.

Here again, the confusions of younger children are seen to relate
to modality – to the failure to distinguish between fiction and reality. The ability to make modality judgments – to identify the special effects, for example, or to reassure yourself (as Jenny does) with
the belief that 'this would never happen' – is regarded as a significant strategy for coping with the unpleasurable aspects of genres
such as horror, although as we shall see it is sometimes an
ambiguous one. Credulity is, in Jenny's terms, part of the condition
of being a child, and was often seen in this way by other children.
Martin (12), for example, spoke about how he had been frightened
when he first saw *Aliens 2*, although he was quick to reassure us
that this was well in the past:

*Martin:* I had to sleep with the lamp on for a week, and then now, at
   this age, I think that's pretty dumb. 'Cause it couldn't, well it might
   happen, there might be some far away planet, but it's not going to
   happen in my lifetime, I don't think ...

*Interviewer:* So it sounds like you were more frightened afterwards?

*Martin:* Yeah, I wouldn't be *now*, it was just like what I was *then*.

In persistently marking the difference between 'now' and 'then',
Martin emphasises the distance from his earlier self: 'that age' is,
by definition, vastly different from 'this age'.

Significantly, however, the confusions Jenny identifies also relate
to adult power, and the possibility that adults (or at least 'bigger'
people) might actively seek to delude children in order to enjoy the
experience of their own superior knowledge. Likewise, the notion

of the 'younger self' is defined partly in relation to adult regulation. One group of twelve-year-old girls, who identified themselves as horror fans, described this as follows:

*Donna:* As I've got older, because when I've got a horror movie, like everyone comes round that I know and we all go and sit down and watch it, and my mum just leaves me. But she sends my little sister up to bed.

*Interviewer:* How old's your sister?

*Donna:* She's nine. / But like when I was little she always used to say 'go to bed, go to bed!' ...

*Sonia:* Now, if I said to my mum I wanted to get a horror movie out, she'll just say 'which one?' and she'll ask what the age group [classification] is. My mum will let me watch some '18' films, 'cause some of them ain't that scary ...

*Carol:* If there's swearing in it, my mum says 'turn it off!' and goes 'go upstairs!' or 'put another video on *now!*' [*laughter*]

These girls' different experiences of regulation led them to position themselves in rather different ways here. Yet these differences were also a result of the different composition of their families. In general, Carol's parents were keener to regulate her viewing, and although she appeared to have seen a great many horror films, she had had to resort to some elaborate forms of deception in order to do so. She also had a sister who was barely a year younger, yet whom she referred to as 'my little sister', clearly attempting to distinguish herself as older and more mature. Significantly, she was the most forceful of the three girls in her attempts to assert that horror films really weren't all that scary: as she said in an earlier discussion, 'we're older, and we can take that kind of stuff'. By contrast, Donna is able to enjoy privileges that are denied to her sister, who is three years younger, and is clearly perceived as less of a threat. Both Donna and Sonia had significantly older siblings, which meant that, unlike Carol, they were not in the 'front line' of the attempt to challenge their parents' authority. It was perhaps for this reason that their need to proclaim their own maturity seemed much less urgent than it was for Carol. As this implies, how children choose to position themselves – as more or less 'adult' or 'childish' – clearly depends upon their social experience, and on the negotiation of power in the home.

## Conclusion

These anecdotes about one's past, and the narratives of personal development that they often entail, are of course not the only means by which individuals seek to define and construct their own identity in talk. Yet perhaps particularly for children, they are bound to be among the most explicit and the most significant. In all societies, children's lives are largely bounded by the constraints imposed by adults – yet these constraints exist not merely in order to sustain adult power, but also in the name of protecting and pre- serving a particular definition of childhood. It is perhaps not too surprising, therefore, that the discourses which serve to define and construct 'the child' should be subject to such intense and often contradictory negotiations.

Since television is such a significant part of children's lives, argu- ments about its effects are inevitably an important part of this broader process. In questioning the ways in which the notion of 'effects' is often used, it has not been my intention merely to sug- gest that television has no effects, or even that it has only beneficial effects. On the contrary, my argument is that the notion of 'cause and effect' is itself a particular discursive construction, which in turn serves particular social purposes. In the kinds of discussions I have been analysing here, for example, the discourse of media effects is often used to support children's attempts to lay claim to 'adult' status, or otherwise to distance themselves from what are seen to be 'childish' inadequacies – although these attempts are inevitably fraught with difficulty. The discourse of media effects is, as I have shown, intimately bound up with the construction of knowledge and with the operation of social power.

These broader arguments also apply to the ways in which chil- dren talk about their own emotional responses to television – and they clearly point to the need for some caution in interpreting what they have to say. People's assertions that they were scared or upset by what they watched, or indeed that they were not, should not be taken at face value. We need to trace the complex relationships between 'emotions' and the social contexts in which they are experienced and discussed; and to be aware of the possibility of multiple interpretations. Yet analysed in this way, children's accounts of their emotional responses can provide a rich and often surprising indication of the complex roles that television plays in their lives.

## Notes

1 The arguments in this section are largely drawn from discourse analysis: see, for example, Potter and Wetherell (1987) and Edwards and Potter (1992). For a development of this approach in relation to children and television, see Buckingham (1993a), particularly Chapters 3 and 4.
2 For examples of this research, see Lewis and Saarni (1985).
3 See, for example, Harré (1986) and Lutz and Abu-Lughod (1990).
4 See Warner (1986), Sarbin (1986) and Averill (1986).
5 See Brunvand (1983).
6 See Buckingham (1992).
7 Buckingham (1993a) Chapter 5; see also Holman and Braithwaite (1982).
8 For a parallel discussion, in relation to data from an earlier project, see Buckingham (1995).
9 This is well-documented, for example by Gans (1974), Huyssens (1984), Ross (1989) and many others.
10 See, for example, Allen (1985) and Hobson (1982).
11 See Barker (1989).
12 See, for example, Campbell (1993) and Segal (1987). It is interesting to note, however, that a number of the precedents that were quoted in relation to the Bulger case involved female killers, most notably Mary Bell.
13 See Bazalgette and Buckingham (1995).
14 For parallel findings, see Cullingford (1984) and Buckingham (1987).
15 See J. Wood (1993).
16 For a wider consideration of 'lay theories' of psychology, see Furnham (1988).
17 This argument derives from the work of Michel Foucault (e.g. 1980). For a more extended discussion of the way in which these discursive positions are marked out in discussions of television, see Buckingham (1994).

# 4

# Distress and delight

## CHILDREN'S EXPERIENCE
## OF HORROR

The origins of the horror genre – and the concerns that have consistently surrounded it – can be traced back to ancient times. Centuries before the violent excesses of the Gothic novel or the morbid preoccupations of Jacobean drama, the Greek philosopher Plato was warning against the dangers of popular representations of the underworld in the dramatic poetry of his time.[1] Of course, stories of Hades and the after-life were a central part of ancient Greek cosmology, and of the moral order on which social stability was based. Yet Plato was concerned that the 'thrill of terror' induced by such tales of ghosts and corpses would encourage moral weaknesses in the future rulers of his ideal Republic, undermining their 'fighting spirit' and making them 'more nervous and less tough than they should be'. At the same time, he argued, the power of dramatic representation could encourage young people to identify with evil characters, and hence to imitate their actions. And as is well-known, he ultimately proposed that such material should be banned.

Contemporary research and public debate have reflected similar concerns about the negative effects of horror. In the James Bulger case, the principal preoccupation was with the dangers of imitative violence – although, as we have seen, there was considerable confusion about the precise mechanism by which such behaviour was assumed to be caused. The murderers were seen to suffer from an unhealthy form of 'identification' – although whether this was with the killers of Chucky, or with the demonic doll himself, remains unclear. The emotional charge of identification was seen to be so powerful and so lasting that it was able to override the killers' ability to distinguish between fiction and reality, long after they had supposedly seen the film. More broadly, it was argued that films like *Child's Play 3* would cultivate a callous and superficial attitude to violence in real life: they would 'desensitise' children to violence, at the same time as 'triggering' copycat behaviour. The films were 'brutalising', yet they would also encourage children to 'brutalise' others.

The problems with these arguments are not simply to do with their inherent contradictions, however. What they signally fail to explain is why people might *choose* to watch such 'vile' material in the first place – and even if one's ultimate intention is to prevent such activity, this would seem to be a logical place to begin. Yet this question is most frequently answered by recourse to a pathological conception of the viewer. From this perspective, a taste for horror is seen to be a symptom of immaturity, lack of intelligence, or more fundamental personality defects. In the end, it would seem, people only watch this stuff because there's something fundamentally wrong with them.

This pathological conception of the viewer is writ large in early research into the effects of horror. Mary Preston's clinical study of children's reactions to 'movie horrors and radio crime', published in *The Journal of Pediatrics* in 1941, offers a symptomatic example.[2] Despite its scientific credentials, the study is suffused with moralistic descriptions of the movies and shows, and of the (implicitly working-class) families who enjoy them. Using the dietary metaphors common in such arguments, Preston describes the movies as 'an indigestible mass forced into [the child's] mental craw', thereby producing 'severe mental indigestion'. 'Addicts' of such material are seen to be unhealthy, nervous, fearful and morbid, and to suffer from 'sleep disturbances' and 'eating disturbances'. They have an 'intense craving for thrills' and abnormal fears of kidnapping and family breakdown. Much of the blame for their state of mind is placed on indifferent parents, and on the 'Fathers and Big Brothers [who] break the monotony of their drab existence by the loudest blood-and-thunder they can manage'. Radio crime and movie horrors are seen as a training in killing and delinquency: they lead to 'an atrophy of such desirable emotions as sympathy and compression [*sic*] towards those in distress'. Ultimately, Preston concludes, repeated exposure to such material leaves 'scar tissue in the form of a hardness, an intense selfishness, even mercilessness': children effectively become the killers and monsters they behold.

These arguments may be unsurprising given the time at which they were written, although they would not have been out of place in many of the newspapers in 1994. Nevertheless, they do illustrate some of the unspoken assumptions that underlie a great deal of more recent psychological research in this field.[3] Such research frequently begins from the assumption that viewers are somehow socially or mentally inadequate, and that horror offers a form of 'sensation seeking' that compensates for the limitations of their pathetic lives. Horror fans, it would seem, are people with problems. Meanwhile, the genre itself is seen as homogeneous and undifferentiated, and there is little attempt to consider the form or content of specific films. There is no recognition of the ways in which children might learn to make sense of the genre, to distinguish between reality and fiction, or to cope with the experiences it offers. Above all, there is no serious consideration of the *pleasures* that must largely explain why viewers choose to watch horror in the first place.

## Approaching the child audience

Arguments about the effects of horror, both in research and in public debate, have tended to characterise its audience in a way that is both patronising and based on an unspoken fear. The 'typical' horror fan is generally seen as a male, working-class adolescent, whose psychological inadequacies find their outlet in an unhealthy appetite for the sick and the depraved. Yet while he is often despised, the fan is also perceived as a threat. Like all potential 'delinquents', he is seen to be in a state of uncertain transition between two disciplinary sites – that of childhood in the home and that of adulthood in the workplace. In pandering to these adolescents' anti-social fantasies and desires, horror may disrupt the smooth process of 'secondary socialisation' and contribute to wider forms of social and psychological deviance.[4]

Yet, as is frequently the case in debates about popular media, the 'bad object' is one that critics of all persuasions can usefully join in condemning. On the moral right, there are those who have accused horror of cultivating an unhealthy preoccupation with Satanism – again, particularly among adolescent boys.[5] Alternatively, from a popular feminist perspective, the taste for horror among this group is seen as further confirmation of their unacceptable misogyny and patriarchal violence. Again, it is through the process of 'identification' with the (male) killer, rather than with the suffering of his victims (presumed to be female), that the negative effects of the genre are seen to operate. Meanwhile, although there are certainly 'horror buffs', it is still quite rare for such films to be subjected to serious critical scrutiny. In the case of *Child's Play 3*, for example, there was very little attempt to refute the suggestion that the film was merely worthless trash – and thus, by implication, that anyone who might enjoy it would be suffering from a serious lack of good taste. Perhaps to a greater extent than any other group of fans, horror enthusiasts are stigmatised from all sides.

Yet the audience for horror is wider than this would suggest. In this research, the genre was popular across the whole range of our sample – with boys and girls, with working-class and middle-class children, and with all age groups from six to sixteen. As we shall see, there were many children who did not like such films, and would go out of their way to avoid them; yet there were also many who actively sought them out. Particularly among the younger children, horror films clearly possessed considerable 'adult' status, and there was a great deal to be gained from claiming to have seen them – even when one had only heard about them from older children, or merely seen a trailer. This much was apparent from the excited whispering and exchanges of looks that often accompanied the initial mention of such films. Yet from their retellings of horror narratives, it was clear that a number of six-year-olds had in fact seen and in some cases actively enjoyed such films. Most children who had developed a taste for the genre at least claimed to have begun their viewing at around the age of eight or nine, and in some cases significantly earlier. Meanwhile, as in the discussions of *Child's Play 3* quoted in Chapter 2, some of the most enthusiastic horror fans were girls – a phenomenon which would be confirmed by the current popularity with early teenage girls of the 'Point Horror' book series.[6] While they remain a minority, the girls' pleasure in horror raises significant questions about the experience of a genre which is all too easily identified as inherently 'male'.

## Horror talk

Talking about horror was an activity that most of the children found very enjoyable in itself, even if their feelings at the point of viewing often appeared to have been rather different. The situation of being withdrawn in groups from their regular lessons and invited to talk about dismembered bodies, flesh-eating monsters and bloodsucking vampires was ripe with all sorts of pleasurable and subversive possibilities. Of course, for many different reasons, they may have been inclined to exaggerate or to underplay or otherwise to misrepresent their experiences. As I have argued, such talk must be seen as a social performance, and not as some form of intimate confession of one's 'true feelings'. Indeed, as I hope to indicate, the social dimensions of the experience are central to its meaning.

The flavour of some of this material, and of the children's engagement with it, is perhaps best conveyed by beginning with some of their retellings of films that they described either as particularly scary and disgusting, or as particularly enjoyable – and, of course, the two often coincide. Here, Liam (12) is describing a film called *Brain Dead*, which he says gave him a nightmare:

*Liam:* It was scary a little bit, 'cause there was this man and he had some horrible like monkey, it never looked like a monkey, it looked really like an ugly beast, and like he was carrying it on his shoulder, and there was these African men chasing him ... And like he got bit on his head, his back and his wrist ... and then like the car stopped, they booted the man off, and they got some like axe, and they chopped off his wrist, then they chopped off his arms, then they chopped off his head, and when they chopped off his head, all blood flew in the air, and then it said like 'Brain Dead'.

Anthony (15), whose graphic comments feature a number of times in this chapter, described his reactions to an unidentified horror film as follows:

*Anthony:* After I've seen it on the TV, I see it in my mind, you know what I mean, like if something like where some girl like, bulges out of her belly and her belly all starts to mess up in the film, and then this kind of like clone kind of thing comes out, it looked like a maggot kind of thing, but it looked big and it was like all gooey and wet and nasty ... the effects were like in *Aliens*, you know what I mean, and it was like, just like some white kind of see-through-ish kind of nasty, it was all jelly, floppy, kind of blops out of her belly, you know what I mean, and she'd dropped dead. And when I went to bed that night, that's all I could see, like blopping out of her belly.

Finally, Lisa (15) describes another unidentified film:

*Lisa:* It was on quite late / couple of Saturdays ago and this woman went into a hospital and someone got strangled and one of the patients went around killing all the doctors and he had this scalpel thing, he just slashed this man's face open, and then the woman had to go, and she was on the run from him, she had to hide in all these bodies, all in embalming fluid, and she had to hide under one, it was just disgusting ... it wasn't that scary but it was just really foul because there were so many half decomposed bodies.

Although they are taken from longer accounts, these extracts illustrate many of the central preoccupations of these discussions, and much of their tone. Retellings of films – sometimes directly invited by the interviewer, but often not – tended to go directly to the key scenes of bodily violation, torture and visceral disgust, with very little by way of explanation or pretext. Questions of characterisation, motivation or narrative plausibility were rarely allowed to get in the way of the ripping out of brains, the tearing of flesh, the spilling of blood and the severing of heads and limbs.

Rather like late-night ghost stories told around the camp fire, these accounts are clearly delivered for an audience. The ability to scare or disgust your listeners guarantees your right to hold the floor; and there is therefore little to be gained from explaining why any of these horrific events might be happening. Furthermore, in the context of a research interview, with a comparatively 'serious' academic interviewer and an audience of one's peers, such accounts may carry a certain subversive charge. In this situation, horror is not an innocent or neutral topic of conversation. On the contrary, this is material which children know they are legally forbidden to obtain, and which they know violates fundamental taboos on violence and bodily display. As in the case of discussions of media effects, what you choose to say about horror – and indeed, to choose to talk about it at all – serves to 'position' you, and hence to define your identity, in a particular way.

### 'It's scary, but I didn't get scared'

Thus, there was often a considerable degree of ambivalence here. On the one hand, the children's accounts of horror films were often accompanied by a good deal of disclaiming. Many vehemently denied that they were scared by horror films, and occasionally mocked those who said they were. As in the accounts described in Chapter 3, many were keen to assert that they were no longer scared by such material, even if they had been when they were younger. Some of the retellings were delivered in a studied deadpan tone, as if to guarantee the speaker's fearlessness.

To some extent, of course, these protestations can be seen as genuine. As we shall see, the children often made quite fine distinctions between films that attempted and failed to be frightening, and those that genuinely succeeded. Yet there were often hesitations and contradictions here. Liam, for example, in the quotation above, says that the film was a 'little bit' scary, although he had earlier admitted that it had given him nightmares. Similarly, Carol (12), began her account of *Pet Sematary* with the claim 'it's quite scary'; yet once she had recounted various stabbings and returns from the dead, concluded 'it's a bit boring, it's not scary at all really, hardly ...'. Even more clearly, Kemal (12) concluded his account of an unidentified film he called 'one of my best scariest films' by saying: 'that's a great film, it's scary but I didn't get scared'. To some extent, this ambivalence could be seen as a function of the social situation. To claim that you were scared is, in some respects, an admission of weakness; yet to argue that the film is not scary is to undermine its 'adult' status, and hence your own status as a viewer. Nevertheless, the ambivalence encapsulated in Kemal's comment is also, I shall argue, indicative of the tensions that are involved in the experience of viewing itself.

To be sure, there is plenty of evidence here that horror films do frighten children, and that such responses are occasionally quite lasting. Anthony, quoted above, described his experience of *The Exorcist* (a film still banned from video distribution in Britain) as follows:

*Anthony:* I'm not quite sure which one I saw, right, but it messed me up, man ... One of them, like where an exorcist was coming into the church or something, and the Jesus was on the cross, and you know where, like they've got the dummy of it yeah, the dummy only turned round and opened his eyes wide and the door flapped open and everything's coming in, and I thought whoa! and my heart was going BANG! ... I'll tell you something, right, for about three weeks, every night I thought about that, and I thought, 'no, man!' And when the girl was sticking the cross in herself, yeah, she was all bleeding and nastiness like that, and she's shouting out 'F me, F me, F me' [*sic*], I thought all that nastiness, you know / it's just not done, you don't think of that stuff naturally, you know what I mean, someone needs help if they're thinking of those sort of things, the way I see it, person needs a lot of help because there's something wrong in their mind.

Anthony's reaction to this film is a combination of shock and disgust; although it is also motivated by a more deep-rooted anxiety about the idea of the supernatural that was shared by a number of other children. The sense in which the film is seen to violate taboos, relating both to sexuality and to violence, is neatly encapsulated in his remark 'it's just not done'. Interestingly, however, Anthony attempts to distance himself from the experience by reflecting upon the *agency* and intentions of the film's producers, and by condemning them as somehow 'unnatural'.[7]

Experiences of this kind were described by many of the children interviewed here. In many cases, they seemed to crystallise around a single decontextualised image or scene, as in the descriptions provided by Lisa and Anthony above. Thus, Liam (12) recounted a scene from *Damien: Omen 2* in which a woman died after looking at a horrific statue of a crow; Elizabeth (9) described how she had cried over an image of a goblin in an unidentified film; while Hannah (6) said she had had nightmares as a result of seeing a poster of Freddy from *Nightmare on Elm Street* on a family visit to a restaurant. According to psychologists, it is these kinds of grotesque images that are likely to be particularly frightening for younger children;[8] although (as we have already seen) such experiences were also comparatively frequent among the oldest age group in our sample.

In some cases, these images had been seen almost accidentally, for example as children wandered into the living room late at night. Yet however fleeting, they often seemed to be impossible to forget. Stella (9) talked about how the 'picture' of a scary film would stay in her head; while Mehtap (12) talked about how she would 'rewind' the images in her head when she went to bed at night. Martin (12), who was keen to assert that he was no longer scared by horror films, described a similar process:

*Martin:* Till I was about eleven, and sometimes now, I don't get nightmares, but I used to, but now, when I go to sleep ... I went through all the horrible films that I've seen, before you go to sleep, and then I slip off to sleep. Like I go through *Aliens, Psycho, Shining, Return of the Living Dead* ... it just comes in my mind, shows the bits I like from each film, all the most goriest bits. Then I click off and go to sleep.

The uncertainty of Martin's position here is reflected in the shifting of tenses (between present and past) and of pronouns (between 'you' and 'I'): he is 'owning up' to being scared, but in a sense he has to do so if the films he claims to have seen are to be accepted as sufficiently 'adult'. Significantly, the 'goriest bits' are also the bits he says he likes; and, like Stella and Mehtap, he seems to conceive of his mind as a projector or a television that 'clicks off' when he goes to sleep.

Such experiences of nightmares, or being scared to go to bed, are very common for young children, and are obviously likely to happen irrespective of whether they have seen horror films. Thus, a number of children described recurrent dreams that had no such apparent origins; while others said they had had nightmares as a result of watching such seemingly innocuous films as *Pinocchio* and the children's TV series *The Moomins*, or reading books like *Little Red Riding Hood*. David (9) described how he was terrified of a picture of the children's book hero Biggles that he had on his bedroom wall, because he felt his eyes were following him around the room; and that he had once had a similar experience with a picture of Robbie from the pop group Take That, which he had seen in a magazine – a truly spine-chilling thought. Ultimately, attempting to psychoanalyse the motivations for such childhood fears on the basis of a single interview would seem unwarranted and voyeuristic. Yet it is clear that such experiences are commonplace, and probably inescapable.

**They're coming to get you ...**

As a number of these accounts have indicated, the experience of fear (although not so much of disgust) frequently appears to intensify after viewing. Many children spoke of the fear of going into a dark bedroom or out to the kitchen to get a drink after they had seen a horror film. Others described how clothes hanging on a door or a shadow on the curtain could temporarily appear like a shape from *Alien* – although again, such fears are commonplace, and do not solely result from viewing. The possibility that, as Lisa (15) put it, '*they* might be upstairs' sometimes resulted in behaviour that was acknowledged to be quite bizarre. Adrian (15), for example, described how he checked his slippers for spiders the morning after seeing *Arachnaphobia*; while Martin (12) took a baseball bat to bed in case his father chose to come for him in the night like Jack Nicholson in *The Shining*. Such fears sometimes transferred to real-life situations that paralleled those in the films: Sonia (12) told how she would recall a scene from *Nightmare on Elm Street* whenever she got into the bath; while Angela (12) described how she was careful not to walk over drains after seeing the Stephen King film *It*. While there was often a considerable degree of self-mocking humour in such anecdotes, it was also acknowledged that the fear had been real at the time.

One possible reason why such fears might intensify in this way is because many of the coping strategies that are available at the point of viewing no longer apply in the darkness and isolation of one's bedroom, where the only option is to hide under the bed-covers. Many children described how, in this situation, they would try to 'think of something nice', but the images would always 'come back in your mind':

*Trevor (15):* The worst is when you're going to sleep at night, that's the worst part ... 'cause you think, like, 'that's nothing', and you chat about something else with your mates or whatever, and when you go to bed you start thinking about it, and all that. [*laughter*]

*Interviewer:* So if you've seen something like that ... is there anything you can do about it, to stop being scared?

*Trevor:* Sleep with your light on. [*laughter*]

*Serena (15):* Put garlic round your neck. [*laughter*]

*Trevor:* See, that's the only thing really, ghosts and supernatural stuff. None of them monster things, 'cause you know they're just rubbish, but the ghosts, there's something more to it.

While it may be easy to dismiss his fears or to distract himself in the company of his friends, Trevor clearly finds this harder on his own. Like many of the children, he was prepared to entertain the idea of the supernatural, or at least to acknowledge the possibility of doubt – and even though Serena mocks the conventional symbolism of vampire movies, she was one of many children who claimed they believed in ghosts, or in some cases claimed to have witnessed them. The laughter and self-mockery that characterise this extract are partly a means of relieving the tensions and uncertainties that are at stake, both in relation to the notion of the supernatural, and in 'owning up' to being scared.

These extracts also raise interesting questions about the notion of 'suspension of disbelief', which is sometimes seen to be a pre-requisite of the experience of horror. Noel Carroll[9] argues that horror does *not* in fact depend upon a belief in the existence of monsters, or even upon such a suspension of disbelief – at least in the sense of a conscious act that happens once and for all. We do not, he suggests, ever give up our belief that the monster is fictional: rather, our fear is in response to the *thought* or the imagination that the monster *might* be real. Thus, throughout these discussions, there was no sense in which the events in horror films were taken to be a documentary record of real events: indeed, they were often condemned as 'fake' and implausible. Yet the distinction that Trevor makes in the above extract is significant in this respect, and it was one that was made by many of the children here. What is frightening is not the possibility that 'they' will actually come out of the television and ambush you as you walk into your bedroom. On the contrary, the fear depends upon a more general *doubt* about the supernatural – and a willingness at least to entertain the possibility of its existence – that is very widely shared, even in apparently secular societies. As Angela said, in relation to her fears of walking over drains, 'I know that it's not real, but at the back of my mind I think that I may as well not chance it.'

In this connection, it was interesting that a number of children commented on the fact that horror books were often more frightening than films, precisely because the books were less explicit, and hence left more to your imagination. As Vanessa (12) said, 'your imagination just runs wild, and you can do anything you like with it'. Here again, the response appears to involve an act of imaginative projection from the fictional world into the real, rather than the mere confusion of the two that is often seen to be the case.

What is perhaps most crucial to emphasise here, however, is that in almost all these accounts, the children take on the position of the victim rather than the 'monster'. There were certainly one or two exceptions here, albeit bizarre ones. Alan (9), for example, claimed to have seen *Hellraiser* at the age of two, and said that the film had given him a nightmare; but since he had played the part of Hellraiser, 'there was nothing to be scared of'. In the large majority of cases, however, it was the children who were menaced and pursued in their dreams, sometimes by horrific mutations of their own parents: Liam (12), for example, became the son of the murdering woman in *Brain Dead*, while Jenny was pursued by her father in the form of the lizard from *V*. Likewise, what the children seemed to imagine as they watched was the experience of victimisation: as Jenny (15) said in relation to watching *Hellraiser*, 'I'm thinking "imagine if this happened, imagine if your skin got ripped off."' Similarly, in fantasy play, it was the revenge on the monster that was often the central aim: Luke (6), for example, said that after watching *Dawn of the Living Dead*, he had ordered a zombie suit and then made his friend wear it, in order that he could pretend to kill him with a fake knife.

Strange as they may be, such anecdotes do begin to question many of the commonsense assumptions about 'identification' on which popular criticisms of horror films are often based. Far from glorying in a sadistic and misogynistic identification with the (male) killer, viewers may in fact be adopting the masochistic position of the (female) victim. As Carol Clover has convincingly argued in her study of the dynamics of 'rape revenge' and 'slasher' movies,[10] contemporary horror is often 'victim-identified': what is perceived as 'good horror', she suggests, may be that which is most successful in 'hurting' its viewers, and playing on fears and desires that are often figured as 'feminine'. The notion that here, as in cinematic spectatorship in general, viewers are necessarily led to adopt the masterful, sadistic 'male gaze' is one that – as I indicate in more detail below – is certainly open to question.

## Parents and peers: the context of viewing

To say the least, the experiences I have discussed so far could all be described as more or less distressing. While there are certainly those who linger fascinated at the scenes of traffic accidents, few people would voluntarily expose themselves to scenes of ritual disembowelling and bloody slaughter if they were to take place in front of their eyes. Yet while some of these experiences may have been accidental or unpredicted, in most cases they arose from a conscious decision to watch a film that actively held out the promise of such a response. So why do children *choose* to expose themselves to such material?

To some degree, this may be explained in terms of 'peer group pressure' – although such teacherly formulations tend to present young people as rather more fickle and easily swayed than they actually are. A number of children here described how they had been persuaded to watch horror films by friends or older siblings, or had done so because they did not want to be left out by their peers. Donald (11) explicitly complained about having to maintain the pretence that he had seen such films, when in fact his parents would not allow him to do so. The fear of mockery was a particular concern. Carol (12), for example, described how she had first seen the *Nightmare on Elm Street* films at the age of eight, in the company of her twelve-year-old cousin:

> Carol: And when I was scared, my cousin said 'oh Carol, what are you so scared for, you wimp?' And I was going to him ... 'shut up Darren, you silly fool, you were scared of this stuff before' and everything. Just 'cause he weren't scared then. He used to be scared of *My Little Pony*. When the my little ponies had fights, he used to scream and go to his mum.

As in this case, watching horror was often taken as proof of one's 'adult' status, which accounts for the force of Carol's riposte about the distinctly 'babyish' cartoon *My Little Pony*. As I have noted, this ability to 'take it' – or at least not to display outward signs of being scared – is frequently seen to be a particular preoccupation for boys, although (as here) it appeared to apply equally to girls.

Carol's anecdote also reveals the degree of sadistic pleasure that children (and not only children) sometimes take in scaring each other. Sarah and Jenny (15) both revealed how their older brothers used to make them kiss a poster of Freddy Kruger, in order that they would be 'safe'; while Sarah went on to describe how, when she was five, her cousins had locked her in the bedroom and made her watch *Evil Dead*. More innocuously perhaps, many children recounted how friends or family had deliberately sought to scare them while they were watching a horror film, for example by jumping on them when they went out to fetch a drink. Of course, such activities are by no means only related to watching horror films. Several children described experiments with fake blood or imitation plastic scars, which reflect a wider interest in the artifice of horror that is most obviously manifested in the yearly ritual of Hallowe'en.

Despite these somewhat negative examples, the social context of viewing is clearly a key factor in the pleasure of horror, and in the ways in which children learn to cope with potentially upsetting responses. A number of children described instances of group viewing, either with family or friends, in which the collective nature of the experience had helped them to deal with their own fear. Carol (12), for example, described sleep-overs in which she and her friends would watch horror videos, 'all just hugging together' at the scary parts. By contrast, while there were one or two enthusiasts who occasionally chose to watch horror alone, this was generally regarded as much more frightening, and to that extent as an experience to be avoided. Even more experienced horror fans such as Anthony and Martha (15) said that they were unlikely to be 'in the mood' for horror when they were on their own.

In such situations, others' display of fear is often a source of amusement in itself. As Alice (12) noted, 'if I'm with my friends, you find a bit more pleasure out of being scared ... some of you are screaming just for the fun of it'. For children, there is often a particular delight when parents appear more scared than they do themselves. Donna (6) related with great hilarity how she had made her mother jump by gripping her leg when they had seen *Nightmare on Elm Street* together; while Lisa (15) mocked the way in which her father had deliberately avoided the scary parts of *Amityville* by making out that he needed to get a drink. On the other hand, Cherie (9) was among a number of children who described how her family would deliberately watch such films in the dark, precisely in order to make them 'scarier' – in her case, using a torch to mimic the projector in the cinema.

This kind of group viewing can provide opportunities for children to 'model' appropriate reactions and emotional displays. In some instances, this took the form of peers or older siblings offering more or less explicit instruction in coping strategies. While the mockery used by Carol's cousin (above) is perhaps the least subtle pedagogical approach. Liam and Donna (12) both described how they would keep reminding their younger siblings that the film wasn't real, or explain to them what was happening.

Similar observations apply to parents. As we shall see in Chapter 8, most parents had experienced situations in which they were surprised by what their children had found frightening, and had attempted to intervene. One mother, for example, described how she had tried to allay the fears of her six-year-old son Luke while watching *Ghostbusters*:

*Brenda:* I was worried about one particular thing, where this thing rushes at you at the screen, so I talked him through that bit and he was all right ... I just said to him, you know, it's just supposed to be a ghost, it's not real, and they've done it with a film and camera and everything, and it's not something that's hiding round a corner coming to get you, you mustn't let it worry you.

*Interviewer:* And do you find that works, if you do that?

*Brenda:* Yes, I think it does help [but] I still think it leaves a little chill there. And I held back on letting him see that for a while as well, 'cause I just thought, I know it made me nearly leap out of my skin when I saw it at the movies. But I knew, I just felt it was the kind of film that he might be at somebody's house and see anyway, 'cause so many of the kids were watching it. And when it came on TV, I think that's the first time that he saw it, and we all sat down together and watched that.

Like many of the other parents, and many of the children, Brenda sees modality judgments as a key element in learning to cope with horror – both in terms of the way she draws attention to the artificial, constructed nature of the text, and in terms of her more general comments on plausibility ('it's not something that's hiding round a corner coming to get you'). While she does attempt to restrict Luke's access to more 'serious' horror (she also has two teenage sons, which makes this difficult at times), she accepts that teaching him to cope with such responses is probably a more realistic strategy, that will prepare him for unexpected experiences in the future.

As I have noted, this process of 'learning to take it' was seen to be a central aspect of gaining experience as a viewer, and of growing into maturity. Becoming a 'true' horror fan meant learning to conquer your fear, and to see the experience through to the bitter end. As Sonia (12), herself an avid viewer, put it:

*Sonia:* You've just got to be, like, ready for anything to come out, out of it. You have to be a person that, like, doesn't care and just wants to watch anything, doesn't care what happens, they want to see the end of it.

While there were many children here who were uncertain of their ability to attain this status, or simply unwilling to undergo such experiences, there was a sense in which the process was regarded as therapeutic. Indeed, Elaine (12) even described how she had forced her father to watch *Arachnaphobia* in order to help him conquer his fear of spiders – 'I kept turning his head round, getting him to watch it.'

This attempt to conquer fear is also an explicit theme in many horror films themselves. In films such as *Nightmare on Elm Street*, the 'last girl' who finally destroys the monster is the one who learns to stand up to her own fears, rather than attempting to escape from them.[11] As Noel Carroll[12] argues, many horror films have an explicitly pedagogical dimension: they effectively direct us in how to respond appropriately to the monster (and hence to the 'dark' side of human experience) by showing how the 'normal', positive human characters respond. At the same time, he suggests, viewers who 'savour the revulsion' of horror may be 'meta-responding' to their own revulsion – that is, indulging in a self-satisfied belief that they are capable of withstanding such heavy doses of shock and disgust. Such 'meta-responses' are of course also encouraged by the marketing of horror, for example in the 'can you take it?' come-ons of the posters and trailers. Yet this self-conscious pleasure in one's ability to cope with such experiences – which is apparent in many of the extracts quoted in this chapter – is crucially dependent on the ability to talk about it with others.

In various respects, then, the social context of viewing is a central aspect of children's experience of horror, and of the ways in which some of them gradually learn to cope with it. 'Peer group pressure' is certainly part of this context, since it is largely at this level that the subversive status of the genre is established, and indeed celebrated – although of course if such material was not officially proscribed for children, its subversive charge would probably be much reduced.[13] Yet while the notion of 'peer group pressure' might explain the reasons why children watch their *first* horror film, it does not adequately explain why many of them continue to do so. Nor does it explain why some children refuse to watch such films, often against the exhortations of their peers, while others actively seek them out – unless we assume that the latter are somehow more gullible and easily influenced, or just fall in with the 'wrong' crowd. If we wish to explain why children choose to watch such films, we must look more closely at their experience of viewing, and in particular at the pleasures that are involved.

## 'I just liked it'

While many of the children described how they had been scared and given nightmares as a result of watching horror, their prime motivation for doing so was clearly to do with pleasure. In fact, many spontaneously mentioned horror in our initial interviews, in response to our open question about what they most enjoyed to watch. Our (somewhat earnest) queries about their feelings about such films were often met with responses such as that of Imran (15) on *Halloween*: 'I just liked it ... I'd watch it again if I could.' Even where it was acknowledged that films were scary, this was often seen to be synonymous with the pleasure. The following discussion of *Arachnaphobia*, with a group of six-year-olds, was typical:

*Interviewer:* What bit did you find really scary?

*Anthony:* / The bit I liked was the bit when the man stepped on the spider ...

*Interviewer:* How did you feel when you were watching that, Luke and / Anthony, when you saw that? /

*Luke:* Normal, actually. Just normal.

Anthony answers our question about the bit he found scary by talking about the bit he liked, as though the two were synonymous; while Luke appears to find strange the implication that he should feel anything other than 'normal'.

Like Imran, many of the children expressed the wish to watch 'scary' things again, even where their first experiences of them appeared to have been quite traumatic. For example, Thomas (9) told how he had first seen *Nightmare on Elm Street* with his teenage brother in a hotel bedroom at the age of six; and despite the fact that he had spent much of the time cowering under the duvet, he now expressed a strong wish to see the film again. Likewise, Samantha (9) claimed that remembering nightmares did not put her off watching such films: 'I say that in my mind, but when it comes on I still watch it ... I don't want to miss it.'

The wish to 'see it again' – and the practice of repeat viewing – is on one level, simply about reliving the pleasure. Many children claimed to have seen favourite horror films 'over and over again'; while others described how they would use the video to fast-forward to the 'best bits' – that is, the scary bits – or to watch those parts again. Carol (12), for example, claimed to have seen *Aliens* 'at least fifty times now':

*Carol:* You know the bit when that robot, it comes through here, and that little alien comes through that woman's body, yeah, I keep rewinding that bit. And also when the big claw comes through that robot's thing, and all that white blood, and he's all twisting round, and then all of a sudden he's chopped in half.

*Interviewer:* So why were you rewinding it?

*Carol:* I don't know. I just liked it ... I like those kind of films.

As Carol later acknowledged, this kind of repeat viewing did help her to cope with her negative feelings: 'I still think that's a bit disgusting, but I don't like hide my face or something like that, like I used to do.' As her friend Sonia noted, rewinding the tape enabled you to 'see how it's done' and hence to conquer your fear. As this extract suggests, repeat viewing can also form part of a conscious

strategy of learning to cope – and hence experiencing the pleasure
of what Carroll calls 'meta-responses'. Like Carol, many children
were keen to boast that they could now cope with material that
was formerly too much for them; and this was generally regarded
as an indication of maturity.

However, it was acknowledged that this was also dependent
upon the context: Lisa and Martha (15), for example, agreed that
even a very frightening film like *Silence of the Lambs* 'becomes less
scary the more times you see it' – although Lisa was still not prepared to take the risk of watching it alone. Both agreed that watching horror films in the cinema was much more scary because of
the 'atmosphere' and the sound quality – and, most significantly,
the fact that 'you can't turn it off'. The fact that both girls had seen
'18'-rated films in the cinema may indicate something of the limits
of the censorship system – although in fact there were hardly any
other children in our sample who claimed to have done the same.
Of course, as I have noted, the 'problem' of video technology is that
it is seen to undermine this form of centralised regulation:
although in fact it may also afford much more positive control for
viewers themselves.

Nevertheless, for many children, there also appeared to be a kind
of calculation here. Was it worth running the risk of being scared
– or, more accurately, of experiencing something that went beyond
your ability to cope[14] – in the hope of gaining some more intense
pleasure? For some children, this was a risk they knew they were
not prepared to take – although this was often reinforced by
parental prohibitions. Richard (9), for example, asserted 'I don't
watch horror movies, my parents hate them, they don't even like
them either.' In other cases, clear distinctions were drawn within
the genre: Lisa (15) was happy to watch *Dracula*, even though
she had found it scary, while she was quite adamant about *Hellraiser*: 'I wouldn't watch that!' Many children reported how they
would leave the room or turn off the TV when things got too
hard to handle. More cautiously, others said they might pretend
to go to the toilet and return when they hoped the scene had
finished.

For the more enthusiastic horror viewers, however, this risk was ultimately worth it – although even here, the pleasure was seen to be inextricably tied up with the possibility of pain. While there was certainly much to be gained from claiming that you were not scared, the experience of viewing a horror film that was *not* scary was also seen to be frustrating: Kemal (12), for example, complained that in the case of *Nightmare on Elm Street*, 'I couldn't get scared from that film, and I watched it and watched it, and I didn't see anything from it.'

In other cases, however, this balance was harder to strike. Stella (9) described a scene from *The Fog* that she acknowledged was 'disgusting', even though she had seen it several times: 'I just had to, I didn't want to go back and watch it, but I wanted to see it again, so I just went and watched it.' Likewise, Jane (15) said of horror films in general: 'They all scare me. I don't like them, they scare me too much. / I like to watch them though.' This kind of contradiction – liking but not liking, wanting to see but not to watch – was common in these interviews, and reflects the fundamental ambivalence of the viewing experience.

This ambivalence is perhaps most clearly manifested in the characteristic pose of the horror viewer, peering over the top of the cushion, or peeking through half-closed fingers, as in Alison's description already quoted in Chapter 2:

*Alison (12):* I sit there with my hands over my eyes, just peeking out, which is really, I know it's really stupid, 'cause you can still see, but I just feel safe ... I have to hide my eyes. but I still watch it all with my eyes covered.

While this pose allows you to feel 'safe' – a term significantly used in this context by other children – it also allows you to fulfil the desire to know the outcome of events, and ultimately the need for narrative closure. As Thomas (9) put it, 'I want to know what happens, or else ... you think about it all night.'

Interestingly, however, many children appeared to be unable to recall the endings of films, even where they had described the films themselves in considerable detail. And, as we have seen, the fear generated by the narrative often appeared to last well beyond the reassurance or safety that might be provided by the ending. As a number of critics have noted, one of the characteristics of contemporary horror is its failure to return to stability and order at the conclusion of the narrative – unlike 'classic' horror, in which the threat is routinely dispatched or neutralised at the end. The bogeyman in *Halloween* and *Nightmare on Elm Street*, for example, keeps rising again, signifying that equilibrium will never be re-established[15] – although of course on one level viewers recognise that this is simply a way of preparing the ground for sequels, and would almost seem to have become a reassuring convention in its own right.

Yet the status of endings remains an interesting issue, both in relation to horror and (as we shall see) in relation to other genres such as melodrama. Psychological researchers,[16] for example, have often argued that the gratifications that are provided by 'just endings' – in which the good character defeats the monster – are a key source of the pleasure of horror. Yet while this argument might be reassuring on a moral level, it tends to imply that the 'pain' of horror is significant only insofar as it builds up a kind of negative emotional charge, which is then released or transferred into positive feelings of relief.[17] Rather like banging your head against a wall, watching horror is only pleasurable when it stops.

Ultimately, this argument would appear to neutralise the forms of transgression and disruption that are central to horror – and which formed the major focus of the children's discussions of the genre. Children did not, by and large, choose to focus on the restoration of order or the demise of the monster, but on the films' violation of social, sexual and physical taboos. It is an enormous leap to suggest, as some critics have done, that these transgressions are somehow politically 'progressive', or indeed psychically therapeutic – that the monster somehow stands in for all the underprivileged social groups, or for the repressed sexual energies, whose inherent threat must be contained by bourgeois society.[18] Nevertheless, much of the appeal of horror must surely lie not only in the pleasure of watching evil destroyed or controlled, but also in watching it triumph. This is not to suggest that viewers simply 'identify' with the monster – if anything, as I shall argue, the opposite is the case. Nevertheless, it is to imply that the 'pain' of viewing should not be seen simply as the polar opposite of the pleasure, as though the presence of one implied the absence or removal of the other.

## Approaching pleasure

Almost inevitably, given the context of these interviews, and given the reliance on talk in the first place, this kind of research can only provide limited insights into these processes. This is not simply to do with the difficulties of *articulating* 'how you feel' – although this could reasonably be presumed to be a particular problem for younger children. On the contrary, observations about one's emotions are bound to depend upon implicit rules of display, and upon conventionalised styles of talk, and should therefore be seen as inherently *social*. Reflecting on such experiences must invariably involve a form of rationalisation or abstraction.

Nevertheless, there are points at which these interviews appear to come closer to the viewing experience, particularly where children choose to retell the narratives of their favourite films. In this section and the following one, I want to discuss some instances of this. The first is a sustained retelling of the film *The Lost Boys*, which was produced spontaneously by Anthony (15), a black (Afro-Caribbean) working-class boy whom we have already met twice in this chapter. This film might be described as a hybrid of a teen movie and a vampire film; and as we shall see, it is particularly notable for its special effects. Space precludes the quotation of the full version, although the following extracts provide a representative selection from Anthony's account of the film:

*Anthony:* I thought that was good, I really thought that was good
   ... the way they done it, and the effects. Like when the people
   at that party in the night and camp fire or whatever, and they
   go down, they swoop down on the people, and the guy gets it
   in his bald head and all that nonsense, all that I thought was    5
   really good.

*Adrian:* They throw them in the fire.

*Anthony:* And you see the blood spurt and everything, yeah, they
   throw them in the fire, I thought the film was A-1 style, I had

to watch that over and over boy, I thought it was good ... I    10
remember when I actually put on a tape, forwarded it to the
middle part where there's the camp fire, and then the end part
and then went out, 'cause I wanted to go out that day, I just
wanted to see that part. That was when I first saw it, a couple
of times, know what I mean, I thought the way they done like,    15
you know when they changed, the vampires' faces actually
change, and like the parts that were swollen up in the face, and
they look more evil, and the red eyes and all that, I thought it
was *crisp* style! I thought it looked really good, you know what
I mean? ...                                                       20

*Interviewer:* So when you're looking at it over and over again,
you're looking to see how it's done?

*Anthony:* Yeah, I like the way they done it. I mean, for instance,
you know when he goes to death by stereo, remember when
he grabs up the boy and he just brings him up in the air, up,     25
and I remember rewinding that film *nuff* times just to see if I
could see the little wires that picked him up, you know what I
mean ... I was just looking, 'cause he just shot up in the air,
and I thought, yeah they done that really good, 'cause sometimes when they do these flying things, they really don't look    30
all that, or they do just a couple of bits of air coming past, you
know what I mean, but they actually showed this person shoot
up in the air with Kerry and somebody, and then afterwards
the boy shot holy water or something like that in his face and
he dropped the boy, you know what I mean, and then he shot       35
an arrow at him, something like that, and it missed and I
thought he was dead. Next thing you know, he see the guy's
going to step on him, and he goes 'missed sucker!' like that and
he takes a second shot and grabs him, and he just gets shot
into the stereo. I thought all that was really, know what I       40
mean? I could tell you that film off by heart, I've watched it so
many times now ... it's only just now thinking of it, I'll probably go home and watch that tonight now, you know what I
mean? 'Cause that is a film that I really thought was good. And
I thought as well um, the way they done it, it wasn't just like    45
the big black cape and the slicked back hair with the triangle
thing going down [on the forehead], and you know what I
mean, and 'I want to zink your blurd' and all that nonsense, it

was really, you know what I mean, it was really just / with it!

*Interviewer:* It was the way they made it in a kind of contempo- 50
rary setting?

*Anthony:* It was here today, you could imagine it happening over
there somewhere, 'cause it was really, you know what I mean,
and when they done like, remember when he stabbed the guy
in the heart, right and all the blood come rushing down, rush- 55
ing down, and you see their feet, they was all shouting, like
they all felt it or something as well [*Adrian is making noises from
film, others laughing*] ...

*Interviewer:* But when you're watching, I mean you're saying that
and you're laughing, but are you laughing when you watch it? 60

*Adrian:* Yeah.

*Anthony:* Yeah, man! I thought it was brilliant, I thought *yes*!!
This is *my part*, you know what I mean, [*laughter*] and like if
people are talking, it's like 'shut up, shut up, shut up, it's my
favourite part', know what I mean, you really want to watch 65
it, and you don't want them opening their mouths because you
might miss something and you have to rewind it back. I always
end up rewinding it back anyway, because I like that part
anyway, you know what I mean. But I liked as well, you know
the top guy, the one with the glasses, the video shop owner, 70
when he dashed the boy up in the air, and his laugh, and it
sounded kind of evil, kind of like a demon laugh, it was sort of
[*Adrian imitates*] yeah, and he's saying 'don't fight, it's so much
easier if you don't fight' and he's got blood there. Exactly, it
was just crisp, I thought the film was *safe*, you know what I 75
mean?

*Adrian:* Know the bit yeah, where the two kids yeah, and they're
going after one of the vampires, and then into the garlic bath,
and he says 'what you doing with my friend?' and you see the
dog 'woof woof woof'. 80

*Anthony:* Just jump up, yeah. And the next thing you know you
just see the boy just melting up, stuff, all garlic in the water.

*Adrian:* Ugh, I just, know what I mean?

*Anthony:* And the next thing you know the whole place was just
blowing up with all the person's blood and that, innit. 85

*Adrian:* And hear the boy 'how much you gonna charge them for
   this?'

*Anthony:* Yeah 'how much, how much would you charge them'
   after they ruined the whole house killing them, they killed the
   vampires, but they ruined the whole house, you know what I  90
   mean, and then afterwards he goes 'how much do you think
   we should charge them?', you know what I mean. But I
   thought the film was really good. And all the time, they all
   thought that they was hiding it from the grandad, the grandad
   knew well, *well*, the grandad knew from *time* that there was  95
   vampires ... I like the way the, what do you call it, like when
   he drove through his house to save them and then afterwards
   the thing just come stabbing ... a stake, stabbed right through
   his stomach and drive it right into like the fireplace and he just
   blew up, just blew up. I thought 'yeah!' And it was not like 100
   blow up and you see blood, it was blow up and like fire.

*Adrian:* Yeah.

*Anthony:* I thought it was brilliant, you know what I mean, and
   the way he tricked them into drinking the blood, he goes 'drink
   this, be one of us', yeah, and they thought, he thought it was 105
   wine at first right, and the girl goes 'don't drink it, it's blood'
   like that, and I thought she's stupid for saying that because he
   ain't going to believe it, you know what I mean, yeah, sure,
   blood, and he drunk it, you know what I mean? Now if she had
   said don't drink it, there's something in there you might, you 110
   know what I mean, maybe try and sly it out, you know what
   I mean, then maybe, but she went 'don't drink it, Michael, you
   don't have to drink it' and then afterwards he goes 'what's
   wrong with it?' and she goes 'it's blood'. He ain't gonna believe
   it's blood, he just saw Deb drinking out of it, so he's not going 115
   to believe it's blood, you know what I mean?

Inevitably, this transcription represents a pale shadow of
Anthony's excitement and enthusiasm. Nevertheless, the sources
of his pleasure in the film are clear. Visceral images of bodily violation and dismembering are absolutely central to his account:
blood pouring and splattering, stabbings in the heart and stomach,
bodies 'melting up' and exploding, faces swelling and transforming,

and manifold forms of violent death seem, at least on one level, to be the essence of the experience. As a number of critics have noted, this emphasis on bodily violation is a key characteristic of contemporary horror, that distinguishes it from the 'classic' films of earlier decades – although the wider significance of what has come to be termed 'the splatter movie' has been interpreted in various ways. Barbara Creed,[19] for example, describes such films as a 'modern defilement rite', that reflects a desire to return to a period of union with the mother, in which bodily wastes were not invested with shame and embarrassment; while Pete Boss[20] relates this tendency to anxieties surrounding the growth of institutionalised modern medicine.

Of course, Anthony's account partly reflects what happens in the film – although *The Lost Boys* is in fact a comparatively 'mild' horror film, and is classified in the UK as a '15'.[21] In choosing to focus on these scenes, he tends to represent the film as 'stronger' than it actually is. What is clear, however, is that Anthony's pleasure in these scenes is much more explicit than his disgust. In fact, Adrian's 'ugh, I just ... ' (line 83) is the only unambiguous expression of disgust in the whole discussion. If Anthony's apparent fascination with these aspects of the film reflects his underlying anxiety about the control of the body or his repressed desire to return to his mother, this is not apparent here – and indeed, it is hard to see what kind of evidence one might use to substantiate such arguments.

On the other hand, it is clear that shock – in the sense of reactions to the unexpected – is central to the experience. For example, the scene of 'death by stereo' (lines 24–40), and perhaps also the garlic bath (lines 77–85), seem to derive their power from the fact that they subvert the viewer's expectations. Humour also plays a very important role here. There is a kind of sardonic verbal humour familiar from action movies – 'missed, sucker!' (line 38) or 'it's so much easier if you don't fight' (lines 73–4) – and a similar feel about the very *excess* of the violence and destruction – most notably in Anthony's account of the final scene (lines 96–101). By contrast, the boy's line 'how much you gonna charge them for this?' (lines 86–94) seems to serve as a form of comic relief once the evil has finally been destroyed.

Yet for all the intensity of his involvement in this account – which is reflected, not simply in its length and detail, but also in the amount of direct quotation – Anthony simultaneously retains a degree of distance. Indeed, many of his judgments about the film are based on what can only be called aesthetic appreciation. Both in the extracts quoted and elsewhere in the discussion, his most fulsome praise is for the quality of the special effects – for example, the animated transformations (lines 15–20) and the flying scenes (lines 24–33). The key criterion here is clearly that of *realism* – although there is of course no sense in which reality and fiction are ever confused. The reason why the flying scenes are so much better than those in other films, for example, is because of the care that has been taken to make the artifice invisible. Like a number of the other children, as we have seen, Anthony uses the flexibility afforded by video, not merely to select out the most pleasurable parts – which are simultaneously the most violent and horrific (lines 10–14, 66–9) – but also to study the text more closely (lines 21–9). Yet his praise for 'the way they done it' (an expression which is repeated in different forms on lines 2, 15, 23, 29, 45 and 54) seems to be based on more than a technical interest in special effects. Thus, while Anthony recognises the film's generic origins in the 'classic' *Dracula*-style vampire movies, he also praises the film-makers for the way in which they have reworked the myth in a contemporary setting, thereby rendering it much more plausible (lines 45–53). He also implicitly praises what might be termed the 'depth' of the film, or at least the unexpected thoroughness with which it has thought through its initial premises – for example, in showing the telepathic connection between the vampires (lines 54–7), or the bodies exploding into smoke rather than blood (line 100–101). Significantly, in the light of Carroll's observations about 'suspension of disbelief', the power of the film in this respect is not that it makes you believe in the reality of what is represented, but that it makes you take seriously the *possibility* that similar events might happen in real life: 'you could imagine it happening over there somewhere' (lines 52–3).

This account also raises interesting questions about the issue of 'identification' – which, as I have noted, is at the heart of moral concerns about the effects of horror. What is clear, however, is that the position from which Anthony reads the film is constantly shifting. At some points, he appears to relate the action from the position of the vampires (for example, in the account of 'death by stereo'); while at others, he appears to take the point of view of the good characters (for example, in his account of the final scenes). Throughout, however, he also talks about his own position as an outside observer, watching, looking and seeing: 'you see the blood spurt' (line 8), 'it looked really good' (line 19), 'you see their feet' (line 56), 'you just see the boy just melting up' (lines 81–2) and so on. Particularly towards the end of the extract, Anthony is also actively generating hypotheses about different characters' points of view. He knows that the grandfather knows about the vampires, even though the other characters had believed they were hiding this (lines 93–6), and (in an extract omitted), he speculates about why he remains so calm. He reads the (comparatively minor) scene in which Michael drinks blood from both characters' point of view, again based on the fact that he knows the truth of the situation in a way Michael does not (lines 104–16). Here, he also hypothesises an alternative outcome, in which Deb might have persuaded Michael not to drink the blood – which positions him on the side of the good victim characters. These extracts clearly point to the limitations of simplistic notions of 'identification', and to the considerable amount of cognitive activity that characterises the viewing process.[22]

Finally, it is important to draw attention to the social nature of this account, and to the elements of performance. In order to hold the floor – as in fact he did for much of this discussion – Anthony has to command the consent of his listeners. Adrian appears to be happy to adopt a supportive role, filling in details and occasional imitations of scenes from the film. As the interviewer, I join in the laughter, and occasionally ask for clarification, but (like the third boy, Randeep, who does not speak here) I do not challenge Anthony's right to speak. Nevertheless, Anthony is clearly working hard: his talk – and indeed his gestures – are very fast and animated, and there is a great deal of emphasis on key terms such as the distinctly subcultural superlatives ('safe', 'crisp style' and 'A-1 style'). Going directly to the 'good bits' is, of course, an important tactic here: lengthy explanations of the setting or the motivations of the characters, or indeed bothering to identify the characters in the first place, would simply detract from this. For this reason, it would be misleading simply to regard Anthony's account at face value, as an honest reflection of his experience of viewing – although (as his brief reference to viewing in the company of others, lines 63–7, would also suggest) the social context, and the experience of talking about the film with others, are a key part of the pleasure. In this respect, it is very significant that the talk leads Anthony to want to relive the experience yet again – 'I'll probably go home and watch that tonight now' (line 42–3).

## Myths and nightmares: the case of Freddy

Many of the characteristics I have identified in this more detailed analysis were apparent across the range of these interviews. In order to develop some of these points, I want now to look more broadly at the children's retellings and discussions of another film (or more accurately, series of films) that recurred on many occasions – namely, the *Nightmare on Elm Street* series.[23] The grotesque figure of Freddy Kruger, the child murderer returning to wreak revenge on the community that attempted to destroy him, appeared to have attained almost archetypal status for many of these children. Many of those who had not actually seen the films appeared to know a great deal about them, and were very keen to discuss them with those who had. While this partly confirms the series' substantial peer group status, it also suggests that children are a significant 'emergent audience' here.[24] In other words, how we respond to Freddy is partly cued by the fame that precedes him; and as in the case of Hannah's chance encounter with a picture of Freddy, or Sarah and Jenny's story of being forced to kiss the poster (see above), even his image appeared to be invested with mythical powers. Martha (15) even described how somebody had sprayed graffiti on a street sign in her neighbourhood, changing 'Elm

Avenue' to 'Elm Street'; and now, she said, she found it 'too freaky' to walk down that road.

Nevertheless, like the *Child's Play* series, these films were also often described as 'unrealistic' and even as laughable, particularly by the older children. As we have seen, many were keen to draw attention to the liberal use of 'tomato ketchup' and make-up. To some extent, the fame of Freddy may have been his undoing in this respect. A number of children had seen documentaries or read newspaper articles about the making of the series, and knew about the private life of Richard Englund, who plays Freddy – although Martha was still disturbed at the prospect that his children would have to live in the knowledge that Freddy Kruger was their dad. As Adam (15) suggested, 'the only reason it's not thought of as scary is 'cause everyone's heard of it, and they know it's not real'. Yet this knowledge did not necessarily assuage the children's fears: as Jenny (15) put it, Freddy might be a joke, but 'he's still a threatening figure'. Indeed, in some cases, the producers were seen to be playing with fears that might prove too dangerous for them to handle. Both Jessica and Hitesh (9) had read in the newspapers that the 'manager' (the director) and Englund himself had had nightmares as a result of making the films, and were reluctant to make any more – although, of course, this kind of story merely serves to perpetuate the myth, and may well be designed to do so.

This ambivalence is characteristic of many of the children's retellings of the *Nightmare on Elm Street* films. On the one hand, as in Anthony's account of *The Lost Boys*, it was the scenes of blood and gore that formed the major preoccupation here. Very few children bothered to explain the setting or the motivation of the characters. On the contrary, they went straight to the scenes of visceral horror – Freddy eating the head of a woman he has killed; the hands and faces of his victims appearing on his face and stomach; Freddy playing with the veins of one of his victims like a puppeteer; and the 'bubbling belly' that erupted with the birth of his child. Freddy's ability not merely to rip and slash his victims' flesh, but also to enter their bodies and minds, makes him a particularly powerful embodiment of the theme of physical violation, which (as I have noted) is central to a great deal of contemporary horror. Yet insofar as the children did appear to 'identify' here, or at least to adopt a position from which the narrative was told, this was clearly that of the victim: Serena (15), for example, said 'I could just picture Freddy coming for me', while in the nightmares recounted by Hannah (6) and Alan (9), it was Freddy who was scratching their faces.

At the same time, *Nightmare on Elm Street* is a film that is almost didactically concerned with the theme of conquering fear. At one point, for example, Nancy (the 'last girl' who eventually defeats Freddy) is given a short lecture on 'dream skills' – that is, on the need to face up to the monster, rather than turning your back on him, since it is this that gives him his energy. Equally literally, we see her in school being taught about Shakespeare's *Hamlet*: Hamlet's response to recognising the rottenness in human nature, we are told, is to dig into it, like the gravedigger, rather than to pretend it is not there. John (9) focused particularly on this kind of resistance in his retelling of the film, as this extract suggests:

*John:* He kept on haunting this girl, she kept on being scared, so she tried trapping him, she put an alarm clock at one time and she put all these traps and all that stuff, and when he came in, she tried burning him, but she didn't succeed ... and then the alarm went on and then they woke up, but then they fell asleep again, and suddenly they tried to get rid of him this time by saying 'you're not true', but it didn't work, and they were still asleep, but they thought they were awake ... and in the morning when she woke up real, she saw a body on her bed all scratched and the blood was spurting out.

John's account is typical in several respects. He clearly takes the position of the victims rather than the killer, focusing on the ways in which they learn to cope with their fear. As in a number of other retellings, the way in which the film blurs the distinction between dream and reality is also crucial here. Dreaming, it could be argued, is seen in the film as a metaphor for viewing: the way to overcome the horror of dreams is to wake up to reality – although (as John's account suggests) the difficulty is in being sure that you are awake and not still asleep. Ultimately, the key to Nancy's survival is that she actively *chooses* to dream – that is, to watch the film.

John's version of the film has all the characteristics of what Hodge and Tripp have termed the 'paratactic' narrative:[25] like *Tom and Jerry* and any number of other children's cartoons, it is read as a series of incidents that are effectively interchangeable. Apart from the necessity of a beginning and an end, it is 'just one damn thing after another'. This recognition of the formula sometimes contributed to a sense of distancing. Joanne (12), for example, confidently dismissed the films as merely 'twenty ways to get killed'. Less explicitly, Thomas (9) described how Freddy 'kept popping up everywhere' – and while he had clearly been scared by this (he admitted that it had given him nightmares), his account increasingly took on the tone of knockabout violence:

*Thomas:* And then in the end she set up all these traps 'cause she was determined to kill him in her dream, and she set up like trip wires and hammers and things that would come down ... and she dreamed that this hammer went [*mimes hammer crashing down*] and he just shook his head and ran after, and then a trip wire had come, because he was just behind her, and then the trip wire came, and he tripped over the wire and smacked his head on the thing again ... [*laughing*] and when he got up to the bathroom, um there's like on *Predator*, there's this like, to kill Predator, Arnie has this huge like mace thing, like huge bit of wood, and it was really heavy, and what she did is ... she slipped through the bathroom door, but Freddy slipped through as well, but then the girl kicked the door open and then this thing came down and squashed him, and that was the end.

While the laughter here may well serve as a way of coping with the emotional tension, there is also a sense in which Thomas seems to perceive the violence as essentially comic – like his friend Alan, who laughed convulsively throughout this account. While he does clearly take pleasure in Nancy's revenge on Freddy – and in that respect, appears to take her position rather than his – Thomas's overall perspective is comparatively distanced, as is apparent from the comically abrupt ending. The intertextual comparison with the sardonic action movie *Predator* is significant here, suggesting that

Thomas recognises the formulaic nature of such violence – although a comparison with *Home Alone* or even *Tom and Jerry* would not have been out of place.

Even for some of the younger children, there was a sense in which the horror of the film merged uneasily with comedy:

*Donna (6):* Well, it's got a boy called Freddy Cooper [*sic*], he's got an actual girlfriend, they're kissing at school. But spikes just come, and went pshoo, right into his girlfriend. He didn't know she was dead until he just looked at her, and he saw spikes, and he said 'I'm a bad guy.' Then he had big lumps of spikes whenever he got really angry ... The bit that scares me really really much is when he um / he takes all the / no, the bit that makes me really sad is when he takes all the girl's friends away from her. The bit I think's really really funny is when she says 'go away, you're just a dream'. That made me laugh.

Interestingly, Donna is one of the few children who draws attention to the sexual dimension of Freddy's threat to the women (both in the 'kissing' and in the rising up of lumps and spikes). While her account is obviously incoherent, it does illustrate some of the mixed emotions that may be at stake here, which partly derive from the way in which the film transgresses taboos on sexuality as well as on the body in general.

As I have indicated, then, many of the children attempted to use their limited knowledge of the genre, and their understandings about modality, to distance themselves from the fears the film had evidently invoked. Yet particularly for the younger or less experienced viewers, this knowledge was uncertain, and its effects could not always be guaranteed:

*Emma (9):* My mum was covering my eyes and I took [her hands] off and all I saw was this, all this blood on the telly, and then I saw this lady flat on the floor, nothing in her, just all her blood was all over the place.

*Peter (9):* Lovely!

*Emma:* And um, my best bit was when he died –

*Peter:* I never knew Freddy could die. Can he die? I didn't think Freddy could die.

*Emma:* He went in this steamer type thing and he come out alive –

*Interviewer:* [*to Peter*] Have you ever seen it?

*Peter:* No, I've heard it, don't want to see it [*laughs*].

*Steven (9):* I've seen the clips of it.

*Peter:* My friend said he's so, there's so much um horrible stuff in it, it makes him laugh, because it's, you, you can't really get someone who goes inside somebody, gets, he goes inside somebody, then, um, he gets his nails and makes a hole in them and then all this stuff starts coming out, all this blood /

*Emma:* Yeah, that's it, yuck.

*Peter:* It's stupid, nothing can really happen like that in real life.

*Emma:* It's funny because I knew that something was going to happen, like just when there was going to be a bang I knew, but I just got scared when there was a bang, just jumped when I knew.

In his expression 'lovely', Peter appears to assume an ironic, 'bloodthirsty' pose, similar to that of Thomas and Alan – a pose which stands in opposition to the (often equally ironic) 'scared child' role we have seen others adopt. Later, he draws on the discourse of the 'critical viewer', asserting that the text is merely implausible. Yet his confidence is shaky; and the fact that he acknowledges that he does not *want* to see the film implies that he is perhaps protesting too much. By contrast, Emma is more explicit about her feelings of disgust, even though she has actively chosen to watch the film. Nevertheless, her (marginally) greater experience of the genre does not appear to afford her much protection: as her final comment suggests, the fact that she is able to predict what will happen does not make her any less scared.

**Learning the genre**

The processes by which children learn to cope with the experience of horror viewing – and in particular, to defend themselves against potentially unwelcome reactions – has been a recurrent theme throughout the discussions recorded in this chapter. In some instances, as we have seen, children simply learn to avoid mater-

ial that they feel they will be unable to cope with, either by refus-
ing to watch it in the first place, or by hiding or leaving the room
or turning it off when it gets too much. In other cases, they look
to comfort in the form of pillows or toys – or indeed people – to
hug; or they attempt to distract themselves with other activities, or
by trying to think 'happy thoughts'. There is ample evidence here
that, in all sorts of ways, children learn to regulate their *own* viewing, and their emotional responses to it – although, as we have
seen, that is not to imply that they are always successful in their
attempts to avoid upsetting experiences.

One particular dimension of this process that is worthy of further comment here is the way in which children use their understanding of television as a medium – or what has been termed their
'television literacy'. As I have noted in my introduction, recent
audience research has tended to present children as much more
critical and sophisticated viewers than they are traditionally
assumed to be. Yet this expertise clearly has its limits, particularly
when it comes to genres such as horror, of which they will generally have only limited experience.

Thus, while a number of the older children here were making
clear distinctions within the genre, these were much less certain
among the younger ones. Most of the fifteen-year-olds, for example, explicitly distinguished between 'monster movies' of the *Nightmare on Elm Street* variety, and what was sometimes termed
'psychological' horror, which was generally seen to be more 'adult'
and more frightening. Sonia, one of the more experienced twelve-
year-olds, made a similar distinction between films that she termed
'scary' and those that were merely 'jumpy' or shocking, such as
*Child's Play 3*. Interestingly, she also condemned films like *Friday
the Thirteenth* on the grounds that they had no 'moral' – which
appeared to mean that the violence had no motivation: 'it's just
rubbish, it doesn't have nothing to it ... 'cause every minute he
kept on coming up and killing people, and that was it!'

As in the case of Anthony's account of *The Lost Boys*, there was
often an aesthetic dimension to these judgments. A number of the
girls, in particular, had read a great many horror books, and were
interested in comparing them with the film adaptations. Lisa and

Martha (15), for example, praised the Brian de Palma film of *Dracula*, which they compared favourably with the book, and with the other 'corny and cheap' versions they had seen: they were most impressed with the quality of the acting, and with the special effects, particularly the spurting blood, which was judged to be much better than the 'Freddy Kruger tomato ketchup sort of thing'. Significantly, they argued that this was an 'adult' film, more on the grounds of the complexity of the plot than because it was especially scary.

Perhaps the most important dimension here, however, was that of modality – or the 'perceived reality' of the text. As we have seen, reminding yourself that 'it isn't real' was generally seen to be one of the most effective ways of coping with horror. The reassurance that 'it's only make-up' – or, as in Lisa and Martha's case, tomato ketchup – seemed to provide a useful means of distancing oneself from the experience. Likewise, as Martha later observed, 'even if you are getting freaked out by a film, you just have to sit there and think of how many cameras and cameramen, you know'. If emphasising the artifice of the text provided one line of defence, accusing it of implausibility offered another.[26] As Martha argued, summarily dismissing *Friday the Thirteenth*, 'you're never going to get anyone running round Ealing Broadway with a chainsaw'. Events that were seen as 'possible', such as those in *Silence of the Lambs*, were generally perceived to be more scary than those that 'would never happen' – and here again, Freddy was widely perceived to have failed the test.

However, these judgments were ultimately dependent upon the beliefs and experiences of the children themselves, and were thus inevitably variable. As I have noted, supernatural horror was regarded by many as more frightening, particularly where the children claimed to have had such experiences themselves. In the case of Serena (15), this appeared to confirm her sense of identification with the victim in *The Exorcist*:

*Serena:* I think it's because I believe that things like that can happen ... and I believe, oh God, this could really happen, would it happen to me, do you know what I mean? And that really frightened me, as well as like the effects and everything.

As in Carroll's arguments about 'suspension of disbelief' (referred to above), Serena clearly does not perceive the text as real (hence her reference to 'effects'), but her fear arises because she is prepared to entertain the possibility of an equivalent experience occurring in real life.

Nevertheless, there is also a sense in which modality judgments can represent a kind of *post hoc* rationalisation – in other words, a way of denying or avoiding unwelcome emotional reactions. The reminder that the film is not real – 'it's just a story', 'it's only make-up' – was one which, as we have seen, many parents and older children used in their attempts to reassure the younger ones. Yet such claims occasionally appeared somewhat hollow. Jessica (12), for example, explained that she did not like horror films in general:

*Jessica:* I don't like them, they're really rubbishy.

*Interviewer:* Why don't you like them?

*Jessica:* Because they're not real at all ... 'cause some of their special effects, they don't make me scared at all, and they just make me want to crack up laughing. [*slight laughter from others*]

*Interviewer:* Have you seen, have you seen one in particular like that / to make you laugh?

*Jessica:* Um / well, I can't remember actually, but some of the, like Freddy Kruger, his make-up, it's so fake, you can just tell that, oh well, and you just watch it.

*Interviewer:* Yeah. Have you seen any one of those films, the *Nightmare on Elm Street* films?

*Jessica:* No, but, 'cause I didn't particularly want to, but when you see like clips on TV and like, whoever thought this up must be a bit ... they can't be very imaginative.

While she is far from alone in criticising the make-up and special effects in these films, Jessica (like Peter, above) is clearly using arguments about modality, as well as notions of cultural value (for example, in her use of the terms 'rubbishy' and 'imaginative'), as a way of rationalising her dislike. At the same time, of course, she wants to claim that she still watches such films ('you just watch it'), since to admit otherwise – as she is eventually obliged to do – clearly undermines her argument.

Furthermore, the consequences of this kind of expertise are not necessarily straightforward: knowing more about the genre does not always mean that you will find it less frightening. Indeed, some of the older children – and even a couple of the parents – suggested that younger children might actually find horror films *less* frightening, since they would be less able to understand them. Some children reported that they would cower with fear while their younger brothers and sisters would watch apparently unaffected; while there were six-year-olds in our sample who at least *claimed* to be much less scared than their older siblings. As Karen (15) argued, in the case of her younger brother and sister, 'because they're younger than me and they don't understand it, they can't get scared'.

Likewise, some more experienced horror viewers suggested that such defences against anxiety were not necessarily effective:

*Laura (15):* You know Freddy Kruger's not real, but he still scares me ... [If I watched it again] it wouldn't have the same effect, but I'd still be scared. I'd still have to sleep with my light on.

Indeed, in some respects, greater familiarity with the conventions of the genre could be seen to *increase* one's fear, as Lisa (15) acknowledged was the case with the use of point-of-view camera:

*Lisa:* If there was like, you know, the camera makes out that there's someone in that place and [*laughs*] I get scared then ... You know, the camera like makes out that someone's staring at them ... I think 'God, something's going to happen', but then, like, I just try and not watch it.

Similarly, for Lisa and her friend Martha, it was the suspense rather than the actual bloody events themselves that caused the most fear:

*Interviewer:* So what bits in horror films do scare you? Is it the gory bits, or –

*Lisa:* No, it's like when something's about to happen and it hasn't happened.

*Martha:* It's the build-up, isn't it, the tension ... before it actually happens, before whoever it is gets killed, when they're walking round
the house, you know, with the gun or whatever, do you know
what I mean? I mean, that's the scariest part for me.

*Interviewer:* But when it actually happens?

*Martha:* When it actually happens, it's like 'oh well'.

As these extracts suggest, the fact that older children – or at least
more experienced viewers – are likely to have a more developed
understanding of generic conventions does not necessarily mean
that they are less likely to be affected than younger ones, even if
they are affected in different ways. The knowledge that the text is
not real, or even that it is edited in such a way as to manipulate
the viewer, does not necessarily help to reduce the fears which it
evokes, and on which the pleasure ultimately depends.

At the same time, it is clear that the genre teaches the compe-
tencies that are required to make sense of it, and indeed to cope
with it – and the didactic moments I have identified in *Nightmare
on Elm Street* are perhaps a rather self-conscious example of this.
As Philip Brophy[27] suggests, horror could be described as a 'genre
about genre': it is suffused with intertextual references, with self-
reflexivity, and with a parodic and deliberately excessive use of
clichés. At the same time, of course, it also has to subvert these
expectations, by providing new and unexpected shocks, if the
pleasure is still to be guaranteed. As Brophy argues:

'Horrorality' involves the construction, deployment and manipulation of horror – in all its various guises – as a textual mode. The
effect of its fiction is not unlike a death-defying carnival ride: the
subject is a willing target that both constructs the horror and is ter-
rorised by its construction. 'Horrorality' is too blunt to bother with
psychology – traditionally the voice of articulation behind horror –
because what is of prime importance is the game one plays *with* the
text, a game that is impervious to any knowledge of its workings.
The contemporary Horror film *knows* that you've seen it before; it
knows that you know what is about to happen; and it knows that
you know it knows you know. And none of it means a thing, as

the cheapest trick in the book will still tense your muscles, quicken your heart and jangle your nerves.[28]

As Brophy and others have suggested,[29] humour and self-parody would appear to be a vital dimension here, partly as a means of relieving tension, but also as a way of drawing attention to the conventions of the text itself. As we have seen, the children's accounts of particularly gory scenes were often accompanied with laughter – which may have functioned partly as a form of distancing or as a release of tension, but also perhaps as an implicit indication of the subversive nature of physical violence. At the same time, the humour also appeared to reflect the sardonic, even satirical, excesses of some of the films themselves. Donna (12), for example, offered an account of *Evil Dead* that dwelt at length upon scenes of severed limbs floating around, and on the summary deaths of several characters, but in a humorous tone which was clearly derived from the 'black' comedy of the film itself. Likewise, as we have seen, Thomas effectively 'rewrote' *Nightmare on Elm Street* as a knockabout farce.

Comedy horror was particularly important in this respect for the younger children, since it seemed to provide more explicit opportunities to balance 'negative' feelings of fear and disgust with 'positive' ones of relief – although, as I have argued, the mutual dependence of these emotions makes it hard to oppose them in quite this way. To be sure, this balance was sometimes an uneasy one. Sam (6), for example, described an incident from *Beetlejuice* as follows:

*Sam:* He says 'it's *showtime!*' and he eats all their skin, leaving out the heart on the floor, and all these yuck, and all the eyes.

*Interviewer:* How do you feel when you see that, then?

*Sam:* [*laughs*] Disgusting.

Likewise, Alice (6) described what appeared to be a satire of *Alien*, in which 'an alien thing burst out of this person's tummy and started dancing': it was, she said, 'funny and horrid and nice'. In a sense, such texts could be seen to function as a kind of preparatory experience, a form of 'coping practice' with comparatively few risks. Like the paraphernalia of Hallowe'en, the ghost masks and plastic skeletons that can be bought from joke shops, and the plethora of humorous versions of *Dracula* and *Frankenstein* that are written for young children, comedy horror appears to provide a relatively safe arena in which the fundamental anxieties with which the genre deals can begin to be addressed.

## Conclusion

As I have begun to indicate in this chapter, the diversity and complexity of children's experiences of horror should lead us to question many of the assumptions that are frequently made about it – assumptions that are often based on ignorance, not merely of children, but also of the genre itself. To be sure, children do often get frightened or disgusted by horror films, but then so do adults. The notion that the experience is therefore necessarily negative and traumatic – or indeed that it inevitably 'depraves and corrupts' – is no more valid than the idea that it is somehow automatically therapeutic. Emotional responses cannot be looked at in isolation in this way. On the contrary, the extent to which children find a film or a television programme frightening will depend upon how they perceive and interpret it; and upon the social contexts in which they watch and subsequently talk about it with others. Their developing understanding of the medium is a crucial dimension of this process, although it does not necessarily help to 'protect' them from harm: more sophisticated or knowledgeable viewers are not necessarily any less scared – although they may well experience more intense pleasure. It may be the case that, as adults, we feel it is our responsibility to intervene, and to help children learn to cope with such experiences. But it is important that we do so in a way that respects the complexity of the process, and that empowers children to make their own decisions.

## Notes

1 Plato *Republic* Book 3, 387 (1987). For a useful, if somewhat sociobiological, history of the horror genre, see Twitchell (1985).

2  Preston (1941).

3  For a brief review, see Buckingham and Allerton (1995).

4  For a somewhat more sympathetic account, albeit one that appears to be grounded in similarly essentialist conceptions of adolescence, see Twitchell (1985).

5  For example, see Phillips and Robie (1988). The same publishers also produce a range of books on the dangers of Hallowe'en.

6  See Charles Sarland (1994a, b).

7  'Agency' is a key concept in media education: it refers to the awareness of the text as a product of an individual or institution, with particular aims or motivations. See Bazalgette (1992).

8  Cantor and Sparks (1984) and Sparks (1986) found that younger children were more likely to be scared by such images, as a result of their 'perceptual boundedness'. Older children, they argue, are able to distinguish between things that may or may not *look* frightening and things that actually *are* frightening.

9  Carroll (1990).

10  Clover (1992).

11  Clover (1992) discusses the convention of the 'last girl' in modern horror.

12  Carroll (1990).

13  In this context, Julian Wood (1993) notes how the ratings system for horror often has precisely the opposite effect to that intended: it appears to mark out 'forbidden fruit', and acts as a gauge against which viewers like to test themselves.

14  See Lazarus and Folkman (1984) and Allerton (1995).

15  See Rathgeb (1991). In the notorious 'video nasties' research (Barlow and Hill, 1985), this apparent lack of narrative resolution was seen as an indication of the moral failings of this new generation of horror films.

16  For example, Zillmann (1980).

17  This is, at least in outline, what Zillmann (1980) describes as his 'excitation transfer model'. Empirical research on this issue, however, has proven inconclusive: see, for example, Tamborini and Stiff (1987) and Sparks (1991) and the review in Buckingham and Allerton (1995).

18  See, for example, Wood (1985). An obvious alternative here would be to see the genre as a kind of psychological 'safety valve' – see, for example, Brummett (1985) and Docherty *et al.* (1987). Carroll (1990) offers a direct refutation of psychoanalytic accounts of horror, not least on the grounds of their generality.

19  Creed (1986).

20  Boss (1986): and see also Brophy (1986).

21  That is, suitable for a fifteen-year-old to watch alone.

22  For an important critique of the concept of 'identification', see Barker (1989). For an account of the cognitive strategies involved in narrative comprehension, see Bordwell (1985).

23  This section also uses material gathered for the Television Literacy

Research Project, funded by the Economic and Social Research Council between 1989 and 1991 (grant no: R000231959). Analyses of some of the other retellings gathered for that project, and a broader theoretical framework for considering narrative retelling, are contained in Buckingham (1993a), Chapter 8. Nearly all the comments and quotations here relate to the first film in the series.

24 James Anderson (1990) defines an emergent audience as one that has not actually seen the programme or film, but whose responses may well condition those of viewers who do. Parents, for example, could be seen as a significant emergent audience for children's cartoons like *Teenage Mutant Hero Turtles*.

25 Hodge and Tripp (1986), particularly Chapter 2.

26 In *Children Talking Television* (Buckingham, 1993a), I follow Hodge and Tripp (1986) in referring to these as 'internal' and 'external' criteria respectively.

27 Brophy (1986). Clover (1992) also notes the parodic excess or 'gross out' of modern horror; although Gledhill (1985) argues that this self-reflexive quality was also apparent in 'classic' Gothic horror, with its rule-bound, 'mythic' approach.

28 Brophy (1986), page 5.

29 Brophy (1987).

# 5

# *Having a good cry*

## THE AMBIGUOUS PLEASURES
## OF MELODRAMA

The experience of being scared or disgusted by a gory horror film might outwardly appear to be very different from that of being moved to tears by a soap opera or a melodrama. Yet there are in fact several striking similarities between the responses analysed in the previous chapter and those to be considered here.

Significantly, both horror and melodrama are genres that attract widespread disdain and critical condemnation. Despite the long tradition of academic work on Hollywood melodrama, and the more recent attention to soap opera, both genres are still broadly dismissed as lacking in serious artistic value. As in the case of horror, this contempt for the genre often appears to reflect an underlying contempt for the people who enjoy it. A taste for 'weepies' or 'tearjerkers' – the terms themselves are suitably dismissive – is seen to be symptomatic of emotional immaturity, or at least of the inadequacies and limitations of viewers' lives. To be sure, there are significant differences here: if horror is generally seen to be the preserve of disturbed adolescent boys, melodrama and soap opera are still often regarded as suitable only for women and young girls. Yet the emotional responses that both genres evoke are widely perceived to be superficial and inauthentic. If horror is about 'cheap thrills' and 'sensation-seeking', melodrama is ultimately defined by its appeal to lachrymose sentimentality. While there are those who seek to defend the pleasures – and indeed the therapeutic benefits – of 'having a good cry', such tears are often seen to indicate a lack of aesthetic discrimination. Melodrama 'tugs on the heart strings', resorting to trite and sensational devices that can be guaranteed to

'bring a tear to the eye'; while the poor deluded viewer merely
reacts automatically and unthinkingly, as though in response to a
conditioned reflex. By contrast, the experience of being moved by
'Great Art' is seen as evidence of true discernment and artistic sen-
sibility: while 'we' are properly emotional, 'they' are merely sentimental.[1]

Yet the similarities between these genres go beyond their critical
condemnation. As I shall argue, children's responses to melodrama
and soap opera also involve a complex combination of 'distress and
delight', in which the masochistic experience of pain and suffering
is balanced by a utopian desire for the joy and pleasure that might
have been. Furthermore, as in the case of horror, these emotional
reactions depend upon complex forms of cognitive or intellectual
judgment, in which children's developing knowledge of the genre,
and of the medium itself, plays a crucial role. And, here again, the
social context of viewing and of talk about viewing significantly
determines the ways in which children make meaning and
pleasure from what they watch.

In this chapter, I define melodrama quite broadly, as a kind of
emotional 'mode' rather than a self-contained 'genre' like horror.[2]
I focus on children's reactions to moments of *pathos* in films and
television programmes from a very broad range of genres, including comedies, science fiction and action movies, as well as those
that they themselves defined as 'weepies'. While soap operas often
include significant elements of melodrama, they appear to function
in a rather different way from feature films, and for this reason are
considered separately towards the end of the chapter. Of course,
non-fictional programmes such as news and documentaries often
evoke similar responses, even if the means that are available to
deal with them are rather different; and these are considered
accordingly in the two chapters that follow.

## Holding it in, letting it out

The large majority of the children we interviewed reported that
they had experienced feelings of sadness over such melodramatic
moments, often to the point of weeping. Yet to an even greater

extent than their feelings of fear and fright, these responses appeared to be surrounded with a sense of stigma. In many cases – and particularly for some of the older boys – 'owning up' to such feelings was often characterised by denial, ambivalence and irony. This was also apparent in many of their accounts of the actual context of viewing. Many of the children here spoke of their attempts to avoid being seen to cry as a result of something they had watched; while others discussed how they had mocked others for doing so, or been mocked themselves.

As a more public venue, the cinema appeared to hold particular hazards here. Kemal (12), for example, described how he had 'bawled' in the cinema during *Turner and Hooch* and *My Girl* – 'everyone just looked at me, they was crying as well, but they just looked at me'. Liam (15) talked about his attempts to 'get out of the cinema just in time' after the tearful happy ending of *Indecent Proposal*; while Caroline (15) reported how she had seen groups of girls coming out the cinema having seen *My Girl* 'with mascara running down their faces'. Many children described how, in such situations, they would attempt to 'hold back the tears', or disguise their crying by pretending to laugh or covering their faces. Yet as Kemal acknowledged, such strategies often failed: 'you're holding yourself, like, keeping it in, and pfhhh!, it's out'.

Such strategies also ran the risk of mockery, both from parents and from peers. Carol (12), one of the most enthusiastic horror fans, reported how she had cried over a video of the cartoon *Winnie the Pooh*, although she was keen to assure us that this had occurred several years ago:

Carol: My dad started laughing at me when I was crying with *Winnie the Pooh*. My dad was going 'what's the matter with you?' I said 'there's something in my eye, my eye's watering, 'cause I've got something in my eye'. I don't like to admit to my dad that I'm crying. He's silly, he always makes fun of me.

Nevertheless, some children were keen to assert their right to such displays of emotion, even in the face of mockery from their peers:

Stella (9): Sometimes some things make me sad, but I don't want to cry because, like, if my mum or my cousins are at the house, I feel ashamed to cry.

*Carl (9):* They call you babies, innit. [*tiny laughs*]

*Stella:* It's true though.

*Carl:* They call you babies, that's why I don't cry. I just go, my face goes all red and I just go [*shows how he stops himself from crying*].

*Stella:* But sometimes I just cry, I don't care. Sometimes I cry, I don't care. Because if that's my feelings, it's not their feelings. If I cry, I cry.

As these anecdotes suggest, emotional displays of this kind were often seen to occur *despite* the constraints of the social context. Yet they were also, in a sense, a kind of social performance, particularly for the girls. As in the case of horror, such films were often viewed collectively: sharing one's responses was frequently seen as an indispensable part of the pleasure, and of the process of learning to cope. Alison (12) even described how she would telephone her friend to 'cry to her' when nobody else was available; while Jessica (12) described how frustrating it was when none of her friends had seen a film that she had found particularly moving. In a number of instances, there appeared to be a kind of 'emotional contagion', in which individuals would take their cues from each other. Tanya (9), for example, described how this had happened when her family had seen an (unidentified) Indian film: 'my cousin, right, he just went [*sniff*] like that, he wasn't really crying, he just sniffed, then my sister started crying, then my brother, then I started crying then'. On the other hand, the attempt to hold back the tears would sometimes result in a rather different kind of contagion, in which children would attempt to outdo each other's mockery, and thereby prevent the possibility of mutual embarrassment:

*Caroline (15):* Like if my little sister's there, like, she cries at films, but she thinks that anyone else crying at films is really funny. So I start going like 'oh, you know what's going to happen next, oh ha ha ha, he's going to die, ha ha ha', like that. And she and I go, 'I bet you'll cry' and all this stuff.

In other cases, however, this kind of mockery occurred in the interviews themselves. Alan and Sam (6), for example, kept up a running battle through their discussion of the children's science fiction series *Doctor Who*. Sam's admission that he had felt sad when one of the 'goodies' had died led Alan to accuse him of crying; which led Sam to retaliate by talking at some length about a scene that he described as particularly 'scary' – although Alan, of course, denied this. This kind of competition between young boys, in which each is keen to accuse the other of emotional vulnerability, is one that I have noted in previous research.[3] Yet while it may be a particular hazard for boys, in each of these instances the shame that is attached to displaying such responses derives primarily from the way in which they are defined in terms of *age* – as something that is only appropriate for 'babies'.

One strategy that was frequently used to resolve this difficulty was that of irony. Some of the teenage girls in particular self-consciously assumed the role of 'the emotional girl' – which allowed them to 'own up' to the shame of being moved to tears, while simultaneously defending the pleasure of such responses. This ironic role was often most apparent in relation to programmes that were generally regarded as self-evidently 'babyish'. Carol's description of her reactions to *Winnie the Pooh* (quoted above) is a case in point, and it was reinforced by her subsequent mention of *Lassie*. In the case of Alice (12), *Little House on the Prairie* appeared to provoke similar reactions:

*Alice:* Every Sunday I'm sitting there at 12 o'clock crying my eyes out. 'Cause every single Sunday, they always do a sad storyline, and it's so, no I like it, I like crying, I like weepy things, but there's all these things about, there was a Jewish man and blind people and miscarriages, and I'm sitting there weeping my eyes out and going through about ten boxes of Kleenex. [*laughter*]

Alice clearly distances herself from the programme, for example by defining it as 'weepy', and by her listing of the storylines; and yet she also distances herself from her own reactions, notably by the mention of the boxes of Kleenex, which occurred more than once in this context. Interestingly, some of her other contributions to the discussion were extremely (and perhaps somewhat self-consciously) 'serious', for example in discussing her responses to a documentary about anti-Semitism. Yet here, apparently aware of the low status of this material, she adopts an ironic pose – albeit one that still enables her to defend her right to cry.

Jenny (15) was another girl who appeared quite comfortable with this role. As we have seen (Chapter 3), she described a number of incidents from her childhood in which she had been publicly shamed for her distraught reactions to cartoons like *Bambi*, *Charlotte's Web* and *The Fox and the Hound*. Yet while she was happy to laugh at her former self, she was also quite willing to admit – and indeed, to celebrate – more recent instances of such reactions:

*Jenny:* If you're sitting in the cinema, and the lights come on, and you're wiping your face, you don't want people to know you've cried. If you're at home, it's all right, but in the cinema, when the lights come on / 'Cause I'll cry at anything. I'll cry at *Beauty and the Beast*, anything [*laughter*] ... Like, I watched *Sommersby*. I knew he was gonna, I knew what was going to happen. You ain't seen it, so I won't say. I knew it was coming, and I got up and got all the tissues, and I was sitting there going, 'cause my dad cries sometimes and he takes a tissue, I was sitting there going [*mimics crying*]. And I looked up and my dad was going [*mimics her dad wiping away tears*], 'cause my dad cries as well. I was just sitting there watching it, I was crying my eyes out, I was still crying when I got in bed. It was really sad. If it's really sad, I cry for ages. /

*Interviewer:* Yeah. You kind of think it's worse afterwards, in a way, or it's worse at the time?

*Jenny:* It makes you think about it. It's like, you know *Dances with Wolves*? You know when they shoot the wolf at the end? I deliberately went to bed so I didn't see that bit, and I still heard it, and I thought about it. I was still sitting there crying, 'cause I thought, 'oh no, they're shooting him'. I started crying.

The elements of irony and performance are perhaps self-evident here, most notably in Jenny's repeated imitations of herself and her father crying, and (of course) in the fetching of the tissues. Her self-conscious adoption of the emotional role is particularly apparent from her generalised self-reflexive comments, which effectively define her as a particular *type* of person – 'I'll cry at anything' and 'If it's really sad, I cry for ages.' Despite her acknowledgement of the shame of crying in public, much of her account seeks to reinforce the idea that crying is acceptable, even pleasurable. It is notable, in this respect, how she avoids revealing the ending of *Sommersby*, for fear of spoiling it for the interviewer (myself).

Jenny's positive validation of crying is also apparent here in her references to the fact that her father cries – although it appeared that her tastes were particularly shared with her mother and sister, and with friends. Indeed, in the interview itself, there was an ironic mutual support between her and Jane (also 15), who describes how they both cried over *My Girl* and *Turner and Hooch*. This was particularly apparent in their discussion of the impossible romance in *Edward Scissorhands*:

*Jane:* There was two [sad] bits. It was when he wanted to cuddle her, and he goes 'I can't.' And um, when she kissed him, she said 'I love you' and he really froze. I knew I was going to cry again. I always cry.

*Jenny:* You're a very sensitive, caring person. [*laughter*] [*To Jane:*] Don't try being nice. [*To interviewer:*] She laughs at me when I cry.

Jenny gets her own back on Jane by satirising her self-conscious presentation of herself as a 'sensitive, caring person' – although, as we have seen, this was an implicit claim in her own contributions. In both cases, what provokes the tears appears to be the *imagination* of something other than what is seen – literally, in the case of *Dances with Wolves*, which Jenny actively avoids watching, and more figuratively perhaps in the case of *Edward Scissorhands*, where the poignancy of both these scenes derives from the recognition that the relationship that is hoped for can never be achieved.

As I have indicated, then, such emotional responses are inextricably bound up with the social contexts in which they are experienced, displayed and discussed. In talking about their responses, children take on 'transitory emotional roles' which are inherently dramatic in nature, and which serve to define their own identities in particular ways.[4] At least in this instance, this process does appear to have a particularly gendered dimension. Thus, while there were certainly many instances of boys talking about how they had cried or felt sad, this was more frequent and (crucially) more *self-conscious* among girls. Broadly speaking, boys were more likely to report that they disliked 'soppy' films, or that they would actively avoid them – although this kind of response was by no means confined to them. Nevertheless, it was almost exclusively the girls who expressed positive enthusiasm for such films, as something they would actively seek out; and it was also the girls who asserted their *right* to 'let it out' – to display their emotions, rather than keeping them under control.

The girls themselves explicitly acknowledged this gendered dimension only rarely, and not always positively: Martha (15), for example, described the way in which she had cried over *My Girl* with her mother and her sister as 'a typical women's thing to do'. On the other hand, later in the above discussion, Jane, Jenny and Sarah spoke about how their class had responded to the film *Threads*, which they had seen in a Humanities lesson. Jane argued that 'a lot of people' had probably been moved by the film, even though they were unlikely to admit it:

*Interviewer:* Why do you think people don't want to admit to it?

*Jane:* Well, people like Trevor, he's really, like 'don't look at me, I'm bad', and he can't admit to something like that. He'd never admit to crying or something like that. We all do it.

*Jenny:* He would jokingly, say 'oh yeah, I've cried', but /

*Sarah:* I think [with] things like that, more girls open up.

*Jane:* I think girls cry more at things like that ... I don't think a man would cry at *The Little Mermaid*.

Interestingly, Trevor did in fact 'admit' to being upset by the ending of *Mary Poppins* – although quite how seriously is hard to evaluate. Yet it is clear that crying – or, more accurately, a willingness to *admit* to crying – is seen positively here, as an indication of girls' greater ability to 'open up'. However ironical and self-mocking it may have been, there was an implicit assumption among the girls that they were indeed more 'sensitive and caring', or at least that they were prepared to display this side of themselves. The key point, though, is not that boys are accused of being 'unfeeling' – as Jane says, 'we all do it' – but that the *public display* of emotion was seen as something that they were keen to avoid.

For one of the mothers, this display of emotion was described as distinctly therapeutic, particularly for her four sons:

*Veronica:* One school holiday, I went and got them from the video shop, one of their karate films / and I also got them *The Incredible Journey*. It's one of my favourite films, and although it was sad, they were on the edge of their seats ... even though they're four boys, they had tears coming down their face, they were shouting at the animals as though they were there. It was wonderful to see ...

*Interviewer:* So you think it's good for them?

*Veronica:* Yes ... I think for us here, I've got four boys, I'm the only female here, and I think the tendency tends to be / macho ... Therefore I try to bring in the female side of it, I suppose. Although I enjoy their karate films when I sit down with them, and some of them are mine anyway. [*laughs*] ... I want them to be able to look after themselves, but I want them to be emotional. I think men should be emotional as well.

Like Jenny and her friends, Veronica argues that women are more in touch with their emotions, and defines this not as a weakness, but as a positive attribute. While she herself is interested in what she implicitly defines as the 'male side' – represented by the karate films – she explicitly argues for a balance between 'male' and 'female'. In this context, melodramatic films have an almost pedagogical function. Here again, the issue is not so much one of internal feelings, but of public *display* – in this instance, in the face of potential mockery from one's siblings. Yet as I shall argue, the question of what it means to 'be emotional', and the wider political dimensions of this argument, are not necessarily straightforward or easily resolved.

## A litany of sorrows

What is it that makes us cry or feel sad in response to what we watch? One obvious way of beginning to answer this question is to look at the *content* of the children's talk. Across these interviews, two broad themes emerged with remarkable consistency.

The first and most prevalent of these concerns the disruption of the family, or of family-like groupings. As critics have frequently noted, the family is often the focus of narrative conflict in melodrama: it acts both as the generator of fundamental psychic problems, and as the means of their resolution.[5] For some early feminist critics, this emphasis was the key to the genre's appeal to women, but also to its ultimate conservatism. The Hollywood family melodramas of the 1950s, for example, were seen to acknowledge the suppressed contradictions at the heart of family relations, and the subversive desires of women, yet ultimately to recuperate these within a patriarchal resolution.[6]

Nevertheless, for children – and particularly younger children – the family may be seen much less ambivalently as a source of safety and security, at least on the level of fiction. The process by which family harmony is lost or destroyed through death or separation was emphasised in the children's accounts of a very wide range of films, many of them quite different from the 'classic' melodramas that have been the focus of so much film criticism. The separation between the sisters in *The Color Purple*, and between E. T. and his alter-ego Elliot; the son regretfully abandoned by his parents in *Running on Empty*; the final departure of Mary Poppins from the family home; the daughter's fear that her father had left at the end of *Curly Sue*; the separation of the boy from his parents in *Empire of the Sun*; the death of the father in *Ghost Dad* and *Terminator*, of the mother in *The Land Before Time*, *Beaches* and *Bambi*, and of the young boy in *Yol* and *Mad Max*; and even the estrangement of Uncle Fester from the Addams Family had all been occasions for tears or sadness. A related theme, which we have already encountered in the case of *Edward Scissorhands*, was that of the impossible romance – in effect, of the family that never was: *Ghost* and *My Girl* were key texts that were mentioned by many children here.

The second major theme that emerged here – and which was also a key issue in relation to non-fictional programmes – was that of pity towards those who are presumed to be vulnerable or defenceless. Again, this theme of the persecution of innocence is one that can be traced throughout the history of melodrama, and is a central aspect of its enactment of eternal struggles between good and evil.[7] As Patricia Holland has observed, the less understanding and power such characters have, the greater the poignancy – and children, dogs, extra-terrestrials and woodland creatures are therefore bound to be prime candidates for such roles.[8] On the other hand, of course, it is on the grounds of its 'exploitation' of these kinds of responses that much of the critical disdain for the genre has been based – as though pity was somehow inherently a suspect emotion, or a sign of emotional immaturity.

A paramount concern in this respect was that of violence towards animals. Again, the range of films here was quite heterogeneous: the killing of the wolf in *Dances with Wolves*, of the otter in *Ring of Bright Water*, of the gorillas in *Gorillas in the Mist* and of miscellaneous animals in *Rookie* and *The Animals of Farthing Wood* were all mentioned. The death (or fake death) of the dogs in the comedies *Turner and Hooch* and *K-9* was also discussed by many. Violence towards children was another theme that recurred here, both in relation to realist texts such as *Threads*, *Child of Rage* and *My Name is Stephen* and (on several occasions) in relation to the child robot Johnny Five in the children's fantasy *Short Circuit*. Finally, pity was also expressed towards those who were physically deformed, as in *Mask* and *Elephant Man*; or who suffered from mental illness, as in the TV movie *Winnie*.

Despite the remarkable consistency in terms of content, there are obviously significant differences between these texts, not least in terms of genre and modality. Suffering in a comedy will evoke very different expectations from suffering in a realist drama, which will be different again from a cartoon or a fairytale fantasy. As in the case of horror, there are also interesting questions about the status of endings here. In many of the comedies, the suffering is eventually overcome (*Turner and Hooch*, *Short Circuit*), while in the more realist dramas, it tends to remain unresolved at the end of the film (*Running on Empty*, *Yol*). 'Children's films' and cartoons are perhaps more likely to offer consolations that continue beyond the moments of suffering or separation (*The Land Before Time, Bambi*); yet there are significant exceptions to this (*E. T., My Girl, Edward Scissorhands*). In contrast to their discussions of horror, the children's accounts of these films often concentrated on the endings: yet interestingly, 'happy' endings in which the suffering was overcome (most notably in *The Color Purple*) seemed to evoke tears just as much as 'sad' ones, in which it was not.

## Tears for what might have been ...

These considerations begin to move us on towards a discussion, not merely of content, but also of form. To a large extent, of course, the things that make us cry in films also make us cry in real life; but to pose the issue in these terms – as a kind of reflex reaction to particular kinds of content – is to oversimplify the ways in which the relationship between the text and the viewer actually *works*.

Among the substantial body of critical work on melodrama, the question of viewers' emotional responses has largely been conspicuous by its absence. The reasons for this may be partly historical: melodrama originally came to attention in Film Studies following the development of the 'auteur theory' and *mise-en-scène* criticism, neither of which displayed much concern with audiences.[9] The focus of much of this criticism was on a narrow 'canon' of Hollywood directors (notably Sirk, Minnelli and Ophuls), and in particular on the family melodramas of the 1950s. Yet even more recent analyses of the ideological and historical dimensions of the genre, while broader in scope, have barely begun to address this fundamental absence.

Perhaps a more significant reason for this neglect, however, is the way in which the question of emotional responses has been bound up with wider political concerns. The films of Douglas Sirk, for example, were praised primarily for their 'irony': the aesthetic 'excess' of the *mise-en-scène* (for example, in the stylised use of lighting) was seen to produce a critical distancing from the 'dominant ideology' the films were said to represent. Yet the question of whether such responses were available to the primary audiences of the films, or merely to a coterie of intellectual film critics, remains unanswered. As Christine Gledhill has observed, this emphasis on irony may continue to denigrate naive 'feminine' responses to the films – such as weeping – in favour of the rationalistic readings of male critics.[10]

Steve Neale[11] offers one of the very few discussions of this issue within the Film Studies tradition. Following an argument developed by Franco Moretti,[12] Neale suggests that melodrama's ability to evoke tears depends upon two key characteristics of its mode of narration. Firstly, he argues, melodrama establishes fundamental discrepancies in knowledge between the characters in the film and the viewer: the viewer *knows more* than the characters, and the narrative must progress towards the point at which the characters' perceptions coincide with those of the viewer. For example, we know that two characters really love each other, but for various reasons, they do not publicly recognise this, and only come to do so when the obstacles in their path are removed. What is crucial for melodrama, however, is Neale's second characteristic, that of timing: the poignancy and pathos that are evoked depend upon the resolution coming *too late* – or at least upon the fear that it *might* come too late (which would explain the fact that we can still cry over a 'happy' ending). The viewer's tears, Neale argues, arise from the discrepancy between our desire for a happy ending, and the recognition of our powerlessness to alter the outcome of events: we know what we want, but we also fear that it may remain forever beyond our reach. In a sense, then, the melodrama is based on a fundamental contradiction. On the one hand, the narrative invites us to occupy a position of mastery, and thereby to recognise the *possibility* of a happy ending. Yet on the other, it invites us into a kind of masochistic empathy with the suffering of the characters, which we fear is ultimately impossible to avoid.[13]

As Neale argues, what motivates the wish for a happy ending often takes the form of adult, heterosexual desire. Yet as he suggests, it might also be seen more broadly, as a reflection of the basic human desire to be loved – or indeed, in more psychoanalytic terms, as a 'nostalgic fantasy of childhood characterised by union with the mother'.[14] It is the articulation of this fantasy, he argues, that accounts for the pleasure of crying:

> tears in childhood arise as a consequence of loss, the loss, particu-
> larly, of a sense of union with the mother. However, crying isn't
> simply an articulation of this loss, it is also a demand for its repa-
> ration – a demand addressed most commonly *to* the mother, who
> is thus situated in fantasy as a figure capable of fulfilling that
> demand. Crying, therefore, is not just an expression of pain or dis-
> pleasure or non-satisfaction. As a demand *for* satisfaction, it is the
> vehicle of a wish – a fantasy – that satisfaction is possible, that the
> object can be restored, the loss eradicated ... Tears, in this sense,
> can be *comforting* in a very fundamental way.[15]

Although Neale's argument is developed primarily in relation to
the classic melodramas of silent cinema, and to the family melodramas of the 1950s, it also provides an interesting insight into the
children's discussions of such moments in a much wider range of
films. What appeared to characterise many of these accounts was
a sense of longing for 'what might have been' – a kind of utopian
search for something that is forever lost.[16]

This was most apparent in the way in which the children chose
to focus on very specific moments or details. Some of these were
clearly concerned with the ultimate impossibility of romantic love,
as in the case of Jane's description of *Edward Scissorhands* (above).
Thus, in *Ghost*, for example, it was the scene in which the lovers
danced for the last time; in *Beauty and the Beast*, it was the slaying
of the Beast; while in *Dracula*, it was the scene in which Mina kills
Dracula, in the knowledge that he can only live as a vampire. Likewise, in the case of family separations, many children emphasised
that the characters *wanted* to stay together or be reunited, but
could not – for example, in the departure of E. T., or the conflicting
desires of the characters in *Separated at Birth*. Even in the case of
characters who evoked pity, it was the recognition that things
might have been otherwise that appeared to evoke the most tears:
in the case of *Mask*, for example, this was apparent in a description of the scene in which the deformed boy visits a hall of mirrors
at a funfair and sees himself as 'normal'.

*My Girl* is a film that evoked similar reactions, as Martha and

Caroline's account illustrates:

*Martha (15):* The little boy, Macaulay Culkin, he's got this really bad allergic reaction to bee stings, and his friend, this girl, loses her ring, and he's got to go and get it from this sort of forest thing. And he knocks over this beehive, and all these bees like attack him, and he gets killed. And then he's got like an open coffin, and the little girl Anna, or something, she was going 'give him his glasses, he can't see without his glasses'. And it's just really sad. Like, they're both really good at acting, 'cause they're both really young.

*Caroline (15):* I think it's really sad when she goes, she's got this doctor, and 'cause like her dad's a funeral director, she's really obsessed with ways of dying ... and they say 'keep her away from the funeral, 'cause she'll get even more obsessed with death'. And she's meant to look after this mad grandmother, except she comes into the funeral and she goes like a bit crazy. And it's really sad, because she's acting like he's still alive, he's just asleep, and it's really sad.

What appears to be most poignant here is the girl's unwillingness or inability to accept that the boy is dead – although what is also at stake is the impossibility of romance, since what has motivated the boy to search for the ring in the first place is his unrequited love for the girl. The discrepancy of knowledge that Neale describes also plays a part here, both in relation to the boy's allergy to bee stings, and in the viewer's knowledge that the funeral is taking place, and that the boy really is dead. The pathos also hinges on specific details, such as the glasses and, in the following extract, the ring:

*Martin (12):* The thing I found was sad was, it says 'this was in his hand, his clutched hand, when he died', and it's the ring. But the thing was, whenever she used to wear it, it was black when he was there, and now it was blue, it was one of those change colour things to your emotion. And I thought that was sad.

This focus on symbolic details, that represent the harmony that has been lost or that can never be attained, was apparent in accounts of other films. Kemal and Jacob (12), for example, gave an extended account of the Turkish epic *Yol*, which they had seen in school, focusing particularly on this scene of the death of a child:

*Kemal:* And like after, they've spent all this money, and they catch all of them, but the kid and the man is left, and they're like freezing to death for one day, and the kid dies, and like –

*Jacob:* Yeah, he had a flower, it was like a drug, kind of thing.

*Kemal:* No, all through the film, you see, he had this kind of stick the he used to suck, and when he finally died, you can see when he dies, the stick fell away. You see, 'cause he always kept it in his mouth. The thing was, he died just before the coach came. He was signalling away, he was like that, he was in his hands ... and it dropped away as soon as the coach came.

Here again, the poignancy of the scene arises from the way in which it is just too late for the boy to be saved, and thus for the family (which has been torn apart through the events of the film) to be reunited. Like the ring in *My Girl*, the flower here seems to symbolise the possibility of a lost harmony.

This focus on poignant detail was also notable in accounts of films that were otherwise far from melodramatic. Here, Sam (6) recounts a scene from *Terminator 2* in which a solution is apparently promised that will overcome the sadness of the moment:

*Sam:* That's sad, because he goes in the lava, and it's sad for the boy. Because he comes alive again, and when he goes into the lava, he puts [his thumb] like that, when he's going down ...

*Interviewer:* He puts his thumb out. Why does he put his thumb out then?

*Sam:* Because he likes the boy, they're his sons.

In this case, the 'thumbs up' gesture appears to symbolise the possibility of continuing family relationships in a world that is otherwise dominated by technology and violence. Indeed, as in many melodramas, the narrative of *Terminator* is one in which the lost harmony of the family is gradually reconstituted, as the hero progressively overcomes such obstacles to fulfilment.

As I have noted, even where the children's fears were resolved at the end of the film, the possibility that the worst *might* have happened often seemed to be enough to evoke tears. This was most obvious in comedies like *Curly Sue*, where the girl's belief that her father had left home proved to be false; or in *K-9*, where the dog turns out to be alive after all. In the case of *The Color Purple*, tears arose not simply because of pity for the sufferings of the vulnerable heroine, but also because of the way in which the obstacles to a happy ending were overcome, and the family reunited. On the other hand, films that appeared to offer such resolutions and then snatched them away were seen to be particularly poignant. Jessica (12), for example, described her responses to the climax of the Channel Four drama *Comics* as follows:

*Jessica:* It wasn't sad until the end, and then, 'cause he was so drunk, there was a delayed shock on his body. So he didn't die in the crash, you see, and then he just died. And I was like, it was so unexpected, 'cause he was, 'cause I got to like the character, you see ... Sometimes when you cry, you just get a lump in your throat, or just a few tears in your eyes, but they were like streaming down my face ... He was like so nice and a good actor, and you're like [*mimics crying*] aaahhh.

As these examples suggest, the form of the eventual resolution – whether 'happy' or 'sad' – does not in itself appear to determine whether or not the viewer is moved to tears. What seems to be more crucial is the way in which the film enables the viewer to entertain the *possibility* of a positive outcome, while reinforcing the fact that such things may be subject to accident and fate. The film allows us the power to imagine, while simultaneously denying us the power to influence what takes place.

### As if it were real

A further dimension of this process relates to the question of modality – that is, of the relationship between the fictional text and reality. Compared with the children's discussions of horror, modality appeared to be much less of an issue here. There were occasional references to the constructed nature of the text, but these were few and far between. Some children described how they would attempt to reassure themselves with the knowledge that the film was 'not real', or that it was 'only acting'. Yet, as in the case of horror, a knowledge of generic or narrative conventions did not necessarily provide protection: for example, as Caroline (15) said of *My Girl*, 'you could tell what was going to happen, you started feeling sad, and then when it did happen, it was worse'. Nevertheless, most references to modality were either neutral or positive. As in Martha's comments on *My Girl* or Jessica's on *Comics*, there was sometimes praise for 'good acting'; yet throughout these discussions, there were no instances of the kind of criticism that were routinely made of horror films – that they were poorly acted, implausible, or simply 'fake'.

At the same time, a number of children expressed a particular interest in films that were believed to be based on 'true stories'. Jane (15), for example, spoke at length about *Child of Rage*, a 'true story' film about child abuse that she described as 'brilliant'. Jenny (12) was another enthusiast for such films, and particularly mentioned *Empire of the Sun* and *The Leaving of Liverpool*: while she was aware of the fictional aspects of such films, she was keen to assert that 'things like that really did happen'. Jenny's major interest in this respect, however, was in what she called 'serious' war films such as *Platoon* and *Born on the Fourth of July*: she described how her father would tell her stories about the war, 'and you think, oh no, it really did happen, and you get really sad about it'. Some other fictional films were also praised in similar terms, particularly *The Color Purple*: Jenny again was keen to confirm the film's plausibility – 'even though you think "oh yeah, it's just a film", it's actually happening today, like there's loads of people who have arranged marriages, and that probably happens to them'. As Serena (15) argued, the recognition that the film is – or at least might be – a 'true story' made it much more upsetting: ''cause you can feel for the person, whereas if it's just a made up fiction story, then you can think "well, it's only made up"'.

On the other hand, in some cases, the acknowledgement of the constructed nature of the text was seen to undermine the pleasures of 'having a good cry':

*Jenny (15):* [You cry] 'cause you've fallen in love with a character, so it means it's a good film. 'Cause if you can believe the character, and cry for the character when he dies, it's a really good film.

*Interviewer:* But you were saying you can try and stop yourself by saying 'oh, it's not real, it's only acting'.

*Jenny:* It doesn't usually work, but you can try ...

*Jane (15):* I try and hold them in, but they just come out.

This question of the reality status of melodrama has been a key issue in the academic debates surrounding the genre. Melodrama has, of course, traditionally been condemned for its implausibility, and its reliance on an accumulation of improbable accidents and coincidences – an impression that the accounts of films like *My Girl* (quoted above) might well confirm. One implication of such criticisms is that audiences read melodramas literally, as though they were some form of surrogate documentary. However, more recent attempts to re-evaluate the genre have suggested that viewers distinguish between the 'unrealistic' outward appearance of events and the more 'realistic' experiences to which they refer. Christian Viviani, for example, argues that underneath its 'outer layer' of baroque complexity and excess, melodrama possesses an 'inner core' which is based on 'situations, feelings and emotions which everyone has experienced at some time or another'.[17] Likewise, in her account of *Dallas*, Ien Ang distinguishes between 'empiricist realism' – which, she argues, functions at a cognitive or intellectual level – and 'emotional realism'.[18] Viewers who enjoy the programme, she asserts, do not judge it in terms of its accuracy, as though it were attempting to provide a literal representation of the 'outside world', but in terms of its *emotional* truth – that is, in terms of whether the personal feelings and dilemmas of the characters are psychologically 'recognisable' in terms of their own experiences.

These observations might partly account for the relative absence of the kinds of modality judgments that were so prevalent in the children's discussions of horror. Nevertheless, some of the arguments introduced in the previous chapter would also seem to apply here. As I have argued, following Noel Carroll,[19] what appears to generate – or at least make possible – the emotional response to horror is the viewer's willingness to entertain the *possibility* that such events might happen, even while acknowledging that they are not real. From this perspective, the viewer does not so much 'suspend disbelief' as imaginatively 'translate' such events into the context of his or her own life.

In some instances here, the children drew a direct connection with their own or others' real-life experiences. Carl (9), for example, said he had been upset by *Turner and Hooch* because it reminded him of how his mother had 'got rid of' his own dog; while Mike (12) described how he had 'felt worse' when his mother told him about a person who had a similar affliction to the boy in *Mask*. While such experiences were somewhat more common in relation to soap operas, as we shall see, they were still quite rare.

On the other hand, many children described a kind of imaginative leap – a recognition that 'this could happen to me' – which appeared to be characteristic of their responses both to melodrama and to horror. Significantly however, the positions the children adopted here were not necessarily those of the immediate victims – those who were killed, for example, or who disappeared – but often seemed to be those of the people who were left behind – the bereaved, or others who had to live with the experience of loss. While this might be described as a form of 'identification', it was much more *hypothetical* than this term tends to suggest. It did not appear to involve 'stepping into the shoes' of the character and simply sharing their responses to the situation. On the contrary, it seemed to depend upon importing the feelings evoked by the situation back into the context of their own everyday lives, and transferring them from the fictional characters to themselves or to people they knew.

In some instances, these accounts were based on what I have termed a 'narrative of the self'. Anthony (15), for example, described how he had seen a 'rags to riches' film about a baseball star called *The Babe* and had been upset at his eventual decline:

*Anthony:* I wouldn't like that to happen to me, from being nobody, you're top, used to everything, you could buy yourself ten cars and all that stuff like that, and then next thing you know, you've got nothing, nothing ... I wouldn't like that to happen to me at all.

Yet if Anthony's account appears to be based on a kind of fantasy 'identification' between himself and the central character, in most cases these accounts reflected more realistic fears of bereavement, and particularly of the death of parents. The death of the mother in *Beaches*, for example, was discussed in this way by a number of girls. Lisa (15) said she had asked herself 'how would I feel if that was my mum?'; while for Alison (12), the film had fed into a more general sense of crisis surrounding her recognition of mortality:

*Alison:* I went through this stage when I was little when I kept on seeing all these films about parents dying and all of this. And every night I would cry myself to sleep, and I would go down and go to my mum 'I don't want you to die' and all of this. But she didn't, she wasn't ill or anything, I just didn't want her to die. 'Cause all the things I'd seen, like *Beaches* ... when her mum dies and she has to go and live with her mum's best friend and everything. And that affected me so much ... It just suddenly came to me that anyone could die at any time.

Similar fears appeared to have been evoked by a number of other films and programmes. Kemal (12), for example, said that after watching *My Girl*, 'I imagined my mum and dad dying, just imagining it, I cried.' Likewise, Jessica (12) reported similar fears that had arisen in relation to scenes showing a man with senile dementia in the TV comedy *If You See God, Tell Him*:

*Jessica:* It's like really upsetting that he's old. 'Cause like my grandma, 'cause she's ill, and you think 'oh that could really happen', even though it's supposed to be a comedy.

As all these accounts suggest, such responses involve an act of *imagination* in order to make the connection between fiction and reality. There is no sense of a confusion between the two: on the contrary, as in Jessica's comment, investing the text with a kind of realism seems to happen *in spite of* its fictional status.

Yet certainly in the case of *Beaches*, there was also a sense in which the emotional responses to such events were partly 'cued' by the responses of the characters in the film – again, in the same way that Noel Carroll argues is the case in relation to horror.[20] The concern here was not so much for the suffering of the mother, but for the bereavement on the part of the daughter, as Lisa (15) made clear:

*Lisa:* You think about it, how would you react if one of your relatives [died] or something. And then I think how her kids must feel, and you think how you'd carry on, like if your mum died or something, how it would change you and everything.

Likewise, Jessica (12) described how she had cried when the Tom Cruise character in *Rain Man* had dropped his 'tough' exterior and wept at the end of the film; while Nancy (12) had cried in response to seeing the family in *Running on Empty* doing the same. Here too, the experience that is imagined is that of the person who is bereaved, or forced to abandon somebody they love. If there is a kind of masochistic 'identification' here, it is not so much with the primary victims themselves (as it often is in the case of horror), as with those who have to live on and suffer in the knowledge that their desires could not be fulfilled.

### Coping and the limits of modality

This discussion raises some interesting questions about how children learn to cope with such experiences – and indeed, whether 'coping' has the same significance here as it does in relation to other genres. In many respects, the coping strategies described here were very similar to those that were applied to horror films. Some children simply avoided material that they felt might make them cry or feel sad; while others said that they would turn off the television, hide under a cushion or walk out of the room. Likewise, in attempting to overcome such feelings, a similarly broad range of strategies was described. Some children would attempt to distract themselves, for example by watching something else or reading a book or drawing, while others would just 'try to forget it'. Some sought comfort from food, or by getting under the bedcovers; while others (as we have seen) would try to find somebody else to talk to.

In other instances, however, the children described how they would seek to re-interpret or intervene in the text in various ways. As with horror, a couple of the younger children described forms of 'fantasy participation', both in relation to the mistreatment of Johnny Five in *Short Circuit*. Luke (6), of zombie suit fame, described how he would imagine that he was inside the film, and would attack the bad characters with a knife; while Stella (9) described a similar response:

*Stella:* What I would have done, I would, if I could, I just always say this in my head, if I could have went through the telly, they wouldn't be alive any more.

*Interviewer:* So if you could jump into the telly, then you'd kill those people, and then the robot would be all right?

*Stella:* Yeah. 'Cause I'd treat him like he was my own, my only best friend, and he's a hero.

While such responses are more likely to be confined to younger children – although there are many adults who regularly talk back to the screen – they cast an interesting light on Neale's observations about the 'powerlessness' of the viewer. Here, the desire to bring about the fantasy of a happy ending leads the children to imagine that they can intervene physically in the text, literally going 'through the telly'.

In other instances, children described how they had used video to manipulate the text, and thereby change their own responses. Donna (6) recounted how her younger sister had helped her to deal with her fears of the death of Prince Eric in *The Little Mermaid* in this way:

*Donna:* 'Cause I said, 'he's gonna die, he's gonna die, he's gonna die'. But I was wrong. My sister said 'no he's not, I've seen this before, he's not gonna die, he's still alive' ... I said 'OK, let me see.' So she winded our video forward and then she went '*see*, he didn't die, he's still alive'.

On the other hand, repeat viewing was not always seen to be an effective strategy: a number of children described how the same feelings recurred on a second or third viewing, even though they were well aware of the outcome. Jenny (12) argued that there was a significant difference in this respect between 'sad films' and 'scary films':

*Jenny:* They're different. Because you don't know what's going to happen in a scary film, but like if you watch it for the second time, you're prepared for it. / In a sad film, a real-life sad film, you're like, you know what's going to happen, but it's just / sad.

As we have seen, there was certainly evidence that, in the case of horror, knowing what was going to happen – or indeed, knowing that it was all make-up and special effects – did not necessarily reduce children's fears. Nevertheless, there was a sense in which the feelings evoked by 'sad films' were seen to be more lasting and perhaps more 'real' than those evoked by horror – particularly where they could be 'translated' to potential or actual experiences in real life. This was explicitly argued by one mother:

*Yasmin:* One thing that upset Nancy was *Stand By Me*. Both her and David were in tears after that. And I mean, it's generally things that you think wouldn't upset them, things that aren't so obvious. Like, 'cause the horror and things like that, the few that they have watched, they might be frightened that very night, but the next day they're fine. But the emotional things really play on their minds ... it's almost like they can see that the horror is just a movie, but it's those emotions that they can actually feel themselves that are more real.

Again, it would be important to distinguish in this respect between what some of the children called 'monster films' like *Nightmare on Elm Street*, whose basic premise was widely regarded as implausible, and those that were based on the supernatural, where the children were more inclined to believe that there might be 'something in it', and thus more likely to be frightened. Nevertheless, the question of which feelings are 'more real', as Yasmin puts it, and thus perhaps more lasting, is an interesting one.

Like Yasmin, many of the other parents said they had been surprised by the films or programmes their children had found upsetting – although, as in the case of Veronica's experience with *The Incredible Journey*, such responses were not necessarily seen as a bad thing. What was striking here, however, was the discrepancy between children's attempts to regulate their own responses and the strategies that parents described, which were almost exclusively based on modality judgments. Thus, for example, a number of parents had tried to deal with their children's distress over *Turner and Hooch* by reminding them that it was 'just a film' and that (as one put it) 'it's only an acting dog'; while similar strategies were described in relation to *Ring of Bright Water* and *Dances with Wolves*. Yet in some respects the feelings that had been evoked by such films appeared to be remarkably resistant to this kind of rationalisation. As I have argued, such feelings may be a consequence not of a belief in the reality of what is shown, but of an imaginative attempt to 'translate' the events of the text across to one's own life. If this is the case, then a response based on demonstrating the fictional nature of the text is unlikely to make very much difference. Once the imaginative leap has been made, it may prove hard to undo; and perceiving the text as unreal may not dispel the fear that something similar might come about in one's own life.

## Playing with the text: soap opera and the critical viewer

Examining the children's discussions of soap operas casts a slightly different light on this relationship between emotional responses and modality judgments. Of course, some soap operas are closer to melodrama than others, yet there are several broad similarities between the two genres. The family, for example, plays a central structuring role in soap opera narratives, although particularly in the more social realist British soaps it often exists alongside, and occasionally comes into conflict with, notions of community.[21] In terms of narrative form, the satisfaction of the happy ending that is constantly promised – and often denied – by melodrama is, in a sense, permanently deferred by the ongoing story of the soap opera. Like the melodrama, the soap opera tends to place the viewer in a position of comparative 'mastery', in which we frequently know more than the protagonists; and yet our recognition of the complex interrelationships of the characters, and the apparently immovable structures in which they are embedded, leads us to accept the futility of fantasy and the inevitability of suffering. In this respect, both genres share what Ien Ang has called 'the tragic structure of feeling'.[22]

Yet despite the dangers of generalisation, there are equally clear differences between the two genres. Soap operas tend to have a much broader range of characters, enabling viewers to shift their 'identifications' as the narrative proceeds. British soaps in particular tend to move between a number of distinct emotional 'modes', as comedy gives way to social realism and thence to melodrama. Furthermore, the extensive coverage of soap operas in the press and on television, and their role in everyday conversation, means that a great deal of additional information is available, for example about future developments in the narrative, about the production process and about the private lives of the stars. In different ways, all these characteristics would tend to undermine the sustained emotional intensity that is generally seen to be required of melodrama.

On the other hand, the fact that the characters in soap operas are often on our screens two, three or even five times a week, and over several years, may well encourage a belief that they are, if not real, then at least people whom we 'know' in the same way as we know friends or acquaintances. Furthermore, at least in the case of the British and Australian soaps, the undemonstrative filming style, the realist sets and the profusion of everyday detail all contribute to a sense of the soap opera as comparatively closer to real life than most other television genres. If the very 'ordinariness' of soaps might also appear to undermine their emotional intensity, it could nevertheless be seen as a kind of guarantee of their emotional authenticity. Melodramatic moments may occur comparatively rarely, although of course with much greater frequency than in most viewers' real lives. Yet when they do occur, they are acted out by people who are very familiar to us, and in settings that we recognise very well. For both reasons, they may appear much more 'real', or at least more authentic, than the more improbable events and the visual 'excess' of the full-blown melodrama.

Research on soap opera audiences has frequently addressed the

fundamental ambivalence that characterises the genre's relationship with reality. As numerous studies have shown,[23] the viewer
typically shifts between an intense involvement with the characters and with the fictional world of the text, and a comparatively
distanced, even playful, recognition of its conventionality and artificiality. In Christine Geraghty's terms, viewing soap opera involves
a kind of 'double vision', an 'oscillation between engagement and
distance'.[24] Crucially, however, this should not be seen as an
either/or relationship, but as a necessary tension that is essential
to the genre. The 'ironic viewing attitude' is not, as Ien Ang[25]
would have it, merely confined to those who regard soap opera
with disdain, yet who watch it as a kind of 'cultural slumming'.
On the contrary, it is characteristic of viewers in general – and not
least of children.

Thus, on the one hand, there were many instances in which
children described sad or moving moments in soaps. As in the films
discussed above, these often appeared to involve threats to the stability of the family, or obstacles to the fulfilment of romance. Here
too, much of the poignancy appeared to derive from the way in
which the viewer was granted superior knowledge to the characters: Alan (6), for example, recounted two storylines from *Neighbours* and *Home and Away* which both depended upon the
characters' inability to speak about their true affections. Likewise,
the death of long-lasting characters was often an occasion for grief,
and for an implicit recognition of 'what might have been'. Again,
in many cases, the children appeared to focus on the emotions of
the bereaved characters, or those who had suffered loss. On the
other hand, moments of resolution – such as the marriage of Scott
and Charlene in *Neighbours* – were also an occasion for tears.

As I have noted, the children appeared to be more able to relate
the events in soaps to their own lived experiences. This was apparent, for example, in Hannah's account of marital breakdown in
*EastEnders* – an account that led on, at first sight quite paradoxically, to a discussion of the film comedy *Home Alone 2*:

*Hannah (6):* Well, Arthur was being horrible to Pauline. I think so.
Pauline didn't let Arthur live there until a long time, and that made

me feel a bit sad, because I like those two. I don't like them fighting
and / when I was watching my video called *Home Alone*, well I
didn't like it because um, I don't because um / Kevin gets lost in
the big city ... and I think that's so horrible, just wanting to be on
his own. And he goes 'oh no, my family's in Florida and I'm in New
York' he goes. Suddenly, then he does that smile, 'cause that's how
he wanted to be, 'cause he didn't trust anyone in his family.

*Interviewer:* But you thought it was a bit sad, though?

*Hannah:* Yeah, because I don't think he would have never done that
... And my daddy, well my mummy / I think my daddy was being
horrible to my mum, right / this is not on telly / well, because I felt
so, and it made me sad because when daddy came up to say bye
bye, because he went to live and stay with his mum ... I thought I
would never see him again. Because who would take me to school?
... I thought now I'm going to be left alone.

The fear of abandonment by one's parents displayed by Hannah in
this extract is, I would argue, the largely unspoken anxiety that
informs a great many of these children's observations – and to this
extent, it would support Steve Neale's assertions about the fantasy
of union with the mother as the driving force of melodrama. Nevertheless, Hannah's fears inform her judgments of these two contrasting texts in interesting ways. Pauline and Arthur clearly
'stand in' for her parents – although her affectionate comment 'I
like those two' seems to suggest that she recognises them not only
as people, but also as fictional characters. On the other hand, Kevin
'stands in' for Hannah – although the fact that his response to
abandonment is so different from her own causes her to question
his plausibility.

Viewers' ability to relate the events in soap operas to their own
situations – despite their recognition of the differences between
them – does support Ang's argument about 'emotional realism'.
While sometimes extremely distressing, this could also be seen as
potentially therapeutic. In the following extract, the mother of
Lewis (10) and Adrian (15) recounts one such instance:

*Ruth:* The most poignant thing was a couple of / two and a half years
ago now, my father died. And there was a character called little

Toby Mangle on *Neighbours*, and what's his name died. Well, Adrian had grieved properly, but Lewis found that quite difficult. Well, when this happened there, it just opened his emotions, and he flooded with tears, and you know, we had long conversations ... We were pleased in a way, but he was really upset. / That did open a door for him.

Interestingly, the issue here is again not so much to do with the 'feeling' of emotion, but with its public *display* – as Ruth's repeated references to 'opening' make clear. One of the uncertainties children face in dealing with bereavement is that of knowing how to behave appropriately, since they are likely to have little experience of such events. They have to been *seen* to 'grieve', and to do so in ways that are accepted as an authentic sign of inner emotions. Dramatic representations of such emotional performances can bring such uncertainties into the public arena and, to this extent, can be seen to provide valuable 'models' of emotional display.

On the other hand, such accounts were frequently hedged around with denials and qualifications, as in Nishith's comments on the death of Daphne in *Neighbours*:

*Nishith (12):* Well, there's nothing that I've really seen which made me sad or made me cry. But probably on *Neighbours*, when Daphne died in that car accident, and she died. It was, like, so sad, because she ran a café and she was so nice to everyone ... and she had a little boy, Jamie, and she just died and she said 'I love you Clarkie' at the end before she died ...

*Interviewer:* What did you do, Nishith?

*Nishith:* Just felt sad, because she died. Because she was a good actress and all that. I think it was my favourite then ... I weren't sad, I weren't crying, I just, because she was a good actress, I think she was the best, the way she acted and all that. And it was like sad to see her leave and all that ... 'cause all the old actors now have nearly left, all the old actors.

Nishith's repeated denials here are fairly familiar; but what is most interesting in this extract are his references to the 'actors'. On one level, this functions as another kind of denial: to say that he is sorry to see Daphne die 'because she was a good actress' is to imply that he does not perceive 'Daphne' as a real person, and that he relates to the programme in a comparatively distanced way, almost as if he were a drama critic. On the other hand, his quotation of the poignant line 'I love you Clarkie' (spoken to her husband) implies a degree of sorrowful empathy with the characters. Yet his final remarks suggest that the sorrow can in fact function on both levels: 'Daphne' has 'died', but the actress who plays Daphne has 'left' – that is, left the company of actors with whom regular viewers like Nishith are familiar. Because of his long-term relationship with the programme, Nishith feels that he 'knows' the actress as well as the character; and he appears to look back, both to the fictional past of the programme, and to his own past, with a kind of nostalgia – 'I think it was my favourite then.' This sense of the parallel development of fiction and reality was also apparent elsewhere. Elaine (12), for example, said that she particularly enjoyed the way in which, when a character died, there would be a sequence of flashbacks from their past. In the case of Jim's death in *Neighbours*, she said, 'it brought back memories, when I was little'.

In many cases, however, the children's knowledge of the conventions of the genre and of the production process enabled them to take a more distanced stance, and in some cases to adopt a degree of cynicism. Many children spoke in a knowing way about how cliffhangers were used to 'make you watch it again'; and about how characters were 'killed off'. Jacob (12), for example, described how he had been able to predict the death of Meg in *Home and Away*: 'you could really tell it, it's like a book – you can just read the TV's mind'. Jane, Jenny and Sarah (15) had read in a magazine that Bobby, one of their favourite characters in *Home and Away*, was about to leave the series, and speculated at some length about how this was going to be achieved:

*Interviewer:* So when that happens, I mean, does it spoil it, if you know how it's going to happen beforehand?

*Jane:* No.

*Interviewer:* It still upsets you then?

*Sarah:* We like Bobby, don't we? I wouldn't mind if it was someone else ...

*Jenny:* She doesn't want to be in it no more, she thinks her character is boring.

*Jane:* And the only way they can get rid of her is to kill her off, 'cause they want Greg to come in ... [But] I'm just sad if anyone dies.

*Jenny:* No, I think she got a bit boring. I liked it when she was first in it, she was a little rebel ...

*Interviewer:* So you don't feel that bad, 'cause she's not so interesting any more?

*Sarah:* It's not real, is it, so you don't really feel that bad.

*Jenny:* But it's still sad, the moral of it's sad ... I mean, if it was a true story, and like it really did happen, Bobby was a good person. It wouldn't be so bad if it was somebody else.

As in Nishith's account, there is a distinct ambivalence here. On the one hand, the girls clearly have a long-term relationship with this character: indeed, much of Bobby's appeal for teenage girls in general appeared to derive from her status as the 'rebel'.[26] On the other hand, their knowledge about the actors, and about future developments in the plot, enables them to adopt a much more distanced approach, in which they effectively 'play god' with the text – although, as Jane's comments suggest, this knowledge does not necessarily prevent them from feeling sad. Jenny's final comment here is particularly interesting: while she appears to entertain the hypothetical possibility that the text *could* be real, her use of the word 'moral' suggests that she also regards it as a kind of fable – in other words, as a fictional story that is consciously constructed in order to achieve a particular didactic purpose.

This more distanced approach was most apparent in the case of characters who, for whatever reason, were particularly *disliked*. The death of Todd in *Neighbours*, which was discussed in several groups, was a case in point. Todd was not, I would argue, constructed by the narrative as a negative character; while he might have been presented at times as a misguided teenager, he was far from a villain. For most of the younger children, his death was a sad event, even if they knew it was coming. As in many of the instances recorded above, the central emphasis here was on 'what might have been': Todd's girlfriend, Phoebe, had been forced to have an abortion, and in his haste to prevent this happening, Todd had been killed in a car accident. While the children knew that the actor playing Todd would be leaving the series,[27] the manner and particularly the timing of his death were still unexpected:

*Simon (6):* I feeled sad because, no, first I didn't know that he ran out and I didn't know if he was going to die. And then it stopped, 'cause it always stops at the bit when it's scary. But he's gonna die, and on the next day I watched it, and they was at the hospital and then he went in the hospital compartment and then the doctors said that he was gonna die.

*Nathan (9):* I thought he was gonna die, 'cause everyone was gonna say that, and then after a couple of minutes when he was all right, he just got knocked, he was just dead.

Even for these children, there was a certain ambivalence. On the one hand, all of them seemed to know that the character was about to be 'killed off', having read about it in magazines or heard from others. Simon, for example, said 'he didn't die for real ... he just wanted to be out of the programme'; while others noted that the actor had already begun to appear in other shows. Such observations often led into a listing of other soap opera characters who were apparently in line for such treatment. Yet on the other hand, the predictions still appeared to leave room for uncertainty: as Lisa (15) pointed out, 'we didn't know *when* it was going to happen'. Perhaps for this reason, the hope remained that somehow Todd would be reprieved, at least temporarily – and this hope was clearly encouraged by the way in which the programme delayed the outcome (via the cliffhanger that Simon describes), and by giving the appearance of recovery (as Nathan notes). This hope was again partly based on the children's long-term relationship with the programme: as Julie (9) suggested, 'it was sad, 'cause he's been in it quite a while'.

However, particularly for some of the older children, Todd's death was a cause for some satisfaction:

*Interviewer:* And how did you feel when Todd died, then?

*Carol (12):* I was happy. I hated him. [*laughter*]

*Interviewer:* Why's that?

*Carol:* He got on my nerves, I don't know why, Probably because of his long hair. He's a fool, I don't like him. He's too soppy.

*Sonia (12):* Yeah, he's an idiot.

*Interviewer:* He's too soppy?

*Sonia:* Yeah, it's like he moulds to everything. Or he's too easy, like, easily led.

In this case, the girls' dissatisfaction is almost exclusively with Todd as a *character* – with the possible exception of Carol's comment about his hairstyle. Interestingly, it is not the programme that is condemned as 'soppy' or sentimental – as soaps frequently are – but the character himself. By contrast, Thomas (9) developed a more stereotypically 'masculine' criticism of soaps on precisely these grounds:

*Thomas:* When Todd died in *Neighbours*, I was laughing. Because it was supposed to make you feel sad, but it didn't, because he's a bit of a show off ... In the whole of the series, he was just a bit of a show off, you know, like jumping and just showing everybody what he could do, and then he finally got killed. So I was laughing.

*Interviewer:* So you think he kind of deserved it really?

*Thomas:* Yeah, a bit. I thought he deserved it.

*Interviewer:* Did you know he was going to get killed?

*Thomas:* Yeah, in the end, because every [time] something happens, like they go away. And I only thought he was going to buzz off and go to a different country. I thought he was going to be killed or drowned or something like that ... 'Cause they're getting in new people now, it's more exciting now anyway. And he wanted to finish it because he wasn't earning enough ... *EastEnders, Eldorado, Home and Away* and *Neighbours*, if they try to make you feel sad, it doesn't. / But my mum always cries over things like that though, *Coronation Street* and *Brookside*.

*Interviewer:* ... So how do they make you try and feel sad?

*Thomas:* Well, they put them on TV, and they go through along life
and things, and show off and things like that, and then by the time
they get killed, they try to make you feel sad. But if they've kept on
putting them on and showing them off, then you don't.

While Thomas did admit to feeling sad over other events in *Neighbours*, his position here is distanced to the point of mockery and
cynicism. His account of how he had predicted the manner of
Todd's departure is quite off-hand, as though this was merely
decided on a whim of the scriptwriters (which of course in some
ways it is). Interestingly, his criticisms of 'Todd' appear to extend
from the character to the actor who plays him, who is implicitly
accused of financial greed. Likewise, it is not clear whether it is
Todd or the actor who is guilty of 'showing off', although it could
well be both. Yet it is particularly the sense of the text as a product which is designed to manipulate the viewer – 'they try to make
you feel sad' – that appears to motivate Thomas's criticisms.

Of course, as in Nishith's account of *Neighbours*, or in a number
of the criticisms of horror films recorded in the previous chapter,
Thomas's use of this critical discourse could be seen as a form of
defence, and indeed of 'impression management'. Gender
inevitably plays a part here: by implication, crying over a soap
opera is something that women (like Thomas's mum) might be
expected to do, although it is certainly not appropriate for boys. On
the other hand, of course, Thomas does appear to watch *Neighbours* regularly, and is sufficiently experienced to be able to recognise formal similarities across the genre as a whole. Yet what is in
it for him, he seems to imply, is 'excitement', rather than anything
that might involve a closer empathy with the characters.

### Conclusion: the politics of tears

Ultimately, this discussion leads us back to the broader question of
the politics of melodrama. On one level, of course, there is a politics of *content*. The central preoccupation with the nuclear family
and with heterosexual romance that characterises the children's
responses here could be regarded as highly conservative. As I have

noted, some early feminist critics of melodrama acknowledged that the genre did articulate the repressed needs of women, but argued that these were simply recuperated back within a patriarchal framework.[28] Despite its appeal to women, therefore, melodrama was seen here as little more than a vindication of heterosexual male power. On the other hand, of course, this kind of criticism could be accused of underestimating the utopian force of 'politically incorrect' desires – such as the desire for romantic love – which more recent feminist theory would be inclined to acknowledge and to build upon. In this context, we would need to take account of *children's* rather different position in relation to the family. As I have noted, what appears to motivate many of the children's observations on this issue is a very genuine fear of abandonment, which arises directly from their material dependency upon adults.

Yet what is in some ways more fundamental here is the question of the politics of *form*. As I have indicated, critical work on Hollywood melodrama has tended to play down the issue of viewers' emotional responses, and to emphasise – indeed, to validate – elements of 'irony'. The irony that is apparently induced by the 'excess' of the *mise-en-scène* (for example, through stylised lighting and decor) has been seen to result in a form of Brechtian 'distanciation': it undermines the emotional appeals of the text, and leads to a more rational ideological critique. It is by reading in this ironical, distanced way that readers are led to challenge the overt ideological values of the text. Yet in this insistence on irony, it would appear that the distinction between 'elite' and 'popular' readings of the genre has been sustained. Those who possess the sophistication that leads them to perceive the opulence of the *mise-en-scène* as a form of 'excess', for example, will have access to this ideological critique. Those naive souls who do not will continue to read the text literally – and hence to empathise, to fantasise and to weep. Tears and sadness thus continue to be perceived as inauthentic, or indeed as a kind of false consciousness – a sign that the viewer has simply swallowed the ideology of the text. As subsequent critics have argued, such arguments tend to validate a suppression of emotionality – or at least of emotional *display* – that is characteristically masculine.[29]

These debates thus give rise to radically different estimations of the political implications of the genre. Patricia Holland, for example, regards the emotional responses produced by melodrama as politically disabling:

> Accepting and even seeking out the role of the tearful spectator may well involve self-hatred and self-tormenting. The tears of the powerless, those associated with 'women, children and fools', partly express hatred and frustrated anger. They are more likely to imply a damaging turning away from the outside world, than to act as an expression of healing and comfort.[30]

For Holland, melodrama's attempts to evoke tears are little more than a form of 'textual rape',[31] an act perpetrated by the powerful against the powerless in order to maintain their consent to a fundamentally regressive social order. Tears are, in this account, both a sign of 'feminine weakness' and a means of sustaining it. Melodrama, Holland argues, is ultimately 'infantilising': it does not deepen viewers' understanding, but on the contrary, drains their energy and reaffirms the futility of political action.

Jane Shattuc,[32] on the other hand, condemns what she calls 'feminist critics' refusal to own up to the political power of affect in melodrama'. The emphasis on a reading strategy based on ironic distance, she argues, derives from European high modernism, and is ultimately based on 'class and racial privilege': it is a form of policing that regards tears as merely a supine surrender to bourgeois ideology. In her analysis of *The Color Purple*, Shattuc points to the ways in which tears may represent a radical and affirmative desire for utopian transcendence. Tears are not, then, a sign of feminine weakness: on the contrary, 'having a good cry represents the potential for the disempowered to negotiate the difficult terrain between resistance and involvement'.

Ultimately, the polarisation between such arguments merely seems to confirm the futility of generalised assertions about the 'power' – or indeed the political consequences – of viewers' emotional responses. As I have attempted to show, 'ironic reading' may well not have the political implications that are often claimed for it[33] – although there are significant distinctions to be made in this respect between melodrama and soap opera. At the same time, there is a definite danger of puritanism here: we need to beware of the assumption that emotional responses are somehow inherently suspect, or indeed that they necessarily have guaranteed political consequences. In this case, however, there are interesting questions to be asked about the relationships between children's emotional responses and the development of their political understanding. To what extent does political understanding require the kind of rational distance that appears to be valued here? Are emotions like pity and empathy somehow inevitably politically compromised or 'unsound'? These issues are among those that are addressed, in relation to quite different material, in the following chapter.

## Notes

1 According to the French sociologist Pierre Bourdieu (1984), those who possess high cultural capital are distinguished by their distanced, contemplative stance towards the emotional appeals of art.
2 The rather fluid boundaries of the term have been discussed by Gledhill (1985), among others.
3 See Buckingham (1993b).
4 See Sarbin (1986).
5 See, among many others, the seminal work of Elsaesser (1987).
6 See, for example, Mulvey (1987).
7 See Gledhill (1987), page 32.
8 Holland (1992), page 6.
9 For a valuable historical overview of this work, see Gledhill (1987). It might be added, however, that this neglect is equally acute in psychological research on media audiences: in our review of the literature (Buckingham and Allerton, 1995), we could locate only one such study, compared with the thousands that have been published on the effects of television violence.
10 Gledhill (1987), pages 11–12. This argument is taken up by Shattuc (1992).
11 Neale (1986). Similar arguments are developed in relation to the 'women's film' by Mary Ann Doane (1987).
12 Moretti (1983).
13 This tension is also discussed briefly by Annette Kuhn (1984), page 27.
14 Neale (1986), page 17. The fact that this explanation has also been offered in some analyses of horror (see Creed, 1986) points to the extraordinary generality and elasticity of such psychoanalytic theories.

15 Neale (1986) pages 21–2.
16 Gledhill (1987) describes the motive force of melodrama as the 'search for something lost, inadmissible, repressed' (page 32).
17 Viviani (1987).
18 Ang (1985), Chapter 2.
19 Carroll (1990): see above, page 103.
20 Carroll (1990): see above, page 108.
21 See, among others, Swanson (1981); Ang (1985), Chapter 2; Buckingham (1987), Chapter 2; Geraghty (1991), Chapter 4.
22 Ang (1985), pages 72–8.
23 See particularly Ang (1985), Chapter 3; Buckingham (1987), Chapter 4; Seiter *et al.* (1989); Liebes and Katz (1990); Buckingham (1993a), Chapter 4.
24 Geraghty (1991), page 24.
25 Ang (1985), Chapter 3.
26 Similar observations are recorded in Buckingham (1993a), Chapter 7.
27 *Neighbours* is screened in Britain eighteen months behind its screening date in Australia, which means that such predictions are generally reliable.
28 See Mulvey (1987).
29 Gledhill (1987).
30 Holland (1992), page 8-9.
31 This phrase is drawn from Doane (1987).
32 Shattuc (1992).
33 For a wider critique of this rationalistic emphasis, in relation both to television audience research and to media education, see Buckingham (1993c).

6

# *Facing facts*

## THE EMOTIONAL POLITICS
## OF NEWS

### News: a case of cognitive bias

The genres of horror and melodrama considered in the previous two chapters are largely defined in terms of the emotional responses they are intended to evoke. By contrast, news could be seen as a genre in which emotional appeals are precisely *suppressed*. The news is about information; and the ways in which viewers make sense of it are assumed to be purely a matter of cognitive understanding. If the emotional responses invoked by horror and melodrama are widely perceived to be problematic or inauthentic, in the case of news they are often regarded as simply irrelevant.

These assumptions are certainly apparent when one examines research on the audience for news. Within Media Studies, much of the emphasis in this field has been on textual analysis, using semiotic methods or more traditional quantitative approaches. Such studies often assume that the ideological 'bias' revealed by such analysis will be simply transferred into the minds of viewers. Where such researchers have analysed audience responses, they have still tended to concentrate on viewers' readings of an ideological 'meaning' that is seen to be inherent in the text. Likewise, psychological research on news has largely focused on *cognitive* processing, for example through studies of viewers' understanding and memory.

Of course, this emphasis on the cognitive dimensions of news is a centrally important one, and it largely reflects viewers' own stated reasons for watching news in the first place – which are primarily to do with seeking information.[1] Yet what remains striking here is that viewers appear to recall and understand relatively little of what they watch. Studies of the comprehension and retention of news have consistently found that television news is a comparatively ineffective means of communicating information – and yet that viewers still tend to *feel* that it is helping to keep them informed.[2] News may, it has been argued, function primarily as a kind of ritual, a way of dividing up the daily routine, which serves to reassure us that the world remains pretty much as it was yesterday.[3] These arguments might lead us to question the idea that the process of seeking information, and of being informed, can be seen as purely rational.

Likewise, research on 'news values' would suggest that the processes whereby certain stories come to be seen as 'news' in the first place are based not only on ideological biases, or indeed on assumptions about how viewers will come to understand and interpret information, but also on assumptions about their emotional reactions.[4] The decision to include or reject a particular item, to tell a story in a certain sequence, or to select accompanying visuals, for example, is based partly on assumptions about what will grab viewers' attention, or what they will find exciting or moving or even upsetting. Yet researchers have tended to analyse these aspects merely in terms of their ability to assist in viewers' understanding of information.[5] Meanwhile, the 'entertainment' dimension of news has generally been condemned as a diversion from its real business, or indeed as a disguise for more covert forms of ideological manipulation.

### Approaching the child audience

Predictably, very little of this research has considered children as a specific audience for news.[6] On one level, this partly reflects the broader definition of the 'problem' of children and television, where the focus of public debate is almost exclusively on the effects of *fictional* material. Yet it also reflects a common perception that children rarely watch the news, and that they are likely to understand very little of it. These are, I would argue, assumptions that should be questioned.

Of course, children do not possess the level of general knowledge that is available to most adults; and they are likely to be mystified by the complex language in which much contemporary political debate is conducted. Yet as I have indicated, adults themselves appear to understand or remember comparatively little of what they watch on the news. Surveys repeatedly discover that high proportions of adults are ignorant of basic facts about recent history, politics, geography and the workings of the economy – and that many express a profound alienation from the 'public sphere' of social and political debate. Lack of understanding – and even of interest – is clearly not a problem that applies only to children.

On the other hand, audience research has indicated that the programmes people say they prefer are not necessarily those they end up watching, and vice versa – and that this is particularly the case for those (such as children) who have less power in the household, and hence less control of the TV set.[7] Dennis Howitt's research with pre-school children,[8] for example, found that although they expressed very little interest in news, and appeared to pay very little attention to it, a significant number were able to recall items that had been shown. Even quite young children may be 'watching' large amounts of news – or at least be in the room when it is on – without actively choosing to do so.

Of course, it is undeniable that children frequently express considerable dislike of the news. In this research, as in previous studies, there were hardly any children who nominated the news as one of their favourite programmes, and many who simply condemned it as 'boring'. Yet most were able to recall incidents that had been shown on the news and that, in some cases, appeared to have upset them a great deal. Nevertheless, the terms in which the children described their alienation from news were significant:

*Interviewer:* Do you ever watch the news?

*Louise (6):* Oh, *boring!* Only *Newsround* ... I don't really like it when there's all this horrible stuff like shooting and killing and bombs shooting and guns. I don't like that one. I only like ones which are quite happy.

*Interviewer:* Yeah, so ... that's one reason why you don't watch the news, 'cause there's all that nasty stuff on it?

*Louise:* My mum and dad normally do, but I go hhhmmm [*hums a tune while sticking her fingers in her ears*] ... and wait for it to be over.

*Interviewer:* So can you think of particular things that you've seen on the news when you've thought 'oh, I really don't want to hear this?'

*Louise:* Oh yeah, when everybody says 'well, in England, people are getting killed by nasty people who put bombs and bomb scares / bomb scares in London' ...

*Interviewer:* Tell me why, when I say the news, why do you all say it's boring?

*Alice (6):* Children don't like the things that grown-ups do.

In direct contrast to horror, the 'adult' nature of news does not appear to invest it with any degree of status – indeed, precisely the opposite. For Alice, it is as though part of the condition of being a child involves a principled rejection of adults' interests as merely 'boring'. For Louise, as for a number of other children, *Newsround*, the BBC children's news programme, represents an exception to this generalised rejection of news. Yet it is clear that her dislike also derives from the emphasis on *bad* news – and particularly on events that may present a personal threat to her. This argument was far from confined to younger children, however:

*Anthony (15):* The majority of the time [the news] is always someone got raped, someone's got this, someone's got that, and it's like I can tell you what it is without watching it. It's always, I know news is to let you know these things, you're not going to get good news on the news, know what I mean. But it tends to just / get on my nerves. I find it boring.

While there was generally more enthusiasm for local news, and for the informal style (or perhaps merely the brevity) of the *Big Breakfast* news, Anthony's rejection of the emphasis on 'bad news' was typical of many discussions. As Adele (9) argued, this in itself could cause children to avoid the news, and hence lose out on important information:

*Adele:* If they were really young and they thought 'oh golly, I don't want to watch this, it shows too much, it shows really horrible things' and they didn't watch it for the rest of their lives, even when there's really interesting things on, that you just have to know about.

Interestingly, however, Adele appears to exempt herself from this argument, which she applies only to children who are 'really young'. While she is critical of the emphasis on 'horrible things' in the news, she also implies that it is important, even essential, to watch – a balance that is discussed in more detail later in this chapter.

On the other hand, it is interesting to note that the group that expressed most enthusiasm for news did so in very similar terms, although not without a considerable degree of ambivalence:

*David (9):* Well, as I like tanks and stuff like that and fighter jets, when I see things like the wars in Bosnia, and I actually like seeing war films, I think, I think this is really stupid, all these adults fighting / and I actually like seeing all these fighter jets, and I can hardly bear to watch people ...

*Owen (9):* You get quite a lot on *Newsround* and *Newsround Extra*, that's quite good ... I saw this thing about / the people, I think it's in Bosnia or somewhere, and they're starving to death and there was, they did a documentary on this boy and he, and they filmed him when the war was about a year into it, and he was literally, you could see all his bones from the outside ... and there was this other kid who'd been in a bomb and he'd got knocked out, and then he came, he woke up, and what happened is, he got back to England and he was blind in one eye ...

*David:* I do like seeing it, I just, sometimes I can't bear to see people getting shot and all those terrible earthquakes in America, where all these people are being buried in the rubble, and you just see, all you see is their legs sticking out with cuts and scars on it.

While there may be a certain element of self-conscious blood-thirstiness about David's comments, his interest in military technology is combined with a rejection of the stupidity of war, and with repeated expressions of empathy for the victims. Significantly, war is defined here as something conducted by *adults*, while the victims Owen describes are children.

Of course, the audience for news is statistically weighted towards men and towards the middle-class, and it might be tempting to 'explain' David and Owen's enthusiasm in such terms, since both are upper-middle-class – although in fact such generalised conclusions would be hard to sustain on the basis of this research. What is more striking is the similarity between their account and those of the children who explicitly said they disliked the news. Both appear to focus on accounts of disaster and suffering that are simultaneously graphic and detailed, and yet strangely decontextualised: Owen, for example, describes a very specific image, yet he locates this only vaguely, 'in Bosnia or somewhere'. As we shall see, this contrast was characteristic of many of the children's accounts of news. They were able to recall highly specific scenes of children or animals being killed, for example, yet they were frequently unable to identify the context or the reasons why such things should have happened.

Obviously, these kinds of responses are partly cued by our questions: these children have not been asked to talk about what they enjoy about the news – although in fact this is where David begins – or indeed to explain the events themselves. The perception of news as an endless parade of suffering and 'bad news' is, on one level, a conversational cliché, rather like the advice that you should never believe what you read in the papers – although it is one that media professionals themselves have been known to assert.[9] Yet for children (and indeed for adults) who lack the background information that might be required to make sense of what is happening in Bosnia, this may be precisely how it appears. Such distressing images are frequently accompanied only by a rapid soundtrack, and by talking heads whose comments may prove hard to comprehend; and then we move swiftly on to the next item, or to the commercial break, apparently without regard to the way in which emotional responses may need to run their course.[10] The time and information we might be given in order to help us understand and deal with what we are seeing are often in very short supply. Viewers – and not only children – may be left feeling upset, but also uncomprehending and helpless.

So what is it about such images that provokes these responses? And, perhaps more significantly, where do such responses *lead* – both politically, and in terms of arguments about the regulation of children's viewing?

## Remembering the starving children: the politics of pity

Despite their frequent expressions of dislike for such programmes, the children were able to describe a great many incidents from news and current affairs broadcasts. Some time after the main interviews, we conducted a further series of discussions using clips from news programmes about the Los Angeles riots, about the James Bulger case (discussed in Chapter 2) and about famines in Africa; and when prompted in this way, many of the children were able to recall these stories in some detail.

In several respects, the *content* the children chose to discuss was quite similar to that which arose in relation to fiction. Death, physical mutilation, cruelty to animals, wars and disasters were the most frequent themes. Issues mentioned on a number of occasions included: babies in Romanian orphanages, animals being killed for trade, famines in Somalia, racist attacks in London, people dying of AIDS, and children being blown up in former Yugoslavia. As this list implies, stories involving 'innocent victims', particularly children and animals, were prominent. Broadly speaking, the more geographically distant stories were seen to provoke feelings of sadness and pity, as in David and Owen's descriptions of the war in Bosnia; those closer to home were described more in terms of fear and personal threat, as in Louise's account of the bomb scares in London. I shall deal with these two broad categories in turn.

The injunction to 'remember the starving children' is probably a well-worn cliché in the lives of children in most affluent countries, as Alice (6) implies:

*Alice:* I don't like hearing about people getting killed ... and people who can't eat. Every time I waste some tiny bit of food, my grandma or my grandpa or my mum or dad say / 'some people would have said that was a ginormous meal!'

Yet however conventionalised such expressions, and however familiar such scenes of death and suffering on our television screens may be, such images do still appear to evoke pity and even physical disgust:

*Anthony (15):* You see them lying down and flies climbing all over their face and in and out of their mouth, and they're too weak to brush it off and all that. / Every time I see one of those things, them sort of people that are hungry and all that, I just turn it over, 'cause I don't like to watch all of that. / It just makes me feel bad.

As I have implied, such responses appear to be premised on a certain distance from those who are the objects of pity – and who are, almost by definition, deemed to be vulnerable and helpless. As in the case of melodrama, the position of victim is most frequently occupied by children and, perhaps to an even greater extent, by animals. The significant question here, however, is not so much *what* evokes these responses, or even *how* they are evoked: this much is fairly obvious. On the contrary, the crucial issue would seem to be where these responses *lead*, and how children deal with them. What does Anthony mean when he says he 'feels bad', and what consequences does this have? Like many other children, he tries to cope with this feeling simply by avoiding such material. Yet what other responses are possible, and what difference might they make?

While pity for the 'less fortunate' is one of the cardinal virtues of Christian charity, it has often been condemned as merely patronising – and indeed as a luxury that simply confirms the self-righteous complacency of the privileged. Images such as those Anthony describes have been criticised for contributing to a negative image of developing countries, which depicts them as wholly dependent upon Western charity, and incapable of helping themselves. They have been accused of encouraging superficial, short-term responses based on guilt, and thereby actively preventing the longer-term structural changes that are required – encouraging people to 'throw money at the problem' rather than to alter the fundamental imbalances of wealth and power between developed and developing nations.

In some cases here, such images did appear to give rise to a kind of complacency. Many children said that these reports made them feel 'lucky' or 'glad that it never happened to us'. Nevertheless, there was often some ambivalence in this respect:

*Interviewer:* When you see something like that [wars in Bosnia], how does that make you feel?

*Miranda (9):* Really sad. You think how lucky you are ... and that you have food and they don't.

Miranda says she feels both 'lucky' and 'sad'; and in both respects, she would seem to display a recognition of the inequalities between herself and the victims of the war, and a sense that she could easily (but for 'luck') have been in the same position. If pity of this kind is premised on a degree of distance from the victims of suffering, it also appears to require a kind of empathy, an ability to imagine what it would be like to be in their position.

Yet for a significant number of children, such responses had led not to self-satisfied inertia, but on the contrary to forms of social action. Many reported that they had donated money or organised charity collections:

*Adele (9):* Seeing just thin skin covering bones, it makes me feel sort of yuck. I wish there was something I could do to help. But on some programmes, they don't say anything about helping, and it's sort of just showing you things that are actually happening, and they don't give you any chance to help.

*Interviewer:* So are there things you can do to help?

*Adele:* Yeah, on some children's programmes, they give out appeals, and some charities advertise ... We went round our flats saying 'could you help the people in Somalia because they're starving?'

As Adele's comments imply, charitable work of this kind could be seen as a way of coping with the unwelcome feelings of pity and disgust such images evoke. Where such opportunities are not available, she suggests, the viewer may be left powerless to change or overcome such feelings.

Yet particularly for some of the older children, there was a sense in which these responses were also seen to be inadequate. Like Anthony (above), Jessica (12) said that she would often avoid such images:

*Jessica:* I try and turn over the channel and try and watch a little cartoon and try and block it out of my mind. / But it's always there, like, wars and things and bombing, and you see all the Ethiopians. Like at Christmas, they always put them on, and you're sitting there and you're like having tons of chocolates and things and you're sitting there and like suddenly / and once my sister, you know 'Feed the World', the video, she just started crying, and she was like really hysterical, 'cause it was so sad ...

*Interviewer:* What can you do about that, how can you handle it, if you feel sad?

*Jessica:* I don't know. 'Cause you can't exactly get a little doggie bag and send it off. But we donate money and stuff ... I just feel like that's unfair, I just think there must be some way, some way. It could just like give them tons of food and fix it, but / I don't know, it's just impossible.

For Jessica, as for many of the older children, these forms of suffering were seen as 'unfair' but inevitable. Her attempts to avoid the feelings of guilt they evoked were only partly successful – as indicated by her repetition of the word 'try', and her off-hand description of donating 'money and stuff'. As she recognises, the scale of the problem overcomes her ability to resolve it – hence the 'little doggy bag'. Ultimately, she argues that charity of this kind is inadequate, and that the attempt to find some other way of dealing with the situation is 'impossible'.

Many of the children appeared to respond in this way, without any profound belief that it might change matters. Adrian (15), for example, described how he had helped his mother collect money for Romania:

*Adrian:* You can try doing something like that. I mean, it's every little helps, doesn't it?

*Interviewer:* Does that change the way you feel about it?

*Adrian:* Well, it feels like you're doing something.

*Liam (15):* Yeah, 'cause you're not sitting there idle, just watching.

While these responses are partly cued by the interviewer's question here, there is a sense in which such action is undertaken as much for the way in which it helps *you* to feel better, as from any belief that it might actually make any difference to the people concerned. Adrian's slightly self-conscious use of the cliché 'every little helps' would seem to imply that such responses are at least partly a matter of social convention.

Nevertheless, many of these observations appear to rely on an implicit *comparison* between oneself and the objects of one's pity. Jessica, for example, seems to feel particularly bad because of the contrast between the diet of the starving children and her own Christmas chocolates; while Miranda is very aware that she could have been in the same position as the children in Bosnia, even though she is not. In some instances, these observations led on to a more explicit political critique of the waste and consumerism of Western societies – although here again, this was not without its contradictions. Here, a group of nine-year-olds has been discussing the starving children in Bosnia:

*Stella:* You see people, like people who're giving away ten thousand pounds on the telly or something. It's stupid, because look how the people who really need it in Bosnia and stuff, and look how poor they are, and they may suffer as well. So they shouldn't really be giving, like GMTV [breakfast TV station], every single day for one simple easy little question. Even I know the question, and they're just giving it away. And when the Bosnian people come over to this country and they ain't got no-one, no family over here. That's what's happening on the news, when I was watching *London Tonight*.

*Interviewer:* So what did that make you feel?

*Stella:* I think it's sad.

*Tanya:* Sad.

*Carl:* I reckon it's so sad ...

*Interviewer:* So if you see something about people in Bosnia ... what can you do?

*Tanya:* I go to the telly ... sometimes I hug the telly.

*Interviewer:* You hug it? [*laughs*] And does that work, does that make you feel better?

*Tanya:* No.

*Stella:* My mum, 'cause we had lots of old, old clothes that were small for me, 'cause I've got loads of clothes, especially summer clothes, and you see that shop, they were doing it for Bosnia people, you bring clothes that were old but in good condition. And my mum gave them about three bags full of clothes for their country as well.

*Interviewer:* What about that, Stella, does that make you feel better?

*Tanya:* No.

*Stella:* Yeah, it does, because it's just going to go to waste, OK ...

*Interviewer:* So if you feel sorry for the people in Bosnia, Carl, what can you do about the way you feel?

*Tanya:* My sister goes to the telly, says sorry.

*Carl:* Look. [*gets coins from pocket*] 70p here, this would be a lot for Bosnia people. [*Tanya starts laughing*] What you laughing at? I'd laugh if you was living there. / Don't laugh at them.

*Stella:* Ten pounds, my mum gave me ... that would be a lot of money for Bosnian people / and the amount of people that's on the street. I think the government should do something about the people on the street, because look at them, like even if there was a horrible house or something, they can still give it to some like drunk people on the street. I saw this old man, he was in a wheelchair, he had no legs and he was just sleeping like on the High Road, sleeping, and all cars were going by him. I just felt sorry for him.

While Stella does argue for a charitable response – most obviously in her account of taking old clothes to the charity shop – her arguments also take on a broader political dimension. The contrast between the conspicuous consumption of GMTV's morning game show and the suffering of the Bosnians – which might well have been featured on the same programme – leads not to complacency but to a direct critique. Likewise, in her final contribution, she leads away from television to her own observations about homeless people in her area – which, while it might appear irrelevant at first, continues her theme of the disparities between rich and poor. The issue of 'waste' serves as an implicit connection between the three topics she raises – the waste of money that is given away when it could go to those who really need it; the potential waste of surplus clothes that can be used; and the waste of empty houses that could accommodate the homeless. In the latter case, it is specifically the government that is being blamed for its failure to act. This kind of connection, while only implicit, suggests a fairly developed understanding of political concepts for a child of her age.

Tanya and Carl's contributions, however, illustrate something of the limits of this discourse. Carl's act with his pocket money (a comparison he had introduced in a section omitted here) seems almost like a parody of the argument, as Tanya's laughter implies. In fact, it was Tanya who first introduced the topic of Bosnia into the conversation (prior to this extract), and yet she tends to take a more self-consciously subversive role here. Her stories about 'hugging the telly' may be intended sincerely, but here they reflect directly on the children's inability to effect change. Both on her own behalf, and on Stella's, she rejects the idea that any response can make a difference to how she feels. Her laughter over Carl's contribution may have other motivations, but it reflects a kind of playground cynicism about such protestations of concern. In my own schooldays, such cynicism was expressed in 'jokes' about Biafra; and it now takes the form of similar references to Bosnia or Somalia – although such taboo humour would of course be unlikely to surface explicitly in these interviews. Carl, meanwhile, strongly rejects Tanya's laughter on the grounds that she is laughing at the Bosnians – although it might be more accurate to suggest that her laughter stems from a rejection of the 'caring' role that is marked out for her in this discourse.

Among some of the older children, however, the more directly political arguments of the kind developed by Stella were even more explicit. Stephen (15), for example, described his reaction to scenes of bombing in Sarajevo as follows:

*Stephen:* I felt pretty bad, 'cause I mean / like, there we are sitting at home, we got a TV, we got a roof over our head and everything, and we don't really care about all those people dying over there, do we? / They're producing all these nuclear weapons that are not necessary. We were never going to fight the Russians, for God's sake / and all this money being wasted on material things, like people driving round in their BMWs and their Mercs, and there's kids who don't even get a chance to live over there ... At the time when you see it, it seems close to you, but when you think about it, it's so far away, if you get my meaning. It's like, it's people you don't even know or anything, so it doesn't really hit you as much as it would if it was like someone in your family or something like that. But it makes you think at the start of it / and also sometimes I see things about like Ethiopian famines and that, so many little children don't even get to eat properly ... and like it's not really on, 'cause all these Western countries, got all this oil business, and like Arabs, rolling in money, and all these little people are just dying. And like it would probably achieve so much if they gave one million to this, or one million to that, they could easily afford it. But they don't.

These kinds of arguments are familiar territory for many adolescents, and they were echoed by a number of the older children in our sample. While some (like Anthony or Jessica, above) responded by trying to avoid such material, others said they would deliberately choose to watch it – although the reasons for these differences were hard to identify. What is clear, however, is that such arguments are premised on the assumption that 'we' could do more to prevent such events – and, certainly in Stephen's case, that we are at least partly responsible for some of what has happened in the first place. Here again, the critique moves on from the comparison between 'us' and 'them', extending not merely to forms of conspicuous consumption ('BMWs and Mercs') but also to government policy. Ultimately, however, Stephen acknowledges a sense of powerlessness: government policy is unlikely to change, he implies, because in the end 'we don't really care'. And while television has the power to bring such images 'close to you', and hence to 'make you think', the suffering that is represented remains distant, and the concern that it evokes does not last.

**Pity the dumb animals ...**

In Stephen's case, as in many of the other extracts quoted here, it is children who are the particular focus of concern. Yet as I have noted, the role of innocent victim was one that was also frequently occupied by animals, particularly in the interviews with younger children. Many children related instances of the killing or mistreatment of animals in news and documentary programmes – most frequently in *Newsround*, where such issues are a recurrent topic of concern. Many spontaneously identified such stories as the most upsetting or disturbing material they had seen – more so, in many cases, than images of human suffering, whether real or fictional.

Of course, representations of animals occupy a central place in the upbringing of children in most industrialised nations. Many children's earliest attempts at linguistic classification involve the naming of animals, many of which they will never have seen in the flesh. The way in which children's affinity with animals is so assiduously cultivated by books, television programmes and films – and, of course, by parents and teachers – probably reflects a Romantic notion of children as somehow 'closer to nature' than adults. In the process, animals themselves are often anthropomorphised: their rituals of courtship and other social relationships – but also, crucially, their suffering – are translated into human terms.

Significantly, however, as in the stories identified in the previous section, the suffering of animals often appeared to provoke social action, and (in a few cases) political critique. Thus, while some of the children were content merely to describe such events, many were keen to condemn the economic motivation of the humans who had brought them about. Barry and Chris (6), for example, challenged the hunters who killed whales 'for their blubber'; while more explicitly, Thomas and Richard (9) attacked the ways in which poachers were killing elephants 'because they want money'. As with stories of wars and famines, such observations also appeared to have led to forms of social action. David, Owen and Miranda (9) had seen a *Newsround* item about the cruel treatment of dancing bears and had organised a sale to raise money for their release. Yet here again, there was a sense in which such action was seen to be less than completely effective: David complained that it had cost so much, and taken so long, for only one of the bears to be released. Here too, there was often a sense of power-lessness. Adele and Miranda (9), for example, described similar stories from *Newsround*, but seemed unconvinced that anybody would listen to their concerns: as Adele said, 'even if you write let-ters to everyone saying "please could you try and stop this", they'll most likely not take any notice of you'.

In the case of one group of nine-year-old boys in particular, these arguments took on a more explicitly political dimension:

*Peter:* When people try and deliberately kill all those animals, it's not very nice. 'Cause people who are saving them at the moment / I like them. But you see, they just don't care about those animals any more ... It makes me sad, because you think, all these animals, espe-cially when all the fishes get killed. You know, you won't have much fishes left ...

*Matthew:* If they could use animals properly, maybe then, maybe the / the world would be a better place.

*Peter:* Yeah, but it's people, people, though. They go into the forest, they either chop down the trees, you know, and make paper and just use it and chuck it away in the bin, or they kill all the animals.

*Matthew:* They just shoot them, and all they do is take all the fur and horns and stuff off them.

*Peter:* And then after they've taken all the things off and it gets too small, what do they do? They just chuck it in the bin. What a waste of an animal.

Again, these kinds of arguments are fairly common among young children, and they are undoubtedly encouraged by the explicit eco-logical focus of programmes like *Newsround*. There is also perhaps a sense in which they are produced to order here: they reflect an attempt on the boys' part to define themselves as 'serious and con-cerned', and hence as worthy of adult attention and respect. Here too, such expressions of concern are partly conventionalised, as in

Matthew's hope that 'the world would be a better place'. Yet, as in Stella's comments above, it is Peter's *connection* between the concern about cruelty to animals and the wider argument about the threat to renewable resources that seems to indicate a more conceptual grasp of the political issues at stake.

Of course, one might reasonably question the way in which such issues have been constructed as a particular concern for children – as though they alone should be forced to bear the responsibility for correcting the mistakes of earlier generations. Yet it would be patronising to regard these instances of developing political awareness as somehow lacking in the rigours of adult analysis, or indeed as merely charming. While pity can certainly reinforce complacency, it can also be seen as a prerequisite for more concerted attempts at political change. What is perhaps most depressing here, in terms of its politics, is not the pity of the younger children but the sense of *powerlessness* that was most clearly manifested among the older ones – and that might well be seen as much more characteristic of adults' approaches to such issues.

## Fears for the self

As we have seen, children's expressions of pity for the victims of wars and disasters were partly motivated by a kind of empathy – an ability to imagine what it would be like to share such experiences themselves. In other instances, however, their observations were motivated by more direct fears for their own safety. In some cases, these fears were comparatively distant. Jessica (12), for example, was one of a number of children who expressed a generalised fear of nuclear war, which she said had been provoked by watching the news:

*Jessica:* Things I really get scared of are like real things in the news, the nuclear wars. 'Cause I was like sitting there, and someone could just ... press a button and the world would be suddenly over. You're just sitting there, and someone could accidentally do that.

It is notable that even in her imagined scenario of accidental nuclear war, Jessica claims that such stories are 'real things'; and that she emphasises her inability to intervene, 'just sitting there' while the world explodes. In the case of Jane and Jenny (15), these fears had been particularly acute at the time of the Gulf War, with the possibility of reprisals against US bases in Britain: Jane described how she would deliberately make an effort to watch the news, in order 'to make sure we're keeping out of it' – although by 'we' she appeared to mean people living in Britain, rather than the British government.

Most observations of this kind, however, related to news stories that were much closer to home. Instances of rapes, murders, racist violence and attacks by dangerous dogs, particularly gleaned from the local news programme *London Tonight*, recurred throughout these discussions. Here again, it was innocent victims – and particularly children – who were the major focus of concern; and threats to the person far outnumbered threats to property. Such observations often involved an imaginative 'translation' from the text into the circumstances of the children's own lives, as in the case of these twelve-year-old girls:

*Alison:* One thing I really remember was when that girl was killed in a caravan ... 'cause it always, when I was younger, it used to really disturb me, anything to do with little children ... I didn't feel safe, because she had been, she'd just been going on holiday, and she was sleeping in the caravan, and they just, I think they took her away and murdered her ... You're not even safe in your own home.

*Jenny:* That one, oh that one was so sad, when that girl went to school ... and then that man went in and started killing all those people in her class, but she died and all those other people survived. It was probably only like a month ago or something. I thought, oh no, that's so sad. 'Cause she probably just got up for school like I do every morning and you sort of like rushed and just left her room in a mess and then went to school and then never came back.

The sense of 'identification' with the victims – both girls of about their own age – is evident enough here; and it is particularly apparent in Jenny's shifting pronouns. As in many other cases, what appears particularly disturbing here is the *random* nature of the crimes – which of course feeds into the girls' general belief that they themselves could just as easily have been the victims.

Feeling 'safe' was a key term in many of these accounts. Many children said they were scared to go out of the house – or that their parents were scared on their behalf – as a result of such reports; while others described how they would constantly look behind them to check that they were not being followed. While these fears were more frequently expressed by girls, they were also described by boys, including some of the oldest in our sample.

As in Alison's case, such instances were often used to support generalised conclusions about the prevalence or growth of crime – 'you're not even safe in your own home'. The fear that, as Sarah (15) put it, 'we're just gonna be like New York' was one that was voiced by a number of children. In discussing the clips of the Los Angeles riots, Alison and Jenny (12) were uncertain that the situation was quite that bad, but argued that showing such incidents on the news might actually serve as a warning:

*Alison:* I just feel lucky that we don't live anywhere where violence is that strong. 'Cause not many people round here, people don't usually bring out guns or anything. I feel lucky that I don't live in America ...

*Jenny:* They don't carry guns, but they carry knives, so it's sort of half way there. And there isn't pure racial hatred, but there is like gangs of whites and blacks that are fighting, 'cause I know from experience. Most people don't know about it, they say we're nowhere near as bad as America, but we are, we're getting closer and closer to being as bad. But this news [of the LA riots] shows that we shouldn't be as bad, so they should show it. 'Cause it's saying this is what happens, so don't you start anything.

Jenny explicitly accepts what she sees as a record of 'what happens'; and confirms her argument about the growth in violence with a generalised reference to her own experience. Yet far from implying that such representations of violence might lead to imitative behaviour, she suggests that they might have precisely the opposite effect – and hence that, however explicit or disturbing they may be, they should be shown.

Throughout these discussions, there was never any doubt that the events that were shown were 'real'. Many children, particularly from the inner-city schools, were keen to confirm such reports with anecdotes from their own experience. Martin (12), for example, said that he had been particularly disturbed by reports of attacks by dangerous dogs, and described a similar incident that had happened in his street. In many cases, fear appeared to be directly related to the geographical proximity of the crime. Liam (12), for example, described how he regularly had to walk down a street in which a murder had been committed, and would always make sure that he was not being followed; while Jane (15) said that she would not leave the house after watching a report about a girl who had been raped in a local park. Jenny (15) acknowledged that such behaviour could be seen as an 'over-reaction'; but she also argued that it was right to be worried.

Some children also knew that the colour of their skin made them more likely to be attacked by racists, or indeed by the police: one of the schools was in an area where the local police have repeatedly been prosecuted for such offences, and this was explicitly discussed in two separate interviews with the older children. Such fears were described in some detail by Adrian and Anthony (15), two Afro-Caribbean boys. As we have seen (Chapter 4), Anthony was a particular enthusiast for what he himself termed 'violent' films, such as *Goodfellas*, *Scarface* and *Predator*; yet the prospect of being the *victim* of real-life violence, as reported on the news, was a considerable concern for him:

*Anthony:* The thing is, how long is it till it comes to you? ... That's why I'm always alert when I'm on the street at night, and it's about half past ten and coming on to them times, and I'm making my way back home or going off somewhere ... I'm always making sure, my eyes are open and watching. 'Cause next thing you know, I bend a corner, two guys jump me and beat the hell out of me, you know what I mean. Specially as it's night, less people are on the streets, and if it's on a quiet street or a little alleyway, how long till someone finds you, you know what I mean? If you're too weak to crawl out and call out or something like that, it might be too late when they find you.

While Anthony's imaginative account may owe something to his taste in movies, it is clear that his taste for *fictional* violence has not 'desensitised' him to *real-life* violence; and his imagined position here is that of the victim, not the perpetrator.

The extent to which such material may contribute to the fear of crime has of course been a central concern for researchers and policy-makers – although findings on this issue have been at best equivocal.[11] On the one hand, it may be that television leads to an unrealistic fear of crime – in other words, one that is out of proportion to the real risk of victimisation. Yet on the other, it may be that such material addresses viewers as people who are *already* fearful – and that, in many cases, it offers them a consoling image of the protection that is offered by the police. And of course, such material may also have the effect of encouraging crime prevention. These issues are addressed in more detail in the following chapter, in relation to crime reconstruction programmes.

### Pity, fear, fact and fantasy

In some respects, the responses described in this chapter are quite similar to those that were expressed in relation to fictional material. This is perhaps most obvious in terms of *content*: threats to children or animals, the danger of bodily violation, the experience of bereavement and loss, seem to provoke similar responses in both fact and fiction. We might choose to define these responses in terms of conventional psychological categories, as feelings of pity, fear and empathy; or in more psychoanalytic terms, as evidence of forms of projection or masochism. As I have indicated at a number of points, these displays of emotion also need to be seen in social terms, as discursive *performances*, in which children attempt to take on particular social roles, and hence to lay claim to a particular identity. Yet in many ways, children's descriptions of their 'feelings' for the victims in horror films or melodramas are quite similar to their descriptions of their 'feelings' for the victims of war or disaster or violent crime shown on the news.

Nevertheless, there remain some significant differences, which were partly evident from the subjective experience of the interview groups. Responses to factual material seemed to be taken much more seriously in the context of the discussion than responses to fiction. As we shifted topic, for example from horror movies to the news, the tone perceptibly changed. Excitement and laughter gave way to a much more subdued and sombre approach, and it was often quite difficult to return to a lighter note. While the children had a great deal to say about factual material, there was much less competition to speak here. As Carl's response to Tanya's laughter (above) suggests, amusement or ridicule were clearly seen as inappropriate responses. Expressions of pity for the starving children in Africa, or anxiety about walking the streets for fear of being raped, were treated with a degree of seriousness and mutual respect that was less likely to be accorded in discussions of responses to *Neighbours* or *Nightmare on Elm Street*.

Of course, this does not in itself imply that such responses were any more powerful or intense than those that arose in relation to fiction. Such findings have in fact been reported from previous research, although there is some disagreement here[12] – and quite how such levels of intensity might meaningfully be measured and compared remains a very difficult question. Furthermore, as I have implied, talking about factual or fictional material presents very different possibilities in terms of the social roles that might be on offer, particularly in the context of a research interview. Choosing to discuss horror films could be seen, in various ways, as a potentially subversive act; while choosing to discuss news or documentary programmes could reflect an attempt to occupy the role of the 'serious student', ever prepared to follow what is perceived to be the teacher's (or in this case, the interviewer's) agenda. Yet while such differences should not be taken at face value, neither can they be 'explained away' in terms of the context. Some striking differences remain, both in terms of the responses themselves, and in terms of how they are dealt with.

As I have indicated, the children's discussions of horror and melodrama were characterised by a fundamental ambivalence – a balance between 'distress and delight'. While this balance was not always successfully achieved, it was clear that much of the motivation for watching such material, and indeed for choosing to experience feelings of fear and grief, was to do with the expectation of *pleasure*. By contrast, the motivation for watching factual material – and particularly the news – was defined primarily in terms of seeking *information*. As we shall see, many children argued that the news was 'important to watch', because it told you about things you needed to know – despite the fact that what was shown was often upsetting. While such stories were sometimes seen as 'interesting', they were never described as pleasurable.

One of the most striking aspects of these discussions was the way in which the status and credibility of the news was hardly ever challenged. Alice and Celia (12), two comparatively 'politicised' girls in one of the inner-city schools, were the only children to question the selection of material that appeared on the news. Celia argued that the news coverage of an anti-racist demonstration had emphasised the violence in order to discredit the motives of the organisers;[13] while Alice accused the BBC of highlighting bombings committed by the IRA, which she saw as a direct result of the Tory bias of its Board of Governors. Yet with these notable exceptions, the news appeared to be universally perceived as an honest and trustworthy reflection of the real world. As we have seen, many children were keen to confirm what they had seen on the news with evidence from their own experience; and yet even where events were shown that were outside their experience, they appeared implicitly to accept these at face value. Adrian (15), for example, described his family's experience of watching footage on the Romanian orphanages as follows:

*Adrian:* When the news went out to Romania the first time, I think the whole of us, my family as well, were all on the seat, and we just, I reckon we were near to tears ... I didn't believe people could be like that ... It just really hit home that people can be in such a bad state.

*Interviewer:* And you say all your family was upset by that?

*Adrian:* Yeah. 'Cause we can't believe that they're like that, really.

The truth of the news is seen here as something that even supersedes what people 'believe': it 'hits home' because it shows facts that we may otherwise wish to ignore.

The case of the Rodney King beating and the Los Angeles riots obviously raised this issue of the truth status of news – and particularly of its *visual* dimensions – very directly. Kevin and Mike (12), for example, acknowledged that the footage of the beating was upsetting, but argued that it was important to show it rather than merely describe it in words, not least in order to overcome any possible bias:

*Kevin:* Actions speak louder than words, really. It's true. / Like if they just tell you about it, you don't know how bad it was, but showing pictures it shows you how they just totally beat him.

*Mike:* 'Cause you know what the guy said when the verdict was [read], he said if only he'd done what they wanted, but he wouldn't give up. When you saw it, it was different, he did give up and they did carry on. So it's completely different ...

*Kevin:* And a media man can interpret it in a different way. The news people could have said that it wasn't that bad and something, about the beating. But when you see the pictures, it was a really bad one.

While the possibility of bias (or 'interpretation') is raised here, the visual dimension of news is seen as a guarantee of its objectivity as a source of evidence – at least for viewers, if not in the trial itself. Images, it would appear, offer a higher truth that goes beyond the limitations and distortions of verbal language.

Of course, as in Stephen's comments (above), there was a recognition that the more distant realities shown on the news were less immediately affecting than those that were closer to home. Even Alison (12), who spoke at length about the fears that had been evoked by news stories about murders and wars (see above), made this basic distinction: 'sometimes it doesn't affect me, the things I see on the news, but when it happens to someone you know, it's really dreadful'. Adele and Emma (9) suggested that such images might eventually lose their power – 'you just get used to them' – yet there was little evidence here that this was the case. Even children who claimed to be unaffected by fictional violence – or indeed actively celebrated it – were among those who were most vocal about their responses to factual material. In fact, if there was a more general criticism of the news, particularly among parents, it was on the grounds that it was '*too* real' – as we shall see below.

This general trust in the truth and credibility of news had particular implications in terms of coping. As I have noted, one of the principal strategies that the children used in dealing with responses to fictional material was to remind themselves that it was not real – for example, by drawing attention to the way in which the text had been produced, or by mocking it for its implausibility. The effects of this strategy were not guaranteed, particularly where the children were prepared to entertain the possibility that the events *might* be real, or to somehow 'translate' them to their own real-life situations. The modality status (or perceived realism) of texts was not something that was simply given or fixed. Nevertheless, particularly in the case of horror, this process of working out the relationship between the text and the real world was a significant part of the process of gaining expertise as a viewer, and hence of learning to cope with potentially unwelcome responses. With news, however, similar strategies were simply not available. There was much less that children could *do* in order to 'handle' their responses.

As in the case of Anthony and Jessica (above), there were those who attempted to avoid such material by turning it off or leaving the room; while others sought to distract themselves, for example by watching something different. Significantly, however, there were children who responded by deliberately seeking out further information. Alison (12), for example, described how she had made her mother buy all the newspapers so that she could read more about the case of the gunman who had shot the schoolgirl in her classroom (see above). Yet she and her friends mocked the school's attempts to cope with these events through prayer:

*Jenny (12):* [The teachers] just thought 'oh well, everyone's thinking about it, so I'll say something about it'. But they don't, like, every assembly, they don't say 'oh, there's so much war, let's pray about it', because it's always happening, so they can't pray for every single day. Well, some people do, but the specific thing, when it affected school children, they thought 'oh, we're a school, let's pray about it'.

As Jenny's comments imply, such conventional responses seem inadequate, both in the light of the random nature of this particular crime, but also in the face of wider problems. War, she implies, is permanent and inevitable. It is impossible to comfort yourself with the argument that it is not real, or indeed with the hope of divine intervention (at least for most of us). As we have seen, many children looked to social action – in the form of donations to charity, for example, or fund-raising – as a means of coping with such responses; yet while the *thought* of such action might temporarily prove to be comforting, it was increasingly recognised as unrealistic and ineffective.

If the children's accounts of their responses to factual material were therefore different from those that arose in relation to fiction, this may well have been because the opportunities and strategies for coping were also rather different. Yet in a sense, 'coping' may not be the issue here. Feeling scared of a fictional monster is different from feeling scared of a real-life rapist – not least because the latter feeling might well be a basis for taking action to protect yourself. Likewise, feeling pity for Celie in *The Color Purple* is different from feeling pity for the starving children in Bosnia: there is nothing we can do for Celie, while there may just be a possibility that we can do something for the children in Bosnia. As Laura (15) explicitly argued, feeling sad about such material was often a more lasting experience: 'you don't *want* to really forget it, you just want to think about it'. Such responses to factual material are not pleasurable; yet as both parents and children argued, they may well be *necessary*.

## Regulation and the need to know

If the experience of fictional genres such as horror and melodrama depends upon a balance between pleasure and 'un-pleasure', the balance in relation to factual material is thus a rather different one. On the one hand, as we have seen, there are feelings of pity and fear that cannot easily be swept aside; yet on the other, there is the argument that such material is important to see and to know about. This balance between the need for information and the need to avoid distress often presents a dilemma for those who are concerned with regulating children's viewing – and that includes not just broadcasters and parents, but also children themselves.

One strategy that is frequently used by broadcasters, particularly in relation to news programmes, is to warn viewers in advance. This was the case with the coverage of the Los Angeles riots which we screened in our later interviews. Taken from the mid-evening news, this report included the video of the Rodney King beating, as well as subsequent scenes in which people were dragged from their cars and attacked or shot. Viewers were warned that such scenes might be 'disturbing' – yet perhaps predictably, most of the children argued that such warnings would be appropriate for those much younger than themselves:

*Emma (9):* Yeah, they usually say that on some programmes ... in case a young child is watching and the parent didn't know about this programme, and it says like, so you've just got time to get them out of the room.

As in other discussions of this issue, Emma explicitly places the responsibility for regulation on parents. Yet while a couple of children did acknowledge that their parents would take heed of such warnings, and sometimes prevent them from watching, most argued that they were well able to cope with such material. Indeed, for many, the warnings seemed to function as an inducement to watch. Richard (9), for example, said that he would watch in order 'to see how gruesome it really is', while Owen (9) agreed: 'you get curious, you know, what's this about?' Warnings could, in this respect, prove quite counter-productive.[14]

Yet as Owen also argued, the need for such information was motivated by more than mere curiosity:

*Owen:* It might be disturbing for me or someone else watching it, but I still think it's important that I know. / Got to face up to it, face up to the facts.

As Owen later emphasised, the news was 'very important' – although he acknowledged that he had only recently begun to watch it regularly, and that it would be less 'interesting' for younger children who were unable to 'understand it properly'. In a sense, watching the news – or at least claiming to do so – functioned here as a guarantee of maturity. Yet Owen's comments also reflect the fundamental tension I have identified; and in his case, the need to 'face up to the facts', to learn about things that are 'important to know', clearly outweighs the potential danger of being upset or disturbed.

This tension was a focus of debate for many parents also. A number of parents argued that factual material was often more upsetting than fiction, and that it was much harder for them to deal with their children's responses to it. In the case of younger children, this was seen to be partly a matter of the complexity of the issues:

*Wendy (parent of children aged 4 and 6):* Well, I'm not particularly / I'm not very good at explaining exactly what's going on in world affairs. I don't know, I tend to be a bit dismissive, and um / I say things like 'well, it's a long way away' and 'this is what happens in war, when wars are on, horrible things happen' ... I change the subject. 'Cause it is very distressing, and you can't / you either start getting into very heavy discussions about it all, or in a way, you dismiss it. I find it very difficult to come in between, on a level that I think they might understand.

The major difficulty here, of course, is that even if such explanations can be provided, they do not necessarily help children to feel any less upset – and indeed, by confirming the reality of what is shown, may even have the opposite effect:

*Sarah (parent of children aged 9 and 7):* The other thing was Somalia ... David [9] was quite struck about that and [asked] why they had such skinny legs and pot bellies and so on and so forth. And of course [I explained] you get worms in the tummy and 'well, what do you mean?' You know "cause they're not part of our life, it's not part of society here', and so, you know, I sort of explained to him. And of course that was fairly horrific ... he was upset by that.

*Interviewer:* What things did he say about it when he saw it?

*Sarah:* You know '*why* does it happen?' It's always the 'whys', isn't it?

Both Sarah and Wendy emphasise the fact that these events are a long way away, but they cannot deny that they exist. As their comments imply, such things may ultimately prove impossible to 'explain' to younger children.

Nevertheless, this also appeared to be an issue for some of the parents of older children, who were otherwise quite willing for their children to watch horror films or programmes featuring fictional violence. Many argued that the news could often be more upsetting than fictional material, and in some cases, this had led them to watch the news later in the evening, when the children would be in bed:

> *Yasmin (parent of children aged 12, 11, 8 and 7):* I think I generally try not to watch the news when they're around, 'cause I know it does upset some children ... because it's a lot more real. It's not like, you can't say to them 'it's only a movie'. And I think they do pick up that, well, they know the news is real ... I think the news plays a lot more on their mind than horror films ... It's too real, isn't it, really?

Yasmin's comments were partly confirmed by her children. Natalie (12), for example, described how she had cried over the Rodney King beating, and was often upset by material about famines; yet she regarded horror films like *Child's Play* with great amusement.

In a number of instances, parents argued that this kind of control should be exercised more carefully by broadcasters themselves. Some asserted that the news programmes shown at breakfast time and in the early evening were too explicit, not only in terms of such upsetting material, but also in terms of reports featuring sex and violence; while others pointed to the double standards whereby fictional films were censored, yet news reports featuring much more horrific scenes would be shown at times when children might well be watching. Yet these concerns were often set against the argument that such things were important for children to see, and that it would be wrong to 'shield' them too much. This dilemma was most clearly identified by Helen, the parent of three children aged ten, eight and six:

> *Helen:* They start asking questions, and some of the stuff, you really

don't want to be fielding those sort of questions ... there'll be an announcement about a dismembered body or something really quite unpleasant, and one of the kids, it will have gone in some-where, and they'll say 'what does that mean?' / You don't really want your children to be sort of exposed to the truth, and I believe very firmly if they ask you a question, you've got to tell them straight and as honestly as possible. And some of the things that come up are things that you don't really want them to know about when they're this young ... I mean, some things, the way the TV people make the decision for you about what's appropriate for chil-dren to see and not [to see] seems to be a bit cock-eyed as well. You get this flash up saying 'you might find some of these scenes dis-tressing'. Now we're talking about famine-ridden Africa. I think children should see that, and I'm sorry if it's quite distressing. I think that's very valuable for them to see that, particularly in such an affluent society that we live in, to actually see that there are people in the world that don't have enough food and who are really suffering. But then in the same thing, they sort of chop that out so that the children aren't exposed to that, but then they expose them to a report about [Fred West, the Gloucester serial killer] who's chopping people up / and racist attacks and things like that. You don't necessarily want them to be exposed to that very violent stuff close to home, that sort of wanton violence. But it would be nice to have them more exposed to things that are actually happening in the world / that we need to know about, and we need to develop a conscience about ... It is difficult, because there's this quandary. There's the wanting your children to develop an awareness of the dangers in the world around them, but at the same time not want-ing your younger children to be frightened to death about that.

This extract points to a number of important distinctions that recurred throughout these interviews. Most clearly in Helen's final comment, there is the tension between the need to educate your children and the need to protect them from harm. Yet Helen also distinguishes, as I have done in this chapter, between material that is 'close to home' – often featuring apparently random violence – and that which is more distant: while the former may evoke fear, the latter is seen to evoke pity, which may lead in turn to the devel-opment of a moral or political 'conscience'. While both are seen to be 'distressing', it is the more distant scenes of famines and wars that children 'need to know about' – and indeed something that Helen argues should be featured more prominently. Both sorts of material represent a kind of 'truth', but some truths are seen to be inappropriate for children before they reach a certain level of maturity. The difficulty, of course, is that educating children necessarily involves developing an understanding of 'the dangers in the world' – including the dangers that they might face in their own lives – as well as of the 'suffering' of others.

Such dilemmas were also identified by the children themselves. Although, as we have seen, many children described incidents where they had been upset or frightened as a result of watching the news, they almost unanimously agreed that such material was important and necessary for them to watch. As Adele (9) said, 'people have a right to know what's going on' – and her views were echoed by many of the children here. As in the case of arguments about 'effects' (Chapter 3), there were expressions of concern for children much younger than themselves, although these were generally identified as 'little kids' or 'five-year-olds'. Some argued that particularly disturbing material should be shown later at night, although in general the responsibility for regulation was seen to lie with parents and with children themselves. In this extract, for example, Jenny and Alison (12) are debating the coverage of a minibus crash, which had led to calls for stricter legislation on seatbelts:

*Interviewer:* Do you think it's right that things like that get talked about in the news?

*Alison:* It lets people know how dangerous the things are ...

*Jenny:* They're trying to campaign for seatbelts, so they want people to know ... But they don't have to show like dead bodies lying everywhere. I mean, they can say 'oh, there was a minibus crash and these people were killed'. They don't have to show pictures of broken glass and blood everywhere.

*Alison:* If little children see it, they'd like say to their school ... 'oh, we need seatbelts' or something like that. It'll just come out of their mouths.

*Interviewer:* Do you think that's a bad thing, then?

*Alison:* I think it's good, but some people may get upset over it.

*Interviewer:* So what kind of age do you think would be a good age to start watching things like that?

*Alison:* / About six. But I think it should be the parents' choice, if they think their child's mature enough to understand.

Typically, Alison displaces the 'effects' of such material onto those younger than herself – although in this case, the effects are as much to do with arguing for change as with becoming upset. Here again, there is little doubt about the credibility of news – in this case, it shows 'how dangerous the things are' – even if it is implicitly accused of a degree of sensationalism. Yet as the girls imply, such coverage may be justified on the grounds that such things are important for people to know.

Similar arguments recurred in the case of the footage of the Los Angeles riots. Here, of course, it was the screening of the Rodney King video that had largely provoked the events in the first place. As we have seen, Kevin and Mike (12) strongly defended the decision to screen the tape, largely on the grounds that it showed a truth that could otherwise have been hidden or distorted. David, Owen and Richard (9) also debated these issues at some length. David maintained that the riots themselves were not justified, arguing that the violence was out of proportion to the initial crime: 'all that for just one man!' Richard took the opposite view, pointing to the bias of the jury and arguing that the rioters 'had all their right to cause some protest'. Owen was somewhat more equivocal, although he also spoke at some length about the injustice of the verdict. These positions led to rather different arguments about the role of television news. David was alone in suggesting that the Rodney King video should have been 'kept a secret': while Owen countered this by arguing that people would have found out about it anyway. More directly, Richard asserted that 'they should have [shown it] because it lets everyone know how brutal the police force are'. Similar concerns arose in relation to the riot footage itself:

*Interviewer:* What about the footage of the riots themselves, do you think that should be shown?

*David:* Well, it's pretty gruesome for the family if they recognise the person being shot.

*Interviewer:* But do you think it's horrible for people in general?

*Owen:* It's horrible, well, not necessarily horrible. I think you need to know what's happening in the world around you, and how bad it is if you ever get caught in a riot like that, and you have to be careful about it.

*David:* If they knew the person who was shot and then it was a couple of weeks later, they'd probably [?be upset].

*Owen:* But it's important that people know what's happening, how bad it is.

While David's expression of concern about the families of the victims raises important issues to do with privacy, it also serves to support his broader position against the rioters. By contrast, Owen's argument that such things were 'important to know' was one that he maintained fairly consistently in relation to other issues; and it was this argument that was much more broadly representative.

As this debate indicates, however, such judgments about what should or should not be shown were – directly or indirectly – recognised to be political. In this respect, the responses evoked by such material cannot be simply relegated to the domain of 'mere emotions'. On the contrary, there is a sense in which such emotions are a central part of children's developing understanding of the social and political world. Here again, familiar divisions between the emotional, the cognitive and the social can obscure the genuine complexity of what is taking place.

## Conclusion: news as fiction?

In arguing here for the importance of considering children's *emotional* responses to news programmes, and in pointing out what they have in common with their responses to fiction, it has not been my intention to imply that the two can – or indeed should – be conflated. Critics who have sought to 'debunk' the authority of news have often made precisely this move. Drawing attention to the narrative or entertainment dimensions of news, or comparing it to fictional genres such as soap operas, has been part of the wider challenge to its claim to truth and objectivity. John Fiske, for example, argues as follows:

> The differences between news and fiction are only ones of modality. Both are discursive means of making meanings of social relations and it is important that readers treat news texts with the same freedom and irreverence they do fictional ones. A wider and more self-confident recognition of this essential fictionality of news might lead its masculine viewers to treat its texts with the same socially motivated creativity as do the feminine viewers of soap opera.[15]

Fiske's monolithic view of audiences as 'free', 'irreverent' and 'creative', and his essentialist notion of the news as 'masculine', are certainly challenged by the data presented here. Yet the implication of his argument is even more profoundly problematic. Of course, it is vital that children learn about the constructed nature of news. Any media education curriculum should include the study of the forms and conventions of news programmes, and raise issues of representation and bias; and students should be encouraged to engage in, and to develop, the debates about the social responsibility and the political consequences of news reporting that have been considered in this chapter. Parents can, of course, also play a vital role in this process, by raising and discussing such issues with their children. Such approaches should induce a degree of scepticism about the claim to truth that is embodied in the conventions of news, and encourage children to adopt a more questioning attitude towards its credibility than was generally in evidence in the discussions recorded here. Yet if this process results in a kind of superficial relativism – or indeed in Fiske's conclusion that the news is merely 'a masculine soap opera' – it will be neglecting the much wider educational potential that is at stake. The news is *not* 'essentially fictional'; and to treat it as such is to trivialise the real issues with which it deals, and which we all need to be informed about. Considering children's emotional responses to news thus raises fundamental questions about the development of their political understanding, and about how they might be given access to the public sphere of social and political debate, which are in need of urgent attention.

Yet the issue of modality to which Fiske refers is also more complex than simply a matter of distinguishing between fact and fiction. In the following chapter, I look at children's responses to three contrasting programmes in which this became a central concern. As I indicate, the consequences of confusing fact and fiction are far from straightforward or easy to predict.

## Notes

1 For a summary of research into motivations for watching news, see Gunter (1991), pp. 229–30.
2 See particularly Gunter (1987a).
3 See Nordenstreng (1972).
4 The classic study here is Galtung and Ruge (1965).
5 See the studies reviewed by Gunter (1991); and, in relation to narrative, Lewis (1985).
6 For our literature review (Buckingham and Allerton, 1995), we were able to locate only a handful of psychological studies, as against a much larger number relating to children's 'fright responses' to fictional material.
7 This is apparent both from statistical research conducted within the industry (e.g. Barwise and Ehrenberg, 1988) and from qualitative academic research (e.g. Morley, 1986).
8 Howitt (1982), pages 43–4.
9 In 1993, British newsreader Martyn Lewis attracted widespread publicity – and no small amount of mockery – for his argument that television news should feature more 'good news'.
10 The psychological dangers of the fast pace of television news are explicitly criticised by Zillmann (1991) – although here again, his central preoccupation is with fiction.
11 For a brief review of this work, see Buckingham and Allerton (1995). More extensive overviews are provided by Gunter (1987a) and Sparks (1992), Chapter 4.
12 See, for example, Feshbach (1972) and von Feilitzen (1975); and for a brief review, see Cantor (1991), pages 184–5.
13 Celia later described how she had read about the demonstration in the left-wing newspaper *Militant*, which may have been the source of this argument. She was also a member of an anti-racist youth organisation.

14 Experimental research on 'forewarning' – while not without its method-ological peculiarities – has come up with similarly ambiguous findings. In some instances, forewarning has been found to reduce stress, while in others it has been found to increase it. For a brief review, see Buckingham and Allerton (1995). There is also an interesting comparison here with the advance information that circulates in relation to storylines in soap operas (see Chapter 5), where the desire to know precisely *how* a particu-lar character is killed off often seems to guarantee success in the ratings.
15 Fiske (1987), page 308.

# 7

# Feels so real

## ON THE BOUNDARIES BETWEEN FACT AND FICTION

In previous chapters, I have argued that children generally respond very differently to factual and to fictional material. Nevertheless, the distinction between these two categories is not always clear cut. In many cases, as we have seen, children's emotional responses appear to depend upon complex judgments about the *degree* of realism of the text. A text may be perceived as 'realistic' in some respects, and not in others. Thus, on the one hand, there is good evidence to suggest that very young children are able to distinguish between fact and fiction on television; and that by the age of five or six they are beginning to develop a knowledge of how programmes and films are made. Children at this age will readily draw attention to bad acting or cheap special effects, and will frequently dismiss programmes as merely 'fake'.[1] On the other hand, as we have seen, viewers may attribute different degrees of *plausibility* to a text that they know to be fictional: they recognise that what is shown did not actually happen, but they accept that something like it might have done, or could do so, under certain circumstances. For example, viewers know that horror films are not documentaries; yet their ability to frighten us (and also to keep us watching) depends upon our willingness to acknowledge that the events they depict might just possibly happen to us. Here again, there is evidence to suggest that by about the age of six or seven children are increasingly comparing what they watch with their own experience, or with what they believe (or have been told) is the case about the real world.[2]

The modality (or perceived reality) of the text is thus the product of a series of *judgments* made by the reader. As I have implied, this process can be seen to have two dimensions. On the one hand, it depends upon our recognition of formal or stylistic properties that are *internal* to the text. For example, most cartoons employ graphic conventions – forms of simplification and exaggeration – that are clearly at a greater remove from 'reality' than the rather different photographic conventions of live action filming.³ However natural they may appear, these conventions are of course subject to historical and cultural variations; and they are learnt rather than innate. 'Realism' is, in this sense, a relative term: texts are defined as 'realistic' in terms of their relationships with other texts that have been perceived as such in the past. On the other hand, our judgments also depend upon criteria that are *external* to the text – that is, upon our own experience of, or beliefs about, the real world. Such experiences and beliefs are of course not without their inconsistencies and contradictions; although, broadly speaking, it should be harder to make reliable judgments where the reality that is depicted is remote from our own experience. Yet the potential for diversity here is clearly enormous, perhaps particularly for children, whose understanding of the conventions of the medium and of the world in general is still rapidly changing.

The implications of these judgments for children's emotional responses to television are equally complex. Psychological research on emotional development suggests that emotion is crucially dependent upon 'appraisal', or cognition: how we respond emotionally to a given stimulus or event depends upon how we understand or interpret it, and vice versa.⁴ Modality judgments could, in this respect, be seen as a crucial dimension of 'appraisal'. Furthermore, we might reasonably expect to find that texts that are perceived to be less realistic have correspondingly less power to produce emotional responses: if you believe it isn't real, then it won't be able to hurt you. As we have seen, many parents sought to reassure their children by trying to convince them of this; and many children attempted to regulate their own responses in the same way. The difficulty with this approach, however, is the underlying implication that rational judgments of this kind are somehow powerful enough to overcome emotional reactions; and that things which are perceived as 'fantasy' will have little impact on people's beliefs or behaviour. Yet attempting to reassure yourself that 'it's only a story' – or indeed laughing at the inadequacies of the special effects – often appeared to prove less than effective. As we have seen, many children reported disturbing reactions to material that they knew very well was not 'real'; and in the case of horror, an 'expert' knowledge of the genre sometimes served to heighten such responses, rather than to reduce them. Both modality judgments and emotional responses – and indeed the relationships between them – are more diverse and complex than this rather one-dimensional argument appears to suggest.

## Relations with the real

In this chapter, I consider children's responses to three programmes that establish rather different relationships with 'reality'. *Casualty* is a broadly social realist hospital drama, albeit with elements of comedy and soap opera. It is a long-running series, shot on video, which regularly deals with social issues such as homelessness, AIDS and child abuse. In more recent years, it has often brought a critical perspective to bear on the reforms of the National Health Service. It is broadcast weekly in series of thirteen episodes, currently at 8.10 in the evening. *Crimewatch UK* is a factual programme which seeks to enlist ordinary viewers in the fight against crime. Broadcast monthly at 9.30 in the evening, it contains reports of unsolved crimes, often using security camera footage, and relies heavily on reconstructions. Viewers are encouraged to phone in with information, and progress on each of the cases is described in an *Update* later in the evening. Finally, *Ghostwatch* was an eighty-minute spoof documentary, broadcast in a 'Screen One' drama slot at 9.30 pm on Hallowe'en in 1992, approximately eighteen months before these interviews took place. Using well-known presenters playing themselves, it purported to provide a 'live' outside broadcast link to a ghost hunt taking place in a house on the outskirts of London.

If *Casualty* represents a comparatively familiar form of social realism, the other two programmes embody a rather more problematic stance towards the relationship between fiction and reality. While it is clearly presented as a factual programme, *Crimewatch* uses some of the visual and narrative conventions of crime fiction, particularly in its reconstruction sequences. By contrast, *Ghostwatch* used many of the devices of documentary reporting and 'live' television coverage in order to present itself as fact, and did not explicitly alert its viewers to its fictional nature until the very end of the programme.

All three programmes have attracted some controversy, perhaps partly as a result of this issue of their relationship with reality: in different ways, they have all been seen as somehow 'too real'. Indeed, as Paul Kerr has argued, this question of the relationship between television and reality has often been a contentious political issue, most obviously in the case of 'drama documentaries': any uncertainty that might surround its 'claim to truth' raises fundamental questions about the credibility and responsibility of television as an institution.[5] Thus, for much of its life, *Casualty* has been a focus of criticism from the political right, largely on the grounds of its direct treatment of social issues – and, most recently, for its unsympathetic representation of the new Health Service managers. In 1993, the final episode of the series was moved to a later time in the schedules, apparently because of scenes in which a gang of hooligans set fire to the hospital; and in response to complaints, this episode was dropped when the series was repeated. These complaints appeared to be motivated primarily by the fear of 'copycat' incidents. For its part, *Crimewatch* has been widely criticised, largely because of its explicit reconstructions, which have been seen both to 'glamorise' crime, and to increase the fear of crime among viewers – although it is probably fair to say that it is somewhat less sensationalist than other examples of the same genre. Finally, as I have noted in Chapter 3, *Ghostwatch* was the focus of a considerable amount of press coverage. Almost a year and a half after the broadcast, two child psychiatrists published a case history of two boys who had suffered 'post-traumatic stress disorder' as a result of watching the programme;[6] while the parents of the boy who allegedly killed himself after watching it were recently given leave to take their case to the high court (see page 60 above).

Each of these programmes featured in our initial discussions with the children here (although not with the youngest age group); and, largely for the reasons I have described, we subsequently chose them as the focus of a series of follow-up interviews.[7] In contrasting ways, these programmes raise interesting questions about the different criteria that children use to define the relationship between the text and the real world; and about the part this plays in regulating their emotional responses. Here again, there is a complex balance to be achieved between the need to avoid distress and the need to be informed, or the desire to experience pleasure.

## *Casualty*: the nasty pleasures of realism

Generally speaking, *Casualty* appeared to be a programme that the mothers of the children interviewed had been interested in first, and that they had subsequently encouraged their daughters to watch – although, as we shall see, it was often regarded as inappropriate for the very young. Some of the older children had a long history of viewing the series, and were able to remember incidents that had happened many years previously; while others made a particular point of watching old episodes on the rerun channel UK Gold. As with soap operas, at least some of the pleasure of the programme appeared to derive from its long-running regular characters, whom many of the children described with great affection and familiarity; while characters long since written out were fondly remembered.

The children's accounts of the narrative pleasures of the programme were also similar to those of soap opera, although the fact that most of the characters last only for a single episode did appear to generate an even greater sense of detachment. The game of prediction that I described in Chapter 1 was one that appeared to be enjoyed by many of the children here:

*Kevin (12):* You know what's going to happen, almost. Because whatever you see someone doing, you know that they're going to have an accident / or cause one. So it's not really suspense ...

*Jenny (15):* It's like, towards the end, there's like five people, or three people, and you're thinking 'one of them's gonna get it' ... it's just the way it goes, there's always one of them gonna die.

Yet while accidents were certainly to be expected, their precise form – and, as Jenny implies, the identity of the victims – could not always be predicted. Indeed, a number of children expressed some irritation at the way in which the narrative would often conclude with a 'cliffhanger' that would not be pursued the following week. Adele (9) even described how she would 'play a good game' if she was unable to get to sleep, imagining endings for the episode she had seen. Yet despite Kevin's comment, these devices were recognised as necessary in order to ensure the suspense that would keep you watching: as a number of children observed, 'you just want to see what happens next'.

Nevertheless, as Jenny's comment implies, the wish to find out who is going to 'get it' this week reflects an almost dispassionate relationship with the characters. Indeed, while some of the children described instances where they had felt sad at the death of characters – or, more particularly, for those who had been bereaved – their suffering was occasionally a cause for pleasure:

*Carl (9):* Sometimes I feel sad, and sometimes I feel they got what they deserve.

*Tanya (9):* Sometimes I feel happy, I go 'good, good, good' ... When someone is telling someone to stop doing this or wants to stop doing this, and then he is just going to do it, and then he gets run over or something bad happens to them, I just go 'good, good, good'. Or like, on the other way right, when the good part is coming on and then they just finish it there, I just throw one of my shoes at the TV.

Yet despite Tanya's sadistic relish, there were numerous instances of scenes or storylines from *Casualty* that the children claimed to find either shocking or disgusting. Such responses encompassed both the means of injury – a girl's hair being torn out by a factory machine, a boy's hand being crushed in a lift, a woman being burnt with hot cooking fat – and the scenes of rescue and treatment – bodies being removed from a train wreck, the performing of a tracheotomy, the bones showing through a severed leg in an operation. The memory of such images was often lasting, as in the case of this recollection of an incident that had happened several years previously:

*Adam (15):* I saw one that's stuck in my head ever since I've seen it. It was um, a lorry had a toxic spillage, loads of like toxic things, and something gets out, and this police[man] runs over and he gets all covered in this toxic stuff. And then you see him lying on the bed, dead. And he's all –

*Lisa (15):* His skin's all peeled.

*Adam:* His skin's all been burnt and it's all purple and yellow / just looks well nasty.

At the same time, such observations often appeared to reflect the 'meta-responses' we have encountered in relation to horror. Children frequently expressed a positive relish for the elements of blood and gore, implying that they were somehow to be congratulated for their ability to 'handle it':

*Matthew (9):* I like the blood, I like looking at the blood, that's my favourite bit in *Casualty* ... because it's exciting.

*Karen (15):* You watch it because it's shocking ... I watch it because I know I'm gonna see gory stuff, and I like it.

For Emma (9), as for Karen, such scenes were central to her expectations of the programme, even if they were not always enjoyable in themselves:

*Emma:* I thought one that wasn't particularly nice was this one with the tractor, and the man who got his leg caught in the tractor. You saw his welly boot or whatever, there was just all blood pouring out.

*Interviewer:* So how did you feel when you saw that?

*Emma:* I just sort of took it as like *Casualty*. 'Cause I knew *Casualty* would have that sort of thing, and if I thought I didn't want to watch it, then I would look away or something. But I quite enjoyed it. It's good stories in *Casualty*, good plots.

Such judgments clearly imply that opposite reactions might be possible (for example, 'looking away'), and as such they serve to distinguish the speaker from other people who might be insufficiently strong-willed to take it. This was most apparent in Adam's comment:

*Adam (12):* I don't mind watching the programme, it doesn't make me feel sick. But other people, they may feel sick from it. Like my mum, when she's watching it, she has to turn away ... It's a thing that makes other people sick.

Nevertheless, there is a sense in which this self-conscious emphasis on 'facing up to reality' is part of the programme's definition of itself, and of the way in which it has been critically received. *Casualty* was generally regarded as a programme that did not flinch from 'reality' – and in a way, the realism of its treatment of injury and painful death served as a kind of guarantee of the realism of its treatment of social issues. However implicitly, the programme was seen as 'quality television' in the great tradition of British social realism.[8] Emma's comment about the 'good plots' is typical of a discourse of critical appreciation that recurred throughout these discussions; and *Casualty* was often defined as a 'well-made' programme, principally in terms of its careful cultivation of the illusion of realism.

Thus, while there were a number of children who described the programme as 'real', this should not be taken to imply that they regarded it as a kind of 'window on the world'. *Casualty* was perceived, not so much as 'real', but as real*ist* – that is, as a well-constructed and accurate imitation of the real. In terms of modality, this was partly to do with the technical or artistic quality of the illusion – 'the way they do it'. Many children, for example, praised the quality of the special effects. The wounds, it was argued, 'look realistic', to the point where they might almost convince you that they are real:

*Trevor (15):* You know when they've got a scalpel, and they're cutting them like that, all the blood's coming out, it's really good ... You think it ain't real, but how can it not be real? 'Cause it does look so real.

Likewise, Adele (9) suggested that such effects were occasionally 'too realistic', and that it was at this point that she was likely to become scared: 'if they look too realistic, you're sort of thinking "ugh, what if that happened to me?"' Jenny (15) even argued that the actors in the series would have to turn away from such scenes – 'they can't watch, because the make-up's so good'.

Indeed, for some of the younger children, the programme's evident success in this respect appeared to have created the possibility of precisely this kind of confusion. David (9), for example, described the 'spray' that was used to give the impression that a character had been burnt; although he went on to argue that the programme was shot in a real hospital, which was why it was 'very realistic'. Peter and Matthew (9) appeared to have learnt about some of the tricks of the trade from a book about the making of the series *London's Burning*:

*Peter:* What they do is, they have each shot, and when this person, say like the person falls down and they don't really hurt themselves, 'cause they just go like that and then they stop the –

*Matthew:* Tape.

*Peter:* No, they stop the camera and what they do is, someone comes along with some of that polish and just puts [it] on someone, so that's the blood, and then they have some wax, say to put on their legs, suppose if they got burned, and on their face.

*Matthew:* Yeah, then they switch, then he goes away, then they switch the camera back on –

*Peter:* And then they rewind the tape, so when he falls down, he gets blood on him ... It's very lifelike, though.

*Matthew:* Yeah, it looks lifelike.

*Interviewer:* Mm, so you think they do it quite well, then?

*Peter:* Yeah, because before I got that book I really thought that it was real blood ... but I'd like to know how they, when someone is in *Casualty* right, and I know how they do all the make-up, but I don't know how they make the doooooo [heart monitor sound] like that ...

*Matthew:* Probably they unhook the things from the body, the heart monitor from the body and then it [the line on the display] just goes straight.

*Peter:* Yeah, and probably they don't really stick them on, you know, after they stick them on, then when it takes a shot of somewhere else, someone pulls them out and just –

*Matthew:* Gets pretend ones and sticks them on.

*Peter:* – and when he's lying down they put the same ones on, but they just don't plug it on, you know what I mean, and then when they come in, the thing goes straight.

Despite the confidence of these boys' initial assertions, they are clearly still working on their attempt to sort out the relationship between the text and reality. While they are certain that the programme does not use real blood, they seem to believe that the heart monitor *is* real; and they seek to explain how the character appears to 'die' by simply extending their knowledge about editing to this illusion as well. Yet even if they are not quite correct about how such effects are achieved, the boys are very clear that the text is fictional. They make definite and consistent distinctions between what is 'really' happening and what is merely 'pretend'. Like Adele, they argue that the programme '*looks*' realistic or 'lifelike'; and they are trying hard to generate some plausible explanation of how this illusion of realism is created.

Comments on the programme's use of make-up and special effects recurred throughout these discussions, yet they were almost wholly positive: only in a couple of cases were there more critical comments about 'fake' scars and implausibly spurting arteries. Yet while the rehearsal of this kind of knowledge certainly serves to display one's critical expertise in the context of discussion, it is nevertheless debatable to what extent it comes into play at the point of viewing itself. Jenny (15), for example, praised the special effects with great enthusiasm, but this did not appear to prevent her from being shocked:

*Jenny:* [When I'm watching it] I feel 'wow, that's brilliant, how do they do that? It must have taken them so long to do that make up.' That's what I think.

*Interviewer:* But does that stop it shocking you?

*Jenny:* No, it still shocks you, like [*mimes shock*]. But it's just good ... I just sit and stare at it. I think 'ooh, that must hurt!' And my dad says 'is it gone yet?'

As in many of the discussions of soap opera, Jenny appears to veer between a position of distanced appreciation, in which she reads the text as artificially constructed, and one of close involvement, in which she imagines such events happening to her. Yet despite her first comment here, it seems doubtful that the former position is one that can be sustained for long – unless one is to believe that viewers perceive the text as merely a self-conscious display of illusionism, like a kind of instructional magic show. On the contrary, I would argue that modality judgments of this kind are much more likely to occur after the event, as a form of *post hoc* reassurance – or indeed, of rationalisation.

However, 'realism' was also seen to reside in the storylines, and in the programme's treatment of social issues – in other words, in terms of 'external' criteria. To be sure, this was partly seen in terms of the care taken by the programme producers. Celia (12), for example, implied that there was a kind of narrative depth here:

*Celia:* The good thing about *Casualty* is it's not all about people getting hurt. They have what happened, why they got hurt, and they also have a storyline with the people in the hospital.

Celia's use of the somewhat technical term 'storyline' – like Emma's use of the word 'plot' above – also seems to derive from the discourse of television appreciation. While there is no implication that the programme is perceived as 'real', it is judged to be 'realistic' in terms of a comparison with what is believed to happen in real life:

*Emma (9):* They set it out well. I know they've got lots of different bits, but I think the style's good, and they show you what's in a hospital, what happens, 'cause you don't really find out about that in, like, normally. It shows you the problems they're facing while they've got to deal with all the customers and that.

Here again, the programme is seen to 'show you what happens', although this is a result of a deliberate decision on the part of the producers ('they'). Emma implicitly acknowledges the unrealistic nature of the multiple storylines ('different bits'), but the 'style' she identifies is essentially that of realism. For her, this has an educational function:

*Emma:* I think it's good, because if it really did happen, someone had an accident, and you were standing right by them and you saw this blood, you probably wouldn't be as used to it as if you'd watched something that looks really realistic ... I mean, I haven't really been to hospital loads and loads of times, so I won't actually know [if it's realistic]. But they do give you some idea of what might happen.

Emma was not alone in arguing that the programme might help to prepare viewers for the experience of witnessing such scenes, or for going into hospital themselves. Yet in Celia's case, this educational dimension extended to the programme's treatment of social issues, and appeared to support her growing political awareness:

*Celia:* All these things that I hear about, like / like people getting abused and things / I like to talk about it. 'Cause if I know more, then I can do more when I grow up, when people will listen to me better.

For some parents, this balance between the entertaining and informative aspects of the programme and the potential distress it might provoke had caused some difficulty. In some cases, the concern was primarily to do with the blood and gore; and in this respect, a straightforward reminder about make-up and special effects appeared to suffice. Liz, for example, whose oldest child was nine, described how she would remind the children that 'they're only acting' and 'it's tomato sauce': while they had been upset at one time, 'once they realised it wasn't real, they were OK about it'. In other cases, however, there was concern about the programme's treatment of social issues. Maurice, for example, whose children were aged between six and thirteen, referred to stories about child abuse, and accused the programme of presenting 'a view of life which is somewhat extreme and unnecessary at this particular time', implying that it should be screened later in the evening. His daughter Adele (9), however, appeared to have entered into a pact with her mother, who was a particular fan of the programme: she described how she would occasionally be sent out of the room during the more 'unsuitable' scenes, but that she would continue to watch through a crack in the door.

Many of the children agreed that *Casualty* could be inappropriate for younger children – although, yet again, this always referred to those younger than themselves. Adele (9) suggested that younger children might find some scenes too scary; while Emma (9) asserted that 'they wouldn't understand what happens, because it's quite a grown up programme' – as of course, by extension, are those who watch it. Nevertheless, the same children described how they had resented – and in some cases, successfully resisted – their parents' attempts to prevent them from watching. Particularly among the older children, there was a strong sense that the programme was important to watch, despite the potential for distress. Here, Karen (15) is discussing the 'banned' episode that had featured a gang setting fire to the hospital:

*Karen:* The point was, it was realistic and it would happen, and I think people need to see that, to be able to kind of get a grasp of stuff like that, which is why I don't understand why they keep moving the time and stuff. I mean, I understand little kids could probably be affected by it, but I think it's a really good thing to watch, 'cause it definitely makes you think more about it, about some of the actions you'll do and you won't think about it, and realise that some people get seriously hurt.

The banning of this episode was also condemned by another group of fifteen-year-olds, who went on to criticise the way in which the series had been 'toned down' in order to make it more acceptable for 'family viewing':

*Jenny:* The one they did where there was loads of complaints, it was on *Points of View* or something, everyone complained that it was unbelievable and they shouldn't have done it and stuff.

*Interviewer:* Why were people complaining then?

*Jenny:* ... I don't know. It's like they don't want to face facts, that things happen ... They didn't repeat it, because the story was too powerful or something like that, it aroused too many feelings ...

*Interviewer:* So you don't think things like that would affect kids, I mean, younger children?

*Jenny:* I think it affects them.

*Jane:* No, I reckon it affects them, it might make them cry and get a bit upset, but it won't affect them.

*Jenny:* They might wonder what the hell is going on. 'Cause, you know, they've got this perfect little world, they don't want to see things like that.

*Interviewer:* Mm. So you think it's important that they see things like that?

*Jenny:* Yeah, they've got to know about –

*Jane:* They've got to know what's going on, know about real life.

*Interviewer:* Yeah. And you think that *Casualty*'s one of those programmes that tells kids about real life?

*Jane:* It used to, but not now ...

*Jenny:* I think the make-up and everything, like, the disasters were more before, but the money issue comes up a lot now, all the time ... it'd be good with both of them, the casualties and the money side, but it's like every week they're always going on about the money, and although it's an important fact, it gets a bit boring. [*laughter*] You need a bit of blood and a bit of guts hanging out, to make it more interesting.

*Interviewer:* Why do you think they've done that, though, why do you think they've changed it in that way?

*Jane:* 'Cause they had too many complaints, yeah.

*Jenny:* Busybodies writing in to *Points of View* and telling them it's too vulgar, stuff like that.

*Interviewer:* But do you think they should listen to those people?

*Jenny:* Yeah, they have their right, but –

*Jane:* But they've got the choice whether they want to put it on.

*Jenny:* Yeah, they don't have to, they're not made to sit and watch *Casualty*, they can turn it over if they don't want to.

This extract encapsulates many of the tensions surrounding *Casualty*, and the debate about the regulation of such material. On the one hand, the girls acknowledge that the programme can 'affect' children – although by the word 'affect' they are clearly referring to short-term emotional responses rather than the copycat violence that appeared to be the central issue in the debate around this episode. On the other hand, they argue that the programme reflects 'real life', and as such it informs children about things that they should know, even if this disrupts their 'perfect little world'. Interestingly, however, they imply that 'real life' also has to be balanced against the demands of what they clearly perceive as a form of entertainment: stories about budget cuts in the National Health Service may be important, but they are not as interesting as a good dose of 'blood and guts'. As we have seen above, Jenny's enthusiasm for the explicitly gory aspects of the programme was characterised by an ambivalence that was typical of these discussions: she appreciates the quality of the 'make-up', yet she also enjoys the 'strong feelings' such scenes evoke.

Meanwhile, the girls' criticisms of the 'busybodies' who seek to regulate their viewing are also typical, particularly of the older children. As we have seen in Chapter 3, the BBC's viewer reaction programme *Points of View* serves as a particular focus of contempt here. The people who write in to such programmes are seen to be unwilling to 'face facts'; and they are accused of interfering in other people's viewing when they should simply turn the programme off. In the case of *Casualty*, the girls argue that this kind of interference has not only reduced the programme's appeal as entertainment, but has also undermined its educational function, particularly for children. Indeed, later in the discussion, the girls argued that the producers should have ignored such complaints, and left the decision to be determined on the basis of the ratings: as Jenny said, 'if they get less viewers, then they know that they must have made the wrong decision'.

As this example shows, the balance between the need to inform, to entertain and to avoid distress invokes much wider questions about 'real life' and the ways in which children should be exposed to it. Children may or may not live in a 'perfect little world', as

Jenny suggests; but it is clear that they will at some point have to face up to unpleasant realities. Yet for all its perceived ability to 'show what really happens', *Casualty* was clearly perceived as a fictional construction of the world, which could be critically assessed in terms of its accuracy to viewers' own knowledge and experience. For different reasons, this possibility was not always available with the other two programmes I discuss below.

### *Crimewatch UK*: realistic fears?

Much of the debate that has surrounded television coverage of real-life crime has focused on the extent to which it blurs the distinction between reality and fiction. *Crimewatch UK* and similar programmes like *Crime Monthly* and *America's Most Wanted* tend to present themselves as promoting the 'public good', both through assisting in the apprehending of criminals, and through instructing viewers in methods of crime prevention. Yet this has often been seen to conflict with the need to maximise ratings, and hence to entertain – particularly through the use of dramatic and potentially disturbing material.[9] There has been particular criticism here of the use of reconstructions, which have been seen to sensationalise the threat of crime, particularly against the person. Here again, what is at stake is a fundamental tension between the imperatives of information and of entertainment, in which the perceived reality of the programme is of central significance.

A majority of the children who had seen *Crimewatch* said that it had made them feel 'scared' or 'worried'. As with horror films, the fear often appeared to intensify after the programme was over, particularly if they were alone in the house. Here again, the children clearly imagined themselves not as the perpetrators of crime, but as the potential victims. While a couple of children jokingly suggested that the programme might 'give people ideas' on how to commit crimes, most agreed that the programme made *them* feel 'unsafe' or 'threatened'. As in the accounts of news, this was most evidently the case in relation to local crime. In one school, for example, a number of children spoke about a *Crimewatch* reconstruction that had featured a murder near a local swimming pool:

*Martha (15):* I think the reason it hit home slightly more was 'cause it was at [the pool] and that's local to a lot of people who live in [this] area. And to actually think that there's someone sick enough, because you always see these things and you think 'oh, that's really bad', you know, sometimes it'll make you upset, but you think 'oh it'll never happen to anyone like me'. But that could have easily been one of us sitting in the car at [the pool], it's the local swimming pool for round here, I suppose.

For many children, reports of such incidents connected with those in their own experience, or that they had heard about from other sources; although they frequently gave rise to more generalised arguments about the likelihood of crime:

*Lisa (15):* When things happen to people when they're in their own homes, you know, like they get raped or whatever, actually in their own homes, you think 'wow, you can't be safe anywhere'.

However exaggerated such fears might appear, there seemed to be a general agreement that such things did happen, and that the programme was simply reporting them:

*Serena (15):* They are [upsetting], but they kind of / open your eyes up to the real world, 'cause it's what's happening.

*Trevor:* It's just life.

*Serena:* And you've got to be aware of those things ...

*Trevor:* Everyone knows, you know they're going on, innit? It's just that they show you it.

*Serena:* Yeah, it is. But it's worrying as well, though.

*Interviewer:* So what do they make you worry about then?

*Serena:* When it's going to happen to you, you know. It's happened to everyone else, why not you?

While Trevor maintains a bluff indifference, Serena (like the other girls quoted above) clearly imagines herself as a potential victim of crime. Nevertheless, there is a firm belief here in the reality of what is shown, which is partly confirmed by the children's own experiences ('you know they're going on'); and Serena's fear is balanced against the need to 'be aware', and hence perhaps to guard against such things happening to you.

As with news, these feelings proved difficult to cope with, largely because the programme could not be dismissed as fictional:

*Liam (15):* Because it's real life, I think you get more frightened. 'Cause you know it could just happen to anybody, which makes it more frightening. There's not really much you can do about it.

As Liam's comment implies, the knowledge that the programme is real makes it much easier to 'translate' it into the circumstances of your own life, and hence much harder to cope with. His argument was echoed by a number of other children:

*Interviewer:* So when you get worried about something on *Crimewatch,* what do you do?

*Lisa (15):* I don't know, because it's different than a film, because it's really happened.

*Adam (15):* There's nothing you can do really, unless you actually know any information.

Adam later described (somewhat facetiously, perhaps) how he would 'watch a comedy' in order to take his mind off such fears, while Laura (15) said she would close her eyes when the photofit pictures came on. Yet the recognition that 'there's nothing you can do' was echoed by a number of other children. This group, in common with others, also explicitly mocked the presenter's sign-off line at the end of the programme, which they saw as a lame attempt to reassure them:[10]

*Lisa:* I hate it when he says um / he goes 'goodnight and sleep well, don't have nightmares', and I think 'oh *shut up!*' ...

*Interviewer:* Why don't you like that then, Lisa?

*Lisa:* I don't know. It's annoying, I think.

*Laura:* It's patronising ... I don't know, it's like [*mocking voice*] 'don't have nightmares', like he's being sarcastic.

On the other hand, the programme was also seen by many to be performing a useful social service. Most obviously, this was to do with catching criminals: some children described instances of cases that had been solved as a result of a *Crimewatch* report, while others referred to the large numbers of viewers who would call in with information – statistics which are of course emphasised in the programme itself. Only in a few cases was there a degree of cynicism here. A couple of older children said they would be worried about informing, for fear of being attacked by the criminals' families or associates; while Jenny (15) was rather critical of the time that the police had taken to solve some of the cases, and accused the programme of giving them opportunities 'to show how clever they are, to show off'.

Yet in general the programme was seen to be offering valuable lessons in crime prevention – 'making people more aware of what's going on around them, so they can be safe', as Lisa (15) put it. A number of children, particularly girls, reported that they would change their behaviour after watching the programme, either by going out less, or by being more careful on their route home, although they acknowledged that this might not last. While there was a sense in one or two cases that this was seen as a restraint on their freedom, it was generally accepted as a sensible response. Laura (15), for example, argued 'it doesn't make me more scared, it makes me more aware'; although Vanessa (12) did suggest that the programme tended to intensify such fears – 'you'd feel like that anyway, but [those programmes] make you feel more unsafe'. In some cases, it was argued that it was necessary for the programme to scare people if its message was to get through: as Sarah (15) said, 'if they didn't do that, most of the crimes wouldn't get solved', while Caroline (15) argued that 'they have to be a bit shocking to jog people's memories'.

As I have noted, the central question for researchers and policy-makers in this area has been whether such reports lead to an *unrealistic* fear of crime, that is out of proportion to the real scale of the problem.[11] Of course, this research cannot tell us whether the programme actually increased the children's fear of crime, only that most of them *said* that it did – and this is a limitation that it shares with most other research on this topic.[12] The crucial question, however, is whether this fear causes people to overestimate their possibilities of victimisation in real life. In this respect, as in the discussions of news, it is notable that such fears were expressed much more consistently by the children living in inner-city areas than by those in suburban areas – although they were also more likely to watch the programme in the first place. Similarly, girls were more likely to express such fears than boys. Such disparities may or may not reflect the likely incidence of victimisation in real life;[13] although of course the fear of crime may itself lead to preventative action which reduces the potential for such occurrences. Ultimately, one of the major difficulties here is in defining what a 'realistic' fear of crime might be in the first place.[14] As I have indicated, fear is partly a result of an act of imagination: it is unlikely ever to represent a rational response to a statistical probability. It may be a mistake to assume that 'unrealistic' fears will be dispelled merely by a good dose of factual information – or indeed by reducing the media coverage of crime.

As the observations above suggest, *Crimewatch UK* was clearly defined by all the children here as a factual programme: indeed, it was primarily for this reason that it was seen as particularly frightening or worrying. Nevertheless, there were some significant ambiguities and tensions in this respect, particularly in relation to the reconstructions. Even the youngest children here were clear about the meaning of the term 'reconstruction':

*Peter (9):* It means that ... they're just playing actors of what happened. It's not the real people, but what you see, what you hear and what they say is what really they said.

However, in one or two instances, children admitted that they had been confused about this. Alison (12) described how she used to believe that 'it was the real people' shown committing the crime, and had only realised that this was not the case when an actor had appeared in a reconstruction playing a friend of hers who had witnessed a local crime. Vanessa (12) described how she had once 'forgotten' that she was watching a reconstruction:

*Vanessa:* It was just so realistic.

*Interviewer:* What was it that made it realistic?

*Vanessa:* I think mainly the acting. You knew that the story was true and the acting was so good and you could just imagine that it was those people that it had happened to.

As these accounts imply, there may be several different levels at which the 'reality' of the reconstruction is situated. Vanessa knows that this is acting, and hence not real; but she also knows that the story itself is true, and is therefore willing to 'imagine' that what she is watching is real.

This kind of ambiguity was discussed further by a group of fifteen-year-olds:

*Adam:* When you watch a reconstruction, though, when you see like a person who committed a crime or whatever on the reconstruction, you'll think 'right, I'm gonna look out for that person there'. You don't look at the sort of artists' sketch or impression. [*laughter*]

*Martha:* Yeah, if I was the actor, I wouldn't do it, you know, 'cause you'd get all these people coming up to you in the street going 'my God, it's him, phone the police', going crazy, and it's just an actor.

*Laura:* What made me laugh was one of the actors who was on it was in *Grange Hill* once, so that kind of ruined the *whole thing*.

*Martha:* What kills me is how they can, like that one, the Chinese delivery man who was delivering the Chinese [food] to this farm ... how can they actually get this actor to portray a dead man. I just think it's kind of gross really. I mean, I think it might have been better with that one to have maybe even blacked out his face or something.

*Interviewer:* What, because you thought –

*Martha:* Because I didn't think it was very nice to have that sort of thing done ... I mean, they had the wife and everyone on and they had the mother and she was all upset, you know, talking about it, and then they've got this actor that is like the spitting image of her son, sort of reconstructing her son's murder. I think it's too much.

*Laura:* But then what happens is when the family are in the reconstruction ... you can always tell them though.

On one level, this group seems to accept the idea that viewers might believe that they are watching a documentary record of real events – although there is some amusement here, and in Martha's first comment, the potential confusion appears to be confined to the more gullible members of society. Nevertheless, particularly in Laura's contributions, they acknowledge that the effectiveness of the method depends upon its not being undermined by anything that might draw attention to its fictional status: the problem with having the real family participating in the reconstruction is that they disrupt the illusion – not least, it would seem, because they are such poor actors. Yet their discussion shifts awkwardly from irreverence to moral condemnation in Martha's story about the family of the murder victim. The potential confusion between fact and fiction is, on one level, just a joke; but on another level, it can be seen as tasteless and an invasion of privacy.

Interestingly, however, the formal differences between *Crimewatch* reconstructions and fictional films seemed to contribute to this, rather than undermining it:

*Caroline (15):* The reconstructions, especially where it's like women getting attacked, and like kids when they're walking down the street. And like you can tell it's gonna happen, but they don't play any music like in films so you don't know exactly when it's gonna happen. It's a bit, like, it's a shock that the person comes out and grabs them. It is quite scary, I think ... They don't actually have much violence, but it's more scary than a really violent film, 'cause you know it's really actually happened once. And it can just scare you if they're just saying things, because you know it actually happened.

As Caroline implies, the comparative *lack* of sensationalism of the reconstructions, and the lack of generic 'clues' that would be provided in a fictional film, could be seen to heighten the fear they provoked. Furthermore, the explicitness of what is shown may be less significant than the knowledge that it has really happened – and indeed that it could happen to *you*. As with horror, the fear may well depend not so much on what is there before our eyes, but on the way in which we are enabled to 'translate' it imaginatively into our own experiences. The 'reality claims' of the text – if they are believed – are seen to carry a remarkable power.

At the same time, much of the pleasure of *Crimewatch* appeared to derive from its analogies with fictional drama, and indeed with other entertainment genres. A number of children described how they had enjoyed the comic moments that feature intermittently in the programme, for example featuring incompetent hold-ups of building societies. In other cases, it was the narratives of detection that were found particularly enjoyable, although here again there was a sense in which this enjoyment was seen to be somewhat 'sick':

*Sarah (15):* I saw the one about the man who hacks with the axe. It was good.

*Interviewer:* It was good. What was good about it, Sarah?

*Jenny (15):* They reconstruct what happens.

*Sarah:* Yeah, the reconstruction was good. [*laughter*]

*Jenny:* It sounds awful to say it's good, but it is. It's like a little film.

*Sarah:* I don't know, you're waiting for them to catch him, isn't it. It's good.

*Jenny:* And how they do it is interesting.

The girls here are aware that there is something inappropriate about reading the programme as though it were fictional, and even about the kind of critical appreciation they adopt (hence the laughter after Sarah's comment 'the reconstruction was good'). Yet the rather irreverent stance adopted here was apparent among other groups of older children:

*Martha (15):* It makes everyone aware, you know, and with the photofits and that.

*Laura (15):* 'Cause you always think you're going to see someone you know and you're like [*imitates hiding*].

*Martha:* Yeah, that's why you always get a bit nervous before they show the photos. I mean, for all you know, your dad's face can be there, you know.

*Laura:* [*laughing*] Your dad's gonna come up!

While on one level, Laura appears to adopt the role of the 'scared child' in this interview, similar fears were expressed by her fourteen-year-old brother Gareth, whom we interviewed later. The children's mother also confirmed that Gareth had been very scared by the programme – and particularly by the 'hideous faces' in the photofits; yet she acknowledged that such fears might have been encouraged by the fact that she herself worked as a counsellor for Victim Support, and would sometimes tell the children about similar cases she had been involved with. Both Gareth and Laura agreed that *Crimewatch* was more frightening than horror films; although Laura acknowledged that much of the pleasure of the reconstructions derived from the fact that 'people like scaring themselves'. As this implies, programmes like *Crimewatch* may provide opportunities for viewers to cope with their *existing* anxieties about crime – although, unlike most crime fiction on television, true crime programmes do not always offer the reassurance that the criminals will be caught and that justice will be seen to be done.

Ultimately, *Crimewatch* was seen to be caught in the balance between the need to inform and the need to entertain. While there was occasionally a sense that the entertainment dimensions of the programme might be somewhat 'sick' or exploitative, it was compared positively in this respect with American live action crime series such as *Cops*:

*Karen (15):* The sick thing is, some of them are filmed, some of them are like home videos ... That's the sick thing in America, it's a big thing to go to an accident and film it with your camera.

Yet here again, the programme was generally seen to be inappropriate for younger children. A couple of parents described how they would not allow their younger children to watch it; while many of the children themselves agreed that younger children would be frightened unnecessarily:

*Martha (15):* I don't think there's any reason for them to be exposed to it. I mean, ninety-nine times out of a hundred they're not gonna know who did what and be able to phone up and give them vital evidence, you know. I don't think there's any point to it really, 'cause it would make them more scared and paranoid when they're going out. I mean, of course you've got to be aware, but you don't have to see some woman being brutally killed, you know.

*Adam (15):* Yeah, but they're not really graphic, are they?

*Martha:* Well, no. But they can understand it to a certain extent.

While Martha accepts that the programme is not 'really graphic', she argues that this is beside the point. The balance between being 'aware' and being 'paranoid' is, she implies, a difficult one to strike, yet it partly depends upon what you *need* to know, and how far that information will actually be of use to you. Thus, a number of children argued that young children did need to 'worry about strangers', but that they should not be scared unnecessarily:

*Alison (12):* I think [those programmes] should only be shown to certain age groups, because I really think that if someone little watched it, then they're gonna be so scared for the rest of their lives that something's gonna happen to them ... . My mum tells me to watch them because she thinks that it's good that I see them, 'Cause she's always telling me that I shouldn't go out by myself and all of this, and I say 'oh don't be so stupid, you're so over-protective' and everything. But then she likes me seeing those things, but then she doesn't like, she likes sort of scaring me, but she doesn't think it's good for me to be scared, but she likes scaring me so I know the dangers of what could happen.

The ambiguities and hesitations in Alison's comment reflect the fundamental difficulties here: being adequately informed ('knowing the dangers') inevitably depends upon being scared. While Alison argues that the programme should not be shown to younger children, she also points to the central dilemma for parents: to be protective may involve scaring your children, yet to be 'over-protective' is to fail to equip them for what may happen to them. As she implies, there may be a very fine line between being too scared and not being scared enough.

## *Ghostwatch*: crossing the boundary

The blurring of boundaries between fact and fiction has been identified as an increasing tendency in contemporary television.

The use of fictional techniques in true crime programmes like *Crimewatch* has been matched by the adoption of a documentary filming style in cop shows like *Homicide: Life on the Streets* and *NYPD Blue*. Meanwhile, documentaries have taken on the form of soap operas and situation comedies (*The Real World*, *Sylvania Waters*); and 'drama documentary' has grown from its origins in the 1960s to become one of the dominant television genres of today.[15] Nevertheless, there can be few programmes that have sought to cross the boundary between fact and fiction with quite such an explicit intention to deceive as the BBC's spoof documentary *Ghostwatch*. Using the techniques of outside broadcast filming and the authority of well-known presenters, *Ghostwatch* sought to persuade millions of viewers that it was presenting scenes from a real-life ghost hunt taking place in an ordinary suburban house on the outskirts of London.

In fact, there is a striking precedent here in the form of Orson Welles's radio production of *The War of the Worlds* – not least in the significant fact that both were broadcast at Hallowe'en.[16] Transmitted by CBS in 1938, Welles's production provoked widespread panic across the United States, in which thousands of people fled their homes. The play included what purported to be live announcements of a Martian invasion that rapidly swept across the country; and while several disclaimers were included in the pre-publicity and in the programme itself, it appears that several million listeners were fooled. Hadley Cantril's study of the panic, *The Invasion From Mars*,[17] suggested that many listeners had either not heard or had ignored the disclaimers, or did not bother to check the story against other sources. According to Cantril, the broadcast's success derived largely from the American public's trust in radio as a news medium; and while certain types of people were found to be more susceptible – such as those with strong religious beliefs – the use of devices from factual reporting such as 'on the spot' reports and 'expert' commentators was seen to have played a major part in the success of the deception.

While *Ghostwatch* was not on quite the same scale, the reasons for its 'success' were probably very similar. For the children who had watched it, there was almost universal agreement that it was the most frightening programme or film they had ever seen. Even horror enthusiasts like Imran (12), who blithely dismissed films like *Halloween* and the *Child's Play* series, admitted that *Ghostwatch* had 'really scared' them. Those who had watched the programme alone appeared to be the worst affected, although some described how friends or members of their family had cried. Here again, many children reported that the fear intensified after they had finished watching – even though it was evident from the credits at the end of the programme that it had been fictional.

As with *The War of the Worlds*, there may well have been an element of 'contagion' here – and this was probably encouraged by the programme's use of a (fake) phone-in, whereby viewers were reported to be experiencing similarly supernatural incidents in their own homes. The fact that the programme went out at Hallowe'en was, of course, not incidental: in some cases, it appeared to serve as a focus for a family party, which in the case of Alison (12) and her friends involved turning all the lights out and using candles instead. Furthermore, as I have noted, the programme has since come to be surrounded by a certain mythology, according to which (as Caroline (15) put it) 'some boy committed suicide because he believed it' – although such stories were also dismissed as reflections of the *Points of View* mentality (see pages 72–3 above).

On the other hand, of course, these interviews were conducted almost eighteen months after the broadcast. At this distance, one might expect memories to have dimmed, and that viewers would be less likely to admit to having been 'fooled'. One should therefore regard the data with a degree of scepticism – although what remains striking is the detail and scope of the children's recollections, and their clear descriptions of being frightened.

As in the case of *Crimewatch*, the key to this fear was undoubtedly the fact that the programme was perceived as 'real', and particularly as 'live':

*Adam (15):* It was just the way it was all supposed to have been real. That's what I thought sort of freaked me out, was that this was all happening and it was live.

In retrospect, of course, the children were able to identify how this illusion of realism had been created. This was seen to be partly to do with the careful pre-publicity for the programme in trailers and in the listings magazine *Radio Times*:

*Laura (15)*: Sometimes, if it is on television and it is fake, something will give it away in the advert, or someone or something in the paper, it will give it away. But nothing – there wasn't even a hint of anything before the credits came up that it was gonna be fake.

*Alison (12)*: They made out in the clips and everything, and when they said about it in the paper, they made out it was going to be a true story.

As I have noted, *Ghostwatch* was in fact transmitted in a 'Screen One' slot normally given over to single plays – which must in itself have alerted some adult viewers that it was not what it claimed to be (it certainly did so for me). But for children, who would be much less used to such scheduling conventions (particularly at this time on a weekday evening), only the announcer's very slightly coy introduction would have given any hint.

Laura, Martha and Adam (15) offered a comprehensive analysis of the ways in which the programme itself had carefully cultivated the illusion of realism – and, in the process, managed to deceive all three of them. The use of well-known presenters such as Sarah Greene and Michael Parkinson 'playing themselves' was seen to be a key factor here:

*Adam*: They were actually presenters, not actors, so you instantly thought it was like some kind of documentary, it wasn't like a drama series.

The programme's use of a phone-in (significantly similar to that in its namesake *Crimewatch*) was a further factor in establishing its credibility. The notion that viewers were calling in to report similar incidents in their own homes, or to provide background information for the case under investigation, was seen to be amusing in retrospect, although at the time it was clearly effective:

*Adam*: I'd love to have been working there at the time, when all the people ring up saying 'my house is haunted', and you could just say 'shut up, you fool'.

*Laura:* [*laughing*] 'I saw the ghost!'

The use of documentary-style camerawork, and of video, was seen to be another guarantee of realism – although interestingly in this case, the programme was compared not with documentary, but with realist drama:

*Martha:* It's the style of how it's filmed. / Like with *The Bill*, it looks like there's just a camera been shoved out in the street, and it's all real and it's all happening. But with something like a movie, because it's so well planned out, it's just so smooth and continuous and nothing ever goes wrong, and the camera never jolts up and down /

*Interviewer:* So was that what made *Ghostwatch* so scary?

*Martha:* Yeah, you could see the mistakes, and if someone dropped the camera, the camera went down.

Significantly, one of the scenes that was repeatedly described as the most frightening involved precisely this kind of 'mistake': the camera had panned past a 'ghost' standing in front of a curtain, and then panned quickly back, as though the camera operator had only just noticed it – only to reveal that it had disappeared. This careful use of the conventions of documentary – and particularly of live outside broadcasts – seemed to undermine any attempt to dismiss the programme as merely fictional or constructed:

*Laura:* You could see all the big lights shining on the house and all the crowds outside ... It looked like a live show, it really looked like one.

*Martha:* Yeah, it really did, 'cause you could see the cameraman running around ... It's different though, when you're watching things like Freddy Kruger, any horror film –

*Adam:* It's just too unbelievable.

*Martha:* 'Cause even if it freaks you out, yeah / Freddy Kruger is too unbelievable for a start, but even if you are getting freaked out by a film, you just have to sit there and think, think of how many cameras and cameramen, and you know.

*Laura:* But this one you could see them and you knew how many there were.

*Martha:* Yeah, that's really what did make it more scary, I think.

In these various ways, therefore, the programme was judged to be particularly successful in constructing the illusion of reality: as Randeep (15) said, 'they made it look 'nuff real'. In some other respects, however, *Ghostwatch* was seen to have failed here. A couple of the older children commented on the unlikely way in which events appeared to happen 'on cue'; and while there were some who disagreed, a number of children commented on the limitations of the acting:

*Alison (12):* It was meant to be a hidden camera, but you could tell. 'Cause you know some children, when they act, you can just tell that they've been reading a script.

*Vanessa (11):* It was a bit stupid because [Sarah Greene] was saying things like 'oh my God, we turned a blind eye to it', and it sounded so stupid because it wasn't in the right sort of tone or pitch or anything.

As I have implied, such observations should be regarded with some suspicion – and in both cases here, the girls' comments appeared to have been cued by parents' observations, which they may have only fully accepted in retrospect (see below). However, it was generally agreed that at a point close to the end, the programme finally 'went over the top':

*Trevor (15):* When the girl was in the hospital, and she's going 'wuuh wuuh wuuh' in this weird voice, I thought 'no, man'. But up until then, it had me going.[18]

*Adam (15):* I believed it until, you know, when she got locked in the cupboard and the studio started shaking about ... It just seemed so stupid, all the lights started shaking, and there was wind and everything / things started falling down.

Nevertheless, even in Adam's case, the illusion was not totally dispelled for most of the children until the final credits began to roll.

In many instances, this whole issue appeared to have been the focus of an ongoing debate while the programme was being watched, although there was often a distinct uncertainty here. On the one hand, there were parents who attempted to reassure their children by trying to convince them that it was not real:

*Amina:* Jaya [14] was asking me questions about what I think about it, can it happen, is it possible, is it true or not, and I was more of the opinion that it was stage managed, because it can't be true, it can't go to that extent. I said 'it's very well done, right' / so I was telling her, you know, 'don't think it's real', right, so I was discounting her fears as she was going along ... I'd say 'don't worry, it's stage managed', and my usual argument, there's a whole bloody crew on the other side of the camera watching it, so how can it be so scary?

On the other hand, as Alison (12) acknowledged, such protestations were not always accepted:

*Alison:* My mum's boyfriend was watching it with us, and everyone was scared at the beginning, but he started us off by saying, 'oh don't be stupid, it's fake, look, can't you see, look at the acting, she just forgot her lines' and all of this / 'and she was just prompted, look, it's so fake' and all of this. So then that made me realise, and my sister. But everyone else was really scared.

*Interviewer:* So he was sure that it was a fake?

*Alison:* Yeah. / Well, I don't know if he actually was really sure, but he had to pretend to us that he was. / But he's the one, while we were watching it, he hides behind the sofa and then suddenly jumps out on us.

Interestingly, the focus of these attempts at demystification is exclusively on what I have termed the 'internal' modality criteria – that is, the evidence (or at least the implicit knowledge) that the programme is constructed. As I have indicated, the programme itself had clearly taken great pains to forestall this kind of criticism, through its careful cultivation of the illusion of 'live' television. Yet there was very little discussion of the 'external' criteria – that is, of the question of the *plausibility* of the programme. Parents instinctively sought to reassure children by convincing them that the programme was 'fake'; but the more awkward question of whether such things really *could* happen – *even if* they were not really happening in this particular instance – was thereby left open.

Thus, in Alison's case, she appeared to accept the notion that the programme was not real, although a fundamental doubt – and hence a degree of fear – remained:

*Interviewer:* What was the scariest bit in it?

*Alison:* The girl, the girl with scratches all over her face ... that's what made me believe it, when she had, 'cause the make-up looked really real, all the scratches. 'Cause she had loads of cuts all over her face, and it looked really nasty.

*Interviewer:* ... But you knew it was a fake, didn't you?

*Alison:* Yeah, but that, just 'cause we weren't certain that it was fake, but when there are people round you that are more scared than you, then you have to make out, you have to try and make them not scared by you being certain that it's all made up.

*Interviewer:* Right, so you have to be really sure and –

*Alison:* [*imitates*] 'I'm not scared!' [*laughs*] ...

*Interviewer:* So what was it about it that gave you that little bit of doubt?

*Alison:* Just some of the make-up and things like that. / 'Cause I've heard ghost stories that friends of the family, things that have happened to them, so – things that, they're not so bad, but they're similar. So I thought it could be real.

In this context, Alison clearly perceives a responsibility to hide her feelings, in order to avoid inducing similar feelings in others – a strategy that she also suspects her mother's boyfriend has adopted. Significantly, the grounds for her doubt relate both to 'internal' and 'external' modality criteria. Thus, she refers to the quality of the make-up, as merely one of the ways in which the programme sought to construct the *illusion* of reality; yet she also refers to evidence about 'real-life' supernatural experiences that she has gleaned from other trusted sources. Despite her confidence (at this distance) about the *artificiality* of the programme, it is this vestige of doubt about its *plausibility* that ultimately provokes the fear:

*Alison:* If they were better actors and actresses, the people who lived in the house, or were meant to have lived in the house, then it would have been more realistic. And then it would have been scarier than any programme like *Freddy's Back* or *Aliens*, because they're just unrealistic ... Then it would have been really scary, because it would have just meant that it could happen to anyone. 'Cause they just said 'someone who lived near the studio in London', and we all live in London. So it could have happened to any of us.

What remains striking here is that, even for children who were more certain than Alison that the programme was not real, it still appeared to evoke a remarkable degree of fear. A number described how they had continued to be scared well after the programme had finished. Some reported that they would not sleep without the light on; others that they would not go into the kitchen on their own; while Imran (12) described how he made sure to put the burglar alarm on, just in case. Alison herself described how, almost per-versely, her friend had suspected that the final credits themselves were fake: 'she still said "yeah, they probably just did that so you wouldn't be so scared"'.

This raises interesting questions, both about the notion of 'sus-pension of disbelief' (see Chapter 4) and about the notion of using modality judgments as a kind of defence or coping strategy. As Alison's comment above suggests, the programme was seen to pos-sess a kind of plausibility *despite* the fact that its artificiality was eventually recognised. The fact that, as she points out, the pro-gramme was situated in London – and in an area near where many of these children lived – was only part of this:

*Gareth (14):* I always think of the circumstances and imagine it hap-pening to me, then I get really sort of [scared].

*Interviewer:* Even though it wasn't real.

*Gareth:* Yeah, even though it wasn't real. 'Cause it was a house in Northolt, a single parent family, which is like an everyday house-hold, and a ghost in there.

Gareth's fear is partly motivated by the proximity of the (fictional) location; and it is also significant that he mentions the fact that the family in the film is a single parent family, like his own. Yet the crucial term here is 'imagine' – and it was one that was echoed elsewhere:

*Vanessa (12):* Even if you know it's a fake, you can still use your imagination and see the things that you saw on the programme.

As I have argued is the case with horror films, much of the power of the text depends upon the extent to which viewers are prepared to grant it plausibility, and hence to 'imagine' themselves in similar situations in their own lives. This is not the same thing as 'suspending disbelief' – at least if this is taken to mean that viewers somehow temporarily agree to accept the text as a kind of window on the world. Certainly in this case, the knowledge that the text is a fictional construction does not appear to preclude a willingness to entertain the possibility that (as all three children here acknowledge) such things might happen to *you*. Obviously, viewers who already believe in ghosts might well be predisposed to such responses – and, as in the case of the *War of the Worlds* research, one might hypothesise that some viewers are more 'gullible' than others.[19] In this case, however, there is no clear correlation between the children who *said* they believed in ghosts and those who admitted that they had believed that *Ghostwatch* was real – although the continuing popularity of such fictional treatments of the supernatural must surely depend upon a lingering doubt, even among the most sceptical of viewers.

Ultimately, it would not seem unreasonable to conclude that *Ghostwatch* was an irresponsible piece of broadcasting. Many of the children here implicitly argued that it was, particularly insofar as it appeared to be targeted partly at younger viewers. There was criticism, for example, of the way in which the programme was trailed in the early evening, and of the use of presenters like Sarah Greene, who was familiar from children's television, and who was also featured in the trailers. Vanessa, Imran and Alison (12) said they chose to watch the programme largely on these grounds, expecting that it would be a fairly anodyne collection of ghost stories like those they had read in books:

*Imran:* Because it was a children's presenter, I thought it would be like a late kind of children's programme, stories and stuff like that ...

*Vanessa:* I thought it was a bit strange, it was on at 9 o'clock, because it's supposed to be, you know, not suitable for children. But I thought it must be OK if it's got Sarah Greene in it.

Particularly on a Hallowe'en night, early bedtime would not have been a possibility in any case:

*Alison:* Also on Hallowe'en, they know that all these kids, they know it's a special night and everyone's going to stay up extra late.

While these children argued that the programme should have been screened later in the evening, the older children placed the responsibility on the parents – although not without some contradictions:

*Adam (15):* If parents didn't want their children watching it –

*Martha (15):* Exactly! What were they doing up at half nine till 11 o'clock, children of that age, that are gonna believe that sort of thing, anyway?

*Laura (15):* Well, I believed it, and I was [fourteen]. Martha, you believed it, and you were up! [*laughter*]

As Laura's comment implies, notions of childhood vulnerability were perhaps not quite so easily applicable in this case – and indeed, there were parents in our sample who also admitted to having been scared by the programme, and who judged it to be much more frightening in this respect than horror films.

However, there was a certain ambivalence on the question of regulation. There is no doubt that the children who saw *Ghostwatch* found it extremely difficult to handle. Some described how they had turned it off, or left the room, or hidden behind a cushion; while Imran (12) even talked about how his cousin had taken comfort from a religious icon – 'he got a picture of god, and started sitting there, just holding it, 'cause he got really scared'. Yet at the same time, many described how the programme appeared to exert a kind of compulsive fascination:

*Vanessa:* It was so strange, because we wanted to go upstairs, get away from the telly, but it was like someone was drawing us closer to it, to watch it more, 'cause it seemed so interesting ...

*Imran:* It was in the papers as well, the next day, so many people watched it, they were scared and they started complaining to the BBC. But all it said in the papers was 'why did they watch it?' They didn't have to watch it, did they? It hooked them in the middle, when they wanted to go upstairs, people got hooked to it so they couldn't go upstairs. Like me, I just wanted to finish watching it and go upstairs.

Of course, the programme did seek to 'hook' viewers, initially by creating doubt about whether there really was a ghost in the house, and subsequently by promising that it would be revealed – although in fact this never really occurred. Yet in these accounts, it is as though the supernatural power of the ghost has passed over into the medium itself, persuading viewers to watch against their better judgment.

Inevitably, many of the children acknowledged that the programme had left them feeling 'cheated' or 'fooled':

*Adam (15):* I felt like an idiot ... 'Cause when they were showing the black silhouette by the window, I was actually going over, sitting by the telly and cranking at it. I was saying 'look, look, I'm sure I can see something there' ... I just felt like an idiot.

Nevertheless, while it was suggested that the programme would no longer 'work' if it was repeated, the older children here did express the wish to see it again – albeit under certain circumstances:

*Martha (15):* I know someone that's recorded it, and I'm always meaning to borrow it, but I never get around to it.

*Laura (15):* Oh, you'll have to let me borrow that.

*Interviewer:* Do you think it would still be scary?

*Martha, Laura:* Yeah!

*Martha:* I'd love to see it now, 'cause I could sit and watch the whole thing.

*Laura:* I mean, I really wish they could repeat it.

*Adam:* I don't know, it'd all be more of a laugh though, when you see it now.

*Laura:* I'd still be scared when I saw that woman in front of the curtains ... I'd still be scared, I'd still have to sleep with my light on.

*Interviewer:* Why is that, then? Why can something scare you like that?

*Laura:* 'Cause it's your imagination.

Even with a programme that they consider to be much more scary than the horror films they also watch, Laura and Martha imply that there is still a balance that can be struck between 'distress and delight'. Yet as Laura's last remark suggests, this cannot be seen merely as a reflex reaction: on the contrary, it depends upon an active response, and a willingness to entertain and to participate in the illusions the text provides. *Ghostwatch* clearly unsettled this balance for many viewers, largely because it sought to deceive them about the terms on which the illusion was being offered. Yet in this case at least, there may be an implicit recognition that being deceived in this way is a necessary learning experience; and that going back to it will enable them to understand more fully how the deception was achieved. To repeat the experience would of course be to do so under different terms, as Adam implies – although quite how much difference this would make remains an open question. Indeed, Laura and Martha even protested that our interview itself had made them feel scared, eighteen months after they had seen the programme:

*Martha:* I tell you something, when I go to bed tonight, I'm gonna remember this conversation. Some blooming black silhouette of a woman's gonna get me in my bedroom now.

## Conclusion

In this chapter, I have considered children's responses to three programmes which have all generated a degree of controversy. While the programmes themselves are very different, they are all ones which come close to – and in some respects, appear to cross – the boundary between fact and fiction. As I have indicated, this often appears to generate debate about the credibility and responsibility of broadcasters, not only among specialist critics but also among viewers themselves. While such material is often condemned, there may be also a sense in which television *has* to cross the boundaries between fact and fiction in order for viewers to learn about them.

Nevertheless, the consequences of this blurring of fact and fiction in terms of children's emotional responses are often problematic, not least because the strategies that parents and children develop for coping with those responses may prove irrelevant or ineffective. For this reason, each of these programmes raises awkward questions about the regulation of children's viewing. On the one hand, there is a difficult balance to be found between the need to provide information and the need to entertain, not least in order to ensure that viewers continue to watch. Yet on the other hand, there is an equally difficult balance between providing information or entertainment and ensuring that viewers are not unnecessarily upset. The problem, of course, is that different viewers will seek to strike these balances in different ways – and that what counts as being 'unnecessarily' upset will therefore vary. As I have suggested, such responses are often hard to predict, and cannot easily be avoided. Yet as they mature, children themselves are becoming aware of these processes, and are learning to regulate their own responses accordingly. At the same time, it is clear that parents can play a significant role in this process; and it is to this issue that I turn in the following chapter.

## Notes

1 See, among others, Hawkins (1977), Hodge and Tripp (1986), Buckingham (1993a). On very young children, see Jaglom and Gardner (1981).
2 Research suggests that this dimension becomes particularly significant in 'middle childhood': see Dorr (1983), Buckingham (1993a).
3 For an analysis, see Hodge and Tripp (1986).
4 See, for example, Harris (1989).
5 Kerr (1990).
6 Simons and Silveira (1994): this story was widely reported in the press.
7 The fact that all three are BBC programmes is purely coincidental.
8 For a relevant discussion of 'quality' in this context, see Brunsdon (1990).
9 For a critical account of the production and aims of *Crimewatch*, see Schlesinger and Tumber (1991). Many of these issues are pursued in relation to viewers' responses in *Women Viewing Violence* (Schlesinger *et al.*,

1992).

10 Similar responses are recorded in Schlesinger *et al.* (1992, page 69).

11 This issue has been most systematically investigated, from different perspectives, by Gunter (1987b) and Gerbner (e.g. Gerbner *et al.*, 1980). Gerbner's work has attracted widespread critical comment: for a very brief review, see Buckingham and Allerton (1995).

12 As Schlesinger *et al.* (1992, pages 44–5) point out, the findings of research on this topic in relation to *Crimewatch* are at least ambiguous.

13 Crime statistics would suggest that young men are much more at risk of being victims of violent crime than young women.

14 This issue has been the focus of a significant amount of debate among criminologists: see Sparks (1992).

15 For a useful history of the genre, see Kerr (1990).

16 Details here are derived from Lowery and de Fleur (1983), Chapter 3.

17 Cantril (1940).

18 The girl is in fact in her bedroom, rather than in a hospital, but otherwise Trevor's recollection is reasonably accurate.

19 Cantril (1940). Quite why viewers with strong religious convictions were predisposed to believe that Martians were taking over America remains an interesting question: on one level, it would seem to support the idea that religious convictions are simply evidence of a more general form of suggestibility.

# 8

# *Screening responses*

## CONTROL AND REGULATION
## IN THE HOME

Public debates about children and television have always been dominated by arguments about the need for stricter regulation. Yet as I have argued, the *site* of regulation has begun to shift in recent years, primarily in response to the advent of the domestic video recorder. As new technologies have steadily undermined the centralised control of moving images, the responsibility for regulating children's viewing has increasingly fallen to parents and to children themselves. In this context, as I have shown, the issue of children's relationship with television has become inextricably bound up with assertions about the nature of 'good' parenting – a theme which itself condenses many broader anxieties about the perceived decline in the social and moral order. 'Good' parents, it is argued, are those who restrict their children's viewing, and prevent them from gaining access to material that will disturb or corrupt them.

Yet the problem with such prescriptions about parental responsibility is that they rarely acknowledge the diversity of family life, or the genuine dilemmas that parents face. The power of parents is very far from absolute, as children know; and parents' ability to control their children's responses to what they watch can only be limited. As I have argued, the possibility that children may be upset or frightened has to be set against the pleasure and the learning that they derive from television. Here, as in many other areas, there is a difficult balance to be struck between regulating your children and enabling them to regulate themselves. To regard parental responsibility in this respect as merely a matter of restricting your children's viewing – or indeed of imposing a fixed set of rules – is to ignore the complex ways in which children make sense of what they watch, and to neglect the possibilities of a more positive approach. As I attempt to show, parents can play a very constructive role in mediating their children's viewing, and in teaching them about television; yet they can also learn a great deal in this respect from their children.

## Learning to handle it: children's self-regulation

The central focus of this chapter, then, is on parents' attempts to regulate their children's viewing. The bulk of the chapter consists of six contrasting case studies of families that illustrate some of the broader issues that are at stake. Before addressing parents' perspectives on this issue, however, it is important to emphasise a key point that has emerged repeatedly in the preceding chapters. Children are not merely passive objects of adults' attempts at regulation – nor indeed do they uniformly resist them. On the contrary, children actively learn to regulate their *own* emotional responses to television. They develop very definite ideas about what they can and cannot 'handle', and hence what they will or will not choose to watch. While parents certainly play a part in this process, these ideas are also developed through trial and error. Children will deliberately choose to test out the limits of what they can cope with; and they will often stop watching when things get too much.

As the preceding chapters have shown, children employ a wide variety of strategies for dealing with such experiences. Most obviously, these involve removing yourself – either partly or completely – or removing the text: leaving the room, hiding your eyes, covering your ears, turning the TV off, turning the sound down, and so on. In other situations, children may choose to change the viewing context, for example by deciding to watch at a different time, or by encouraging other people to watch with them. Other strategies might be termed 'psychological': some children will seek comfort from another person or an object such as a cushion or a toy; some will attempt to distract themselves, or to control the display of emotion; while some will even have recourse to prayer. In relation to factual material, as we have seen, children often look to forms of social action, for example in undertaking charity work, or (in response to crime programmes) by seeking to protect themselves from potential danger. Finally, children also employ their knowledge of television as a medium – their 'television literacy' – as a form of coping: they may challenge or question the reality status of the text; they may use their understanding of generic or narrative conventions to predict what might happen, or to imagine alternative outcomes; and they may draw on their knowledge of the processes of television production. While video is often seen to be a problematic technology insofar as it gives children access to 'forbidden' material, it can also play a vital role in the development of such coping strategies – for example, by giving children the power to select when they watch, to rewind or skip over certain sequences, and to study the text in more detail.

Of course, some of these strategies could be seen to be more 'natural' or more specific to the medium than others. Hiding your eyes when faced with a disturbing or gory scene is a response that obviously occurs in real life, and could be seen as a more or less automatic 'flight reaction'. By contrast, drawing attention to the special effects or being able to predict what will happen next in a horror movie is a response that is learnt, both through the accumulated experience of viewing and through direct instruction (for example, by reading books or magazines about the genre, or by talking to more experienced viewers). Learning which strategy might be most effective – or simply easier to apply – in which situation is a complex process; but it depends crucially upon how the text itself is initially perceived and then interpreted. On the other hand, as I have shown, it is often hard to predict what one will find upsetting or frightening; and such responses are often inextricably tied up with the experience of pleasure, or with the desire for information. As psychological research has increasingly indicated, 'coping' needs to be seen not as a matter of applying fixed and predetermined strategies to a given stimulus, but as a flexible and socially situated activity.[1]

If children are progressively learning to regulate their own viewing experiences, it is clear that they do so partly in relation to external definitions of what is suitable for them to watch. Even the youngest children in our sample here knew about censorship categories and (in some cases) about the 'watershed' for family viewing – although, like their parents, they often claimed the right to make such decisions on their own behalf. These definitions were used 'negatively', as a means of warning children off material they might find upsetting; yet they were also used 'positively', as a means of marking out material that might be seen as 'stronger' or more exciting. As Julian Wood[2] has noted, the classification system often has the unintended consequence of identifying 'forbidden fruit' which children will then actively seek out. Yet in many cases, children also challenged the validity of such classifications, in both directions: some argued, for example, that *Jurassic Park* should have been rated at '12' or even '15' rather than 'PG', while others suggested that the category '18' was simply redundant, and that children should have the right to watch what they liked at a younger age. Many said that they could not understand why certain films had been classified in a particular category. At best, the classification system was seen as an approximate guide, rather than as a definitive source of information.

At least on the surface, children appeared to be more willing to accept their parents' authority on such matters – although here too, there was a fair amount of questioning and resistance. As we have seen, children often argued explicitly for the need for parental regulation; and asserted that, if they were parents themselves, they would exert a considerable degree of control over their own children's viewing. Yet while the need for parental control was accepted in general terms, such arguments were frequently displaced onto 'little kids', much younger than themselves. Particularly among the older age groups, most children asserted that they were mature enough to make their own decisions about what they should watch, and to take the consequences. Meanwhile, as in the case of censorship categories, parental disapproval also appeared to serve as a powerful indicator of forbidden fruit – a fact which many parents were bound to recognise. In many families, there had been some very explicit debates about what was and was not 'appropriate' for children to watch. Parents often seemed to have changed their views on this in the light of experience; and the rules applied to first-born children frequently seemed to have become more flexible with subsequent ones. As I have argued (Chapter 3), such debates often invoke much broader assumptions about what it means to be a child – and, by extension, an adult.[3]

In this respect, of course, television viewing is merely part of the broader struggle for power and control between parents and children – a struggle which has generally been resolved some years before children reach the legal age of majority. As previous research has suggested,[4] the strategies that children use in attempting to evade or undermine their parents' authority are diverse and often ingenious. In some cases here, they described how they would exploit differences between the parents in terms of attitudes or tastes, or rely on older siblings or willing baby-sitters; while in others, they would capitalise on the parents' ignorance of the material concerned, arguing that it was really quite all right for them to watch. Some children described how they would sneak downstairs to watch the TV after their parents were asleep, or hide offending tapes in the hope of watching them later. Many claimed to have seen films or programmes that they knew their parents would not have wanted them to see, either at friends' houses or when the parents were out – although, as we shall see, many parents claimed to know about such behaviour, or at least to recognise the possibility that it might occur.

Yet despite such attempts at evading parental control, children also looked to their parents for guidance, and largely accepted their right to offer it. Like the guidance provided by broadcasters and censors, this was often regarded with a degree of scepticism; yet (particularly for the younger children) it did seem to inform their attempts to regulate their own responses to what they watched. While children often argued that their parents underestimated their ability to cope with more 'adult' material, they also recognised that they were right to protect them in this way: as Carol (12) said, 'they're only trying to stop us being disturbed'. As we shall see, many parents had played a very positive role in helping their children to understand and to cope with what they watched. As previous research has suggested, talk around the television set can create a powerful 'learning context', which enables children to interpret and make informed judgments about what is presented. For example, Paul Messaris[5] has shown how parents can help their children to sort out the relationships between television and the real world, for example by drawing attention to generic conventions, by confirming or questioning the accuracy of TV representations, and by supplementing television with background information. This kind of conversation, it is argued, can encourage children to 'go beyond the information given', and thus assist them in their encounters with media of all kinds. Likewise, in this research, many parents described how they had attempted to teach their children ways of coping with upsetting responses, not least by drawing their attention to the constructed nature of the text. 'Regulation' should in this respect be seen as much more than simply a matter of restricting children's access to television.

## Concerned parents: some broad themes

Against the background of public debates on the issue, interviewing parents about their children's viewing is bound to be problematic. In my previous research in this area,[6] I found that parents tended to offer idealised accounts of family viewing: in an attempt to present themselves as 'responsible' for the benefit of other parents and of the academic interviewer, parents tended to exaggerate the degree of their control over their children's viewing. Yet if parents have an investment in presenting themselves in this way, children may have an equal investment in the claim that they, and not their parents, call the shots. To be sure, at least some of the discrepancy here may be genuine: parents can obviously exercise control in ways that children do not know about, just as children may evade that control in ways that their parents never discover. Yet, as other researchers have found,[7] there is inevitably a 'social desirability bias' built in to such encounters, which should encourage us to treat the data with a degree of scepticism.

In this case, however, the parents appeared to be rather more open about such issues, perhaps partly because they were interviewed in their own homes, rather than in the company of other parents in school. They were comparatively frank about the limitations on their power, and the ways in which their attempts at control were inclined to break down. Having said this, it was clear that parents in all social groups across the sample were concerned to control their children's viewing: while we did interview parents living in very difficult circumstances, and some whose children had seen so-called 'video nasties', we did not encounter any of the feckless and uncaring parents so prevalent in the press coverage that followed the James Bulger case.

As we shall see, the strategies that parents used here were many and various. Particularly with younger children, it was possible to maintain a degree of ignorance, by attempting to ensure that they did not know of the existence of films or programmes that might become the focus of dispute. Parents of such children often maintained that 'discipline' in such matters was quite straightforward: they just said no. For the parents of teenagers, such strategies were seen to be less effective, for obvious reasons. As children got older, outright banning tended to give way to forms of negotiation: some parents previewed films or programmes their children wanted to watch before reaching a decision; while others made a point of watching with their children so that they could mediate or intervene at points that were potentially upsetting. At a certain stage, children were seen to have attained a level of maturity beyond which parents no longer felt they had the right to restrict their viewing: while this was occasionally as high as sixteen, in most cases it was put at between twelve and fourteen – well below the age at which centralised classification officially ends.

Broadly speaking, the grounds for regulation were also remarkably consistent. In some instances, restrictions were seen to be necessary partly as a result of concerns external to television: certainly for the younger children, bedtime was the main constraint on their viewing,[8] while homework was also an important factor for many of the older ones. In other cases, the parents intervened or banned programmes in order to settle conflicts of taste. Yet in terms of television content, it was the predictable issues of violence, sex and (to a lesser extent) 'bad' language that were discussed most frequently. Particular instances of these concerns are addressed in the detailed case studies below; but it is worth emphasising some general tendencies at this stage.

As I have noted in Chapter 3, parents' principal concerns about violence were not to do with the dangers of imitative behaviour, but with the possibility of their children being frightened or upset. While some parents acknowledged that children would copy fighting (such as martial arts 'moves') from the TV, many directly refuted the implication that television would make their children more violent. On the contrary, their main anxiety was that such material would give their children nightmares, or otherwise 'stick in their mind'. Similarly, although many parents sought to distinguish between 'gratuitous' (or 'wanton') violence and 'necessary' violence, the terms that were used to describe such material were all concerned with emotional responses, such as 'gross', 'disgusting', 'gruesome', 'horrific' and 'shocking'. Like many of the children, most parents also made distinctions here in terms of modality: the violence in popular films like *Terminator*, for example, was generally seen to be 'unrealistic' or 'not serious', and hence not something most parents would choose to ban.

In relation to sexually explicit material, the principal concern appeared to be that of embarrassment, on the part of both parents and children. In the case of some younger children, it was argued that sex was something they did not yet understand, and that they did not need to cope with at this stage – an argument that was also applied in some cases to the treatment of social problems such as child abuse, both in realist dramas and in non-fictional programmes. Two parents expressed a rather different but related concern about the representation of women as 'sex objects', and about violent rape scenes, that they felt might have a particular influence upon their sons. In relation to 'bad' language, there was rather more ambivalence. On the one hand, it was argued that children already knew such words, and knew well enough not to imitate them; while on the other, it was argued that they heard enough of such language at school, and that it was not wanted in the home. While this was a particular concern for the parents of younger children, it was (like the other issues mentioned here) one that recurred across the boundaries of social class.[9] The only concerns that appeared to be more class-specific were those that were broadly concerned with cultural value: it was largely the middle-class parents who argued that children should not watch 'trashy' soap operas, or that they were spending 'too much' time watching television and not enough on 'better' pursuits like reading.

Yet apart from this latter area, it is hard to detect a consistent pattern of social class differences here – despite the underlying class dimension of the debate about media effects. Parents who explicitly expressed religious convictions were likely to be less permissive; and mothers were marginally more likely to express concern about such issues than fathers.[10] But by far the most significant determinants of parental regulation – or at least, of parental expressions of concern about such issues – were the age of the children and the size of the family. As I have noted, regulation was much more of an issue for the parents of younger children, and much less so with teenagers. Broadly speaking, larger families offered greater opportunities for children to evade parental regulation, not least because older children were often left in charge of younger ones, and because such families were likely to have more TV sets in the first place. In these families, it often appeared that the battles had been won by the older children, leaving the younger ones to enjoy the benefits of a more permissive regime.

Furthermore, the focus of such concerns was even less consistently distributed. For some parents, sexual content presented much more of a problem than violence, while for others, the opposite was the case. In some instances, violent action movies were acceptable, but horror films were not, and vice versa. A bigger sample and a more straightforward style of attitude survey would almost certainly have yielded more consistent responses, or at least more reliable averages; but it would also tend to iron out many of the complexities that are apparent from the case studies that follow.

As these general observations imply, parents' ideas about the regulation of television viewing reflect broader theories about child development and child-rearing. Arguments about when children are 'ready' for certain experiences, or about the balance between freedom and constraint, inevitably relate to parents' moral or ideological convictions; and of course parents also learn about such matters from their own family backgrounds, as well as from their experience with their children. Yet the relationship between protecting one's children and encouraging their autonomy is inevitably problematic, particularly as they grow older. Children have to learn to make their own decisions; and simply telling them what to do does not necessarily help them with this. Few parents would argue that children should simply be left to their own devices; yet most would also accept that it is not in their long-term interests for them to be unnecessarily 'sheltered'.

In negotiating their way through such dilemmas, parents frequently suggested that they had very little information or support. While all the parents appeared to understand the classification system and the principle of the watershed, they often argued that such blanket rulings based on age were much too crude – and in a number of cases, that they were inaccurate or outdated. Like the children, parents used these forms of regulation as a rough guideline, but ultimately they reserved the right to make their own decisions. In discussing their children's responses to television, they frequently emphasised individual personality differences: it was often suggested that some children were more sensitive or impressionable than others, or that they had matured at different rates, and that different strategies needed to be used in each case. They also acknowledged that their children's responses had sometimes been quite unexpected; and that they themselves had occasionally made mistakes, either in allowing them to watch certain programmes, or indeed in preventing them from doing so. In the end, it was argued, using television successfully came down to a matter of 'knowing your children': it was not something that could easily be reduced to a set of abstract rules and prescriptions.

## Family viewing: six case studies

A great deal of previous research on family viewing has tended to adopt an implicitly normative approach. As in other areas of child-rearing, the discourse about parental responsibility here is one that serves to construct norms of 'healthy' family interaction and of 'good parenting'. Parents who do not conform to such norms are implicitly seen to be in need of remedial training in 'parenting skills'.[11] Meanwhile, Cultural Studies research in this field has tended to concentrate on a rather limited range of families, and (in some cases) to ignore the role of children altogether.[12] In different ways, both approaches would appear to have oversimplified the diversity of family life, and the complex negotiations that take place within families themselves.

In the following sections of this chapter, I offer a series of six brief case studies which illustrate some of the broader themes that emerged across these interviews. These accounts are not intended to be exhaustive, nor are they necessarily representative. Nevertheless, they do indicate something of the diversity and the commonality of approaches across a group of families which in many respects are quite different.

### Family 1

This family consisted of two parents (Mushtaq and Amina) and three children: two girls (Jaya, 14, and Shila, 9) and a boy (Nabeel, 12). Both parents came from first generation immigrant families, and described themselves as 'British of Asian origin': they were Muslims. Both had left school at 16, and worked at home as self-employed garment manufacturers. They owned the house, which was situated in a run-down inner-city area. They had two televisions, one in the main living room (with VCR) and one in the parents' bedroom.

These parents claimed to operate definite 'viewing rules', which appeared to be broadly accepted by the children. The children were not allowed to do their homework with the TV on; and bedtime was fairly strictly enforced, although there was some flexibility for programmes that were favourites with the whole family, such as the sitcom *Roseanne*. The children were also not allowed to watch '18'-rated videos – a ruling which Jaya described as follows:

*Jaya:* Some films do tend to influence children, especially if they're not the right age. 'Cause some parents allow their children to watch '18' films. My dad doesn't let me do that, and I see his point of view.

Mushtaq described how they had consciously decided not to buy an additional TV set for the children: 'I won't allow that because it's too easy to get around the rules.'

At the same time, the parents perceived clear differences between the children, both in terms of their preferences, and in terms of their responses to television. Nabeel's tastes were for violent action movies and horror, while Jaya was more interested in comedies and romances. Both parents were horror enthusiasts, and while Jaya would often avoid such films, Nabeel was seen to be much more able to cope:

*Mushtaq:* He's laid-back.

*Amina:* He's just laid-back. [He'll] watch it, 'oh, that's just a film'.

*Mushtaq:* His nature's like that, so he tends to handle it better, I think.

Nevertheless, the parents distinguished here between older horror films and what they described as the 'more serious' or 'gory' ones, which they were reluctant for the children to watch. In general, mainstream horror films were not seen as a cause for concern. For example, Mushtaq dismissed *Halloween* as 'a load of rubbish': 'I think all the kids have seen that one, they're not bothered at all with that film.'

On the other hand, the parents did express concern about Nabeel's taste in action movies. In one instance, he had got hold of a copy of *Robocop*, and it was this experience that had led to the parents' ruling on '18'-rated videos:

*Mushtaq: Robocop*, that was the first one I think Nabeel watched which I wasn't too keen on. 'Cause there's that one scene in the beginning where they beat the man, the group of them actually shoot him to pieces and I felt quite, I wasn't too keen. I'm not much on violence. I don't like gratuitous violence and I thought that was gratuitous. And at the time also he must have been about nine, something like that, it was quite a while ago and he was quite young and I didn't want too many repeats of that ...

*Interviewer:* Why don't you like them to watch violence?

*Amina:* I don't know, it's like, you know, kids are gonna pick up the bad things very quickly. So I don't let them watch it.

*Mushtaq:* That enactment, to a degree. I don't think TV / affects you as much as what the media's been saying lately, that you know, TV does a lot. I wouldn't say it does a lot but there are children – because you can see a group of kids playing, you can tell they're doing the kung fu and all these kicks to your head and all that. Basically I think parents don't have enough control over their children, they don't put their foot down and say 'look, this is wrong, you mustn't do that'. And what happens is then that carries on and they grow up with that sort of idea. And I think parents fail there.

As in Jaya's comment above, there is a clear distinction here between parents who do exercise control and those (others) who do not. The effects of television violence are defined both in general terms – as a matter of 'picking up bad things' – and specifically in terms of imitation. Nevertheless, Mushtaq also qualifies this argument – and indeed, he subsequently challenged the evidence in the Bulger case, suggesting that it had been 'hyped up', and that 'the background of the kids was more important'. He also distinguishes between 'gratuitous' violence and violence that is somehow justified, a point that was taken up later in relation to Nabeel's viewing of the film *Goodfellas*:

*Mushtaq:* Nabeel watched it, right, and I understood afterwards that it was quite violent and I didn't realise at the time / I wouldn't have / I don't know whether I would make a stand on it.

*Interviewer:* It's interesting, because you said earlier that you didn't really like him watching *Robocop* but *Goodfellas* you'd be OK about.

*Mushtaq:* I think with *Goodfellas*, that has more reality, from my understanding of what the Twenties were like, and also the Mafia and that sort of thing, they are quite, violence as part of life right / I know it's a bit contradictory, but you know compared –

*Interviewer:* So you think if it's based in reality rather than fantasy –

*Mushtaq:* It is basically you can't shield them to the extent that they're gonna be so green that they don't know what goes on in the world. You know, it's so difficult to get a balance / you know, so like I say / I wouldn't make a stand on it, and he got away with it and watched it / I don't think he will become into a violent monster because of it.

Here again, Mushtaq refutes the argument that television alone will turn children into 'violent monsters' – although he also makes a familiar distinction in this respect between his own children and the children of parents whom he perceives to be 'failing'. Screen violence is seen to be justified insofar as it tells you about 'life', and (in this case) offers a reasonably accurate reflection of a particular historical context.

This argument also extended to violence in factual programmes. For example, the parents described how Jaya had been upset by a news story about a kidnapping in the local area, but agreed that this was a necessary process of learning how to protect oneself – 'wherever you go, that's part of life, you've got to learn to discriminate and think for yourself'. Although there was perceived to be a double standard here, the need to present 'reality' was a paramount concern:

*Mushtaq:* I think the news is, they always show the worst of the worst, you know. You get half an hour of news with all the killing, maiming that's going on in the world and you'll get thirty seconds of a nice story / and I'm always, you know when they say that watershed and censors and all the rest of it, and I say, well, you know this film can't be shown because it's this, that or the other. And then I quite vividly remember there was a scene in Burma, I think, and they showed a scene where these guys just picked him up and shot him in the head, right. And I thought that's reality, and they showed that right. And there were complaints but not as much as if that sort of thing was shown on a film version you know, as a film for entertainment / there may be more uproar you see.

Despite this final observation, Mushtaq himself was clearly opposed to what he termed the 'glorification' of violence for the purposes of entertainment:

*Mushtaq:* I think the way rape is portrayed ... usually it's portrayed from a male point of view, so you get a one-sided view. And I think it's a very vile crime and kids should understand that it is bad / I'm quite strong on my views on punishment and law and order, so from that point of view I look at it, I'd rather not let them see that sort of thing ...

*Interviewer:* Rape's been featured in soap operas, hasn't it?

*Mushtaq:* Yes, but it's not graphic, it's suggestive. So OK, fair enough. Again, these things do happen, they hear it on the news, they read it in the papers / it does go on, so you can't shield them to that extent. But I think a glorified scene of rape for the sake of it in a film, I don't think that's something that kids should watch.

What is most significant in all these extracts, however, is the way in which arguments about the children's viewing are located within more general observations about child-rearing. These are partly to do with the need to find a 'balance' between 'shielding' your children and letting them know 'what goes on in the world'. Children, Mushtaq argues, need to know about real-life issues such as rape and violence, and they will find out about them anyway, irrespective of whether they are shown on television. The crucial distinction is between the 'gratuitous' use of such scenes – where they are included 'for the sake of it' – and the necessary treatment of such issues in factual programmes or in realist drama.

At the same time, Mushtaq implicitly acknowledges the dangers of adopting an approach that is seen to be too disciplinarian – an approach which both parents see as a failing of their own upbringing. He argued that such an approach is not only unrealistic, but can also be counter-productive:

*Mushtaq:* I found out that [Nabeel had seen an '18' rated film]. I didn't say much. You can't really, you can't screw them down to the ground really.

*Interviewer:* But it sounds like you have quite tight control over films that they –

*Mushtaq:* Yeah, reasonable. You can't, if you go too far with control then it backfires, then it encourages you to actually do it for the sake of doing it. So if I'm too strict or too tight on them, then I think they'll go the other way. So I will allow the odd indiscretion here or there ...

*Interviewer:* Is that something that you both agree about?

*Amina:* Yes.

*Mushtaq:* I think that's also cultural background as well, because in our culture things are quite restrictive and parents do try to control too much and I found that in my own [upbringing] ... My parents were very restrictive, they were always drilling, that's bad, that's good, that's bad, that's good ... You see my kids are second generation, 'cause I was born and brought up here, so I find that my attitudes and that are a lot different to all my / other Asian people that I know who come from India who have lived here for twenty years or twenty-five years. Again, with my parents and my brother who was born in India, right, my view and outlook are a lot, lot different to what theirs is. So whereas they will say no to this, that and the other I'll be more flexible on / my attitude's much different / the way my brother brought up his kids to me bringing up mine is completely different.

Here again, Mushtaq attempts to define his approach by contrast with that of others, in this case his own family. Yet it was also clear that the parents had adjusted their approach on the basis of experience. For example, Mushtaq described how he had been 'a bit disturbed' by the film *Predator*, but that it had not had the expected effect on Nabeel: 'it didn't bother him, I was quite surprised'.

As in this case, however, there was a particular emphasis here on watching together as a family. *Ghostwatch*, for example, was a programme the family had seen together, and where the parents had made a particular effort to reassure the children that it was not real (see page 240 above). Likewise, while Shila and Jaya were likely to avoid horror films, Mushtaq described how he would try to intervene to make sure that they were not frightened:

*Mushtaq:* I think I pride myself with my kids that I do *not* frighten them, right. I will try and explain if they are frightened of anything. I will explain to them why it's frightening and what takes place and what's the reason for it. Because I've seen a lot of kids that won't go in the dark because they're scared and this, that and the other, and I don't like that. I like my kids to be independent and confident, so I will explain and reassure them that it does not happen, so don't be afraid, don't be afraid to go anywhere. / Again, I think it's back to when I was growing up and I used to, I think I watched *Quatermass* when I was about, I still remember, I must have been about seven / eight ... I watched it in black and white and my dad was quite strict and they all went to bed and I crept in and watched

*Quatermass* and I thought it was absolutely frightening but I had nobody to tell me that it's not true.

While they agreed that it was important to have clear rules, the parents argued that these had to be set against an understanding of the individual children themselves. The fact that both parents worked at home was seen to be a significant advantage in this respect:

*Interviewer:* So what do you base that judgement on, whether you think they should watch something?

*Mushtaq:* Well, knowing them and experience, I suppose / knowing how they are and how confident they are.

*Amina:* And you know, we work at home, so most of the time we're with the kids, like soon as they come home from school ... That way you can experience your kids more.

*Mushtaq:* I think they grow up with more balance. That's the trouble with society to a big degree, it's parental time. People, either they're not bothered or they haven't got the time, one or the other. And kids grow up just / they've got no guidance basically of right and wrong / you build up a knowledge of what your child is capable of and not capable of and what they will do and what they will not do and what they can take and what they can't take, what upsets them, what doesn't upset them, so that's why something different will upset Shila and something different will upset Jaya so / you know, that again is experience. You can't do that without knowing your child and that's all to do with time and consideration and effort.

Ultimately, then, these parents have sought to achieve a series of balances. On the one hand, they are concerned about the possibility of their children being upset by what they watch – and, to some extent, of them 'picking up bad things'. Yet on the other hand, they are making clear distinctions between material that they regard as 'gratuitous' and that which they regard either as not 'serious', or alternatively as important for their children to see. Likewise, they are seeking to balance the need to protect their children against the need to prepare them to be independent. While they recognise the necessity for consistent 'viewing rules', they also acknowledge the dangers of being too inflexible or authoritarian, and the need to take account of individual differences between the children.

### Family 2

This was a white, working-class single parent family, consisting of a mother (Jill) and two daughters (Donna, 7, and Colette, 5). The children's father, a painter and decorator, had only recently moved out of the family's council flat. Jill had left school at sixteen, and described herself as a 'housewife'. There were four TV sets in the house, in the living room (with VCR), kitchen, adults' bedroom (with VCR) and children's bedroom. There was also a satellite dish connected to the main set in the living room, and to the adults' bedroom.

Jill had very definite ideas about what was appropriate for her children to watch, although it became evident that she was not always able to follow these through. According to her, the children usually went to bed at about 8 pm, and their viewing at home was largely confined to cartoons and game shows. The children had an extensive collection of Disney videos, and regularly tuned in to the children's satellite channel Nickelodeon, on which they watched a large number of cartoons. It was this kind of material that Jill preferred them to watch; and they made a particular point of watching game shows together. On the other hand, both girls had watched a number of '15'- and '18'-rated horror films, both on satellite TV and on video; and while they had seen many of these at a childminder's, they had also seen some of them at home. As Jill acknowledged, this was partly her own fault. Yet it was clear that the two girls had responded to these films in very different ways, which Jill saw as a reflection of their differences in personality rather than simply their age. Indeed, the striking differences between the two girls' responses appeared to make it quite difficult for her to make consistent judgments about what they should and should not watch.

On one level, Jill seemed to exercise considerable care about what the children saw: for example, she described how she had been to the cinema to preview *Jurassic Park* before deciding that it was not too frightening for the children to watch. However, even when it came to material aimed at children, this did not seem to have prevented them from watching material that had upset them. For example, Colette had been particularly disturbed by the fantasy *Edward Scissorhands*, another film which Jill had seen first:

*Jill: Edward Scissorhands*, I couldn't believe it. I just couldn't believe it, I was just totally dumbfounded. I thought it's a weepie, the film is a weepie film, it's not, I don't think it's scary at all, just a weepie film and / I was taken aback, and I said 'why do you find it [scary]?' 'Got them big hands, big things on his, big pointed scissors on his hands' ... It isn't scary, 'cause I tried to say to Colette 'he won't hurt you, he's not a person that will hurt somebody, he's just been made that way'. 'Well, how can he be made that way?' Well, I said 'he's made that way, that's the way he is, someone made him like that, he can't help that'. But it doesn't seem to go into Colette. Like if I said it to Donna, she would just say 'oh right' and carry on. / But Colette is very easily frightened.

This report was confirmed in our interview with the two girls, where Donna repeatedly attempted to scare her sister by mentioning the film and screaming with laughter. The crucial point here, however, is the difference between the two girls, both in terms of their responses and in terms of the coping strategies they are able to adopt: Donna is easily reassured by the notion that the character has been 'made that way' (and is hence an object of pity rather than fear), whereas it seems to make little difference to Colette. As I have argued, it is often hard to predict what children will find upsetting; and, as Jill implicitly acknowledges, it may even be a mistake to generalise from one sibling to another. Her sense of the differences between the two girls recurred throughout the interview, to the point where generalisation appeared to become impossible: as she said at one point, 'I think all kids are different anyway, kids look at things in different ways.'

At the same time, it was clear that Jill had not always been able to exercise such control, partly as a result of the availability of TV sets elsewhere in the house. When we interviewed her in school, Donna spoke with great hilarity about the Steven King film *It*, a '15'-rated horror, which she had seen at home. Yet as with *Edward Scissorhands*, Colette's reaction had been rather different:

*Jill:* That's when I was a bit slack with them, they could go upstairs and watch the telly in my bedroom / and I think it started on Sunday night on Sky, it was about 8 o'clock, and I said they could go to sleep in my bed, and I was watching *It* on the telly, and that [the satellite line] goes through and up into my room and what they done is, they put it on to Sky, and they sat there and started to watch it. Well, Donna was staying up there for a good while, and then all of a sudden Colette came flying down, 'I don't want to watch that up there, what she's watching', she went mental! [*laughs*] ...

*Interviewer:* But Donna was all right over it?

*Jill:* Yeah, when she finally come down, she said to me, 'what's this?', and I said 'it's called *It*' and I said, 'you shouldn't be watching it'. She said 'it's all right' and I said 'no, it ain't, you shouldn't be watching it'. But she didn't seem to be all that bothered about it. But Colette, as I said before, Colette's very, she's not as laid-back as Donna, not as hard to scare.

In this case, Jill admits that she has not exercised enough control. While she insists that the film is not appropriate, Donna's apparent indifference to it appears to qualify this judgment; and it is almost as though it is Colette's reaction that requires an explanation – hence perhaps the laughter.

Nevertheless, Jill did express considerable concern about the fact that both girls had seen horror films at their childminder's. While she argued again that Donna did not appear to have been 'affected' by these experiences, she felt very strongly that this kind of material was not appropriate:

*Jill:* There's a couple of horror films that Donna's seen that she hasn't seen in this house. And when she's seen them, I've gone mental ... I know she [the childminder] lets her kids watch them, but I don't allow it, I don't like it, 'cause I think it's frightening for the kids. But when I go to get them the next day, 'oh mum, guess what, we watched, *Aliens 3*'. I gone off my head. And they've watched *Fright Night*, they've watched *Elm Street* there, what they haven't watched there. I've gone mental, I've actually gone up the wall about it, because I don't think kids should see it.

Despite Jill's definite views, and her protests to the childminder, the girls did appear to have seen a fair number of such films. Interestingly, Jill in fact described herself as a 'horror merchant' – that is, a fan – although she did acknowledge that 'heavy horror movies' such as these had frightened her too. Yet the central problem here, she argued, was to do with the children's inability to distinguish between fact and fiction:

*Jill:* I mean, for me, it's different, I know it's not reality, it's just there on the telly, but they don't understand that yet. And it don't matter how much you try to explain it to them, they don't understand ... It's like if [Donna] sat there and watched *Nightmare on Elm Street*, as far as I'm concerned, she could go to bed and have a nightmare about it. That's because her mind, to me, is not old enough to cope with the fact that it is just fictional, it's not real.

Like many parents, Jill argued that a time would come when the children were mature enough to watch such films. Indeed, she suspected that Donna would eventually become a horror fan like herself: 'Donna is a lot like me, and when she's thirteen or fourteen, she'll want to watch the horror films, and I won't stop her.' Nevertheless, she also acknowledged that Donna had enjoyed the horror films she had seen, or at least that she had now learnt to cope with them:

*Jill:* She wasn't really bothered by [*It*], because as I said, she's seen things like *Alien 3* and *Aliens*, and she's seen *Fright Night* and she's seen *Nightmare on Elm Street* and it doesn't seem to bother her ... but I don't think *It* was as scary as *Nightmare on Elm Street* or anything like that.

While Jill would clearly have preferred that her children had not seen these films, Donna's apparently 'laid-back' approach to them appears to have encouraged her to take a more relaxed approach. She described, for example, how they had watched *Arachnaphobia* together:

*Jill:* She's got no fear of spiders, and that film, she loves it, it doesn't frighten her. / It does me ... when it was on, I must have sat in about twenty different places. And Donna said to me 'why do you keep moving, mum?' I was going over here and over there, how can she sit there? But she hasn't got a fear of spiders, whereas I have, you know, so I didn't mind her watching that ... She sat there and went 'look, mum, look at all them spiders'. It didn't bother her, she didn't bat an eyelid.

With Donna, there is a sense in which Jill feels she is able to make reasonably confident judgments; and while Donna herself acknowledged that such films were 'scary', she too said that she had not suffered from nightmares. With Colette, on the other hand, there was a sense that Jill's predictions were less reliable, as the *Edward Scissorhands* episode clearly suggests. Similarly, while she asserted that violence in general did not bother her, she clearly regretted her decision to let Colette watch the action movie *Predator 2*:

*Jill:* I'll tell you another thing she woke up to / was um / *Predator 2*. She went mental / she went mental. And that to me isn't really a horror film, *Predator*'s not really a horror film, it's a bit bloodthirsty, but it's not a horror film. She went mental, and she was literally petrified.

While *Predator 2* is a film that few parents would consider appropriate for their five-year-olds, Jill clearly perceives herself to be making distinctions here about what might frighten her children – and, as I have suggested, these distinctions were partly borne out by her experience with Donna.

As this case study suggests, the attempt to make consistent judgments about what is appropriate for children is often complicated by the different ways in which they respond to what they watch. Even if parents were able to exert complete control over their children's viewing, it would still be impossible to prevent them from becoming frightened or upset, since such experiences are often unpredictable. 'Knowing your children' is clearly essential here: but it is a process that takes time, and no small amount of trial and error.

### Family 3

This family consisted of two parents (Josie and James) and four children, two girls (Sally, 14, and Alice, 7) and two boys (Jake, 16, and Toby, 3). Both parents were white and middle-class, with several years of further education. James worked as an independent television producer, while Josie was a part-time teacher. They lived in a large suburban house. There were four television sets in the house, two in downstairs living rooms (one with VCR) and one in each of the older children's bedrooms.

By contrast with the first two case studies, these parents' primary concerns about television were much less to do with violence. James in fact nominated *Terminator 2* as 'the best film I've ever seen', and while both parents agreed that it would not be appropriate for Alice, it was seen as sufficiently 'tongue in cheek' to be acceptable for the older children. Horror was barely mentioned either: Jake and Sally had seen films like *Child's Play* – which they judged to be 'crap' – but both had been very frightened by *Twin Peaks*, and tended to avoid horror in general.

On the other hand, the parents did express some concern about what they called 'smut' and 'innuendo' in programmes like *Blind Date*, and about 'bad language', which they felt was starting to 'slip in' before the watershed – although in this case, the concern was as much to do with their own parents as with the children:

*James:* I couldn't believe the language in [the film *How To Get Ahead In Advertising*]. My mother-in-law was here and it was about quarter past nine and to be quite frank the language on it was – well, I'm a broad minded person but I was embarrassed sitting next to my mother-in-law who's –

*Josie:* A fairly innocent sixty-year-old.

*James:* An innocent church-going lady of late years. I was absolutely embarrassed ... you know there were words in it beginning in 'c' and ending in 't' and I thought, hang on a minute, *no*, that should not be on television.

In this area, like many parents, they argued that the classification system for videos was not particularly useful:

*Josie:* I don't find [the certificates] particularly accurate a lot of the time.

*James:* I'm quite surprised at some that have come in the house that
have been '15', I've gone 'cor'. And some that are '18' ... some of
them are obviously a joke and tongue in cheek, and how anyone
can see anything wrong with it, I don't know. And yet some 'PG'
ones are frightening, you know ...

*Josie:* As far as the sex content, some of the 'PG's, you don't actually
have scenes of sex going on, but some of the innuendo is just as
bad, I think.

Similar arguments were made about the watershed; and while they
claimed that they would 'take notice' of this, the parents said they
generally preferred to use their own discretion.

Rather more concern was expressed, however, about the issue of
cultural value – which, as I have noted, was almost exclusively a
preoccupation among middle-class families. James was particularly
adamant about his refusal to subscribe to cable TV, even though
this was something that his company would have paid for: he
argued that this would mean programmes with 'poor taste' and
'poor content'. Although (as we shall see) he regretted the fact that
the older children had TV sets in their bedrooms, he appeared reasonably confident that the programmes on terrestrial channels
were acceptable for them to watch:

*James:* On the terrestrial channels, there's nothing really that [Jake]
can watch that can in any way damage him / There's nothing on
there that can 'affect' the way he thinks or the way he'll behave.

Josie was rather less convinced about this. She did express some
concern about the moral lessons of soap operas like *Neighbours*,
and had actually banned the school series *Grange Hill* when the
children were younger. As the children had got older, however, she
increasingly preferred to mediate such programmes by watching
with them, and offering a 'running commentary', rather than
simply preventing them from viewing:

*Josie:* I was much sterner with Jake and Sally. I can remember them
wanting to watch *Grange Hill* and I wouldn't let them because I felt
they weren't old enough. There's a sort of point with children
where they can understand what's going on at one level but they

haven't got the emotional maturity to understand the other bits. And even with *Neighbours*, that was why I used to sit and watch it with them at first. And as I say, that's where I suppose my standards are slipping, in that Alice will now watch *Neighbours* with the older ones who probably don't bother to give her a running commentary, whereas I would be sort of butting in with / Well, say there was somebody planning on sleeping with their boyfriend or whatever, I might try and chat about what reasons there might be for not doing it or trying to ascribe motives or reasons for what was happening.

This kind of pedagogical approach also applied where the younger children had become upset – as Alice had done over programmes like *The Borrowers* and *The Animals of Farthing Wood*. For example, Josie described how she would attempt to reassure them that it was not real, and help them to imagine an alternative ending:

*Josie:* There's been the occasional thing where [Alice] hasn't liked the ending and I've said what I can remember doing with my sister when we were little, which is 'well let's think of another ending, then let's pretend this didn't happen'. And sort of / you know, make your own story. Because that's what they are anyway.

Yet as Josie acknowledged, her approach had changed as the children had grown older – and while this may partly have reflected 'slipping standards', it also appeared to derive from a changing estimation of what constituted 'emotional maturity'. As in the majority of other families, it seemed to be agreed that children should be able to make their own choices about what they watched from about the age of twelve or thirteen – although (as in this case) it was acknowledged that this would be more relaxed with subsequent children.

In this family, however, these questions came to a head around the issue of children having televisions in their bedrooms, which was a major focus of concern for both parents:

*James:* I don't think there's much that Sally can't watch, but I wouldn't want anybody younger than about twelve or thirteen to have choice of what they were viewing and the times they were viewing it ...

*Interviewer:* But do you think that the pressure will come from Alice at some time, to have her own TV?

*Josie:* Oh, she's already asked and I've said 'nobody in this house has their own television in their bedroom till they're thirteen'. And she says 'can't I have it when I'm twelve?' So she's trying to sort of /

*Interviewer:* Chip away.

*Josie:* – and probably, the way things go, she will be younger. 'Cause it just tends to happen that way with subsequent children, you sort of cave in a bit sooner on things ...

*Interviewer:* So why twelve or thirteen?

*Josie:* Well, because –

*James:* It's far enough away. [*laughter*]

*Josie:* Yes / I think by that stage / they are perhaps more able to sort of pick and choose / sensibly and also by that stage, they're wanting to spend more time on their own anyway. 'Cause ... it's not even so much that I think she'd be watching things I didn't approve of, but that I don't want her sitting watching it non-stop. / And I think it probably would cut, if she had one now she might well go up and watch it there and it would cut back on the family time. / Because there are, I mean one of the times when the four children come together is after school with the kids' TV programmes. I mean, even Jake will sometimes sit and watch the cartoons, so they're all in the room together. Now that doesn't happen very often, because normally the big ones are doing something else. So that's really why.

The parents' concerns about the children having televisions in their bedrooms were thus not principally to do with content. Later in the interview, they described how (some years ago) the children had seen '18'-rated videos at friends' houses; but they reasoned that it was impossible to prevent this, and unrealistic to expect the children to refuse to watch them. This had led them to permit the children to watch such material at home as well, albeit initially in the company of the parents: as Josie said, 'I started thinking I'd rather [Jake] watched it here with me than round at a friend's house.' While James in particular was adamant that the children would not have cable TV or video in their bedrooms, the attempt to control their viewing of mainstream TV had also largely been abandoned by the age of twelve.

While Josie does refer to their concern that the children would watch television 'non-stop' – a concern that again was voiced much more frequently in middle-class families – it was agreed that this had not in fact been a significant problem. On the contrary, as she explains, the major concern here was that providing the children with televisions in their bedrooms would reduce their 'family time':

*Josie:* We both regret the television in the bedroom thing. It happened accidentally, in the sense that Jake first had one up there for his computer and then started watching more and more television up there. And then Sally said it's not fair, 'cause there's only eighteen months between them, so she's ended up with one.

*James:* So we don't really see a lot of them in the evenings. They're up there making their own selections.

*Josie:* But having said that, I don't know if people of that age spend much time with their parents anyway ... I think probably the patch that I've regretted most we've probably passed, in the sense that Jake's sixteen now, I feel it doesn't really make any difference whether he's watching it up there or downstairs, he's sort of old enough to make his / I think initially perhaps it meant they were watching things which we wouldn't have encouraged them to watch and perhaps watching later, because you go up and say goodnight and sometimes it goes on again. But again, he's sixteen now, so he'd be awake anyway.

Despite regretting this decision, Josie argues that it is inevitable that adolescents will want to spend less time with their parents, and that it would be simplistic merely to blame television (a point with which Jake himself agreed). However, James suggested that television could provide an excuse for avoiding conflict, and that it might actively prevent communication – although Josie questioned this:

*James:* I think they disappear up there when the going gets tough within the family, and there's an easy route out where they can entertain themselves ... they have with the television something to focus on, so if there's an argument going on they'll storm off and that'll be it. Whereas if there wasn't a television there, I believe they'd come back down and we could –

*Josie:* No, I don't think they would / 'Cause I used to storm off to my room and I would listen to the radio and read, 'cause I didn't have a television then. I still never came down again.

*James:* But I do think it's an easy option for them to get out of a situation within the family group. I do very much regret it.

Despite the differences between them, it is clear that neither parent here regards television viewing in itself as a major problem, or as a primary cause of undesirable 'effects'. The problem is with *privatised* viewing, which is seen both as symptomatic of tensions within the family, and (particularly by James) as a way of evading those tensions, rather than confronting them. While it was acknowledged that 'family viewing' was a comparatively rare event with such a wide age range among the children, it was seen as a desirable ideal. Significantly, however, the older children tried to resist these attempts to make them 'communicate': for example, they described how they had rejected their parents' attempts to encourage them to watch a series about parents and teenagers, symptomatically entitled *Living with the Enemy* – although, ironically, Sally did admit that she had watched some of it alone in her bedroom.

In comparison with the previous two case studies, the issue of parental regulation takes a rather different form here, not least because of the age of the children (or at least the older ones). Concerns about the potential influence of television *content* are secondary to concerns about the role of the medium in the broader context of family relationships. The way in which television is used here is seen to be symptomatic of other tensions – although there is a sense in which it may also make it harder to resolve them. On the other hand, of course, it may well be the case that blaming television can provide a convenient vehicle for anxieties that are an inevitable part of family life.

### Family 4

This was a working-class single parent family, consisting of a mother (Joan) and two daughters (Donna, 12, and Samantha, 9). Their sister, who was in her early twenties, also lived 'in the top of the house'; and there were two older brothers, who had both left home. The mother had left school at sixteen, and worked as a childminder. She described herself as 'black British', and had migrated from the Caribbean in the 1960s: she was a Methodist. They lived in a council house in the inner city. There were two televisions, one in the living room (with VCR and satellite) and one in the mother's bedroom.

Joan appeared to operate fairly strict 'viewing rules', partly in order to ensure that the children found time for other activities. They had to do their homework and 'chores round the house' before they were allowed to watch TV; and on weekdays, bedtime was enforced at 9 pm. Family viewing consisted mainly of soap operas, sitcoms and wildlife documentaries; although the girls also watched MTV and films on the satellite channels. Joan was fairly insistent on the fact that she had 'control' of her children. For example, she was adamant that the girls would not be getting television sets in their bedrooms, for reasons that were similar to those expressed by Josie and James:

Joan: Because then I feel they'd just be watching TV blankly all the time and I would have no control. / When they're old enough or left school, they can get their own. But I will not get my kids a TV in their room, because I think that's a lazy way, right. Your kids are just gonna be there, you're never gonna see them – especially in a house like this, where one of us is up the top. [With] somebody somewhere else, there ain't no family life.

Nevertheless, Joan's concerns about television *content* were fairly limited. She said that she was not particularly bothered about her children watching horror or violent films, and admitted that she rarely paid much attention to the certificates on video rentals. She predicted that the girls would tell us stories about how they watched television late at night, although she insisted that this was not true. Donna and Samantha did indeed describe how they would 'sneak downstairs' after their mother had gone to bed, in order to watch horror films on the satellite channels – although Donna acknowledged that she would sometimes fall asleep too soon. Nevertheless, both girls had seen a number of horror films such as *Evil Dead* and *Fright Night*, and while Joan knew about this, it did not appear to be a major concern. While she acknowledged that Samantha had occasionally been frightened by such films some years ago, she argued that she was now able to cope.

On the other hand, she did describe how Samantha had been much more disturbed by a documentary they had seen one afternoon:

*Joan:* It didn't bother her at the time, but it bothered her afterwards ... It was a documentary about the West Indies, and they had a professor going around telling, you know, like we have folk stories about beings that live in the bushes and they were going on about this woman who was a Diablesse in it, which is a mythical thing, like a beautiful woman and she's got one normal foot and a hoof on the other one. And she watched this thing, and because I found it interesting I'm going 'yeah, I used to hear these stories, and he used to tell me about Jumbies', which is like a ghost. She looked at it all, and she's interested and that. And the next day, 'mummy', we were in the kitchen, it's just me and her alone, and 'is that real?' I said 'what do you mean, is it real?' 'You know, what we were watching on telly, is there really something like that?' I said 'I don't know, Samantha'. Then I realised that she's really sort of, you know, frightened of it all. / That sort of thing frightens her more than blood and gore ... It's not just the visual, it's the thought factor that frightens her.

Here again, it is hard for the mother to predict what will prove to be upsetting – in this case, a *factual* programme transmitted well before the watershed. Significantly, Samantha's response is as much to the 'thought' as it is to the image itself, which might partly account for the fact that she did not appear upset at the time of viewing. In this respect, Joan argued, there was a difference between the two girls. Although she did not make many distinctions between them in terms of what they were allowed to watch, she did acknowledge that Samantha would sometimes try to hide her fears: 'she doesn't want you to know that she's afraid of something, so she'll tend to stay in the room and pretend she's not scared, and then probably look to me for some sort of reassurance that this was what was really happening'. Here again, the key to Samantha's fear is her doubt about what is 'really happening' – which in the case of the folk stories was partly fed by the way in which her mother related similar stories, and appeared to share the doubt herself.

If Joan was not particularly worried about horror or violence, she was much more concerned about explicit sexual material – even though Samantha and Donna maintained that they were not interested in such material anyway. While she argued that the watershed was not widely observed, it did seem to provide some guidance in this area at least:

*Joan:* To say that after 9 o'clock kids can't watch TV any more is a joke really, because 90% of kids watch TV till whenever they feel like it. And I mean, what do you get after nine really that you don't get before? At the same time, I know after nine, I know there's more chances of something sexual. Because I don't worry too much about the violence as such but I do feel embarrassed if something like we're watching a film and suddenly a part comes on and then I find I'm in a bit of a spot. Because I don't want to send them out of the room, but I will if I'm embarrassed enough, I will send them out because I find it difficult to sit there and watch that sort of thing with kids.

As this account suggests, Joan does experience some ambivalence here. On the one hand, she is embarrassed; yet on the other, she does not want to prevent her children from watching. Later in the interview, she described how she had sometimes regretted sending the girls out of the room: 'I'm shutting Donna out of the room, and then I find afterwards that it might be only one scene ... but it's the embarrassment probably, to me at the time.' However, she also traced some of these attitudes to her own upbringing, and suggested that she had changed somewhat as her children had grown up:

*Joan:* The older ones tell me all the time, I've changed as a person, right. I've got more confidence now than I did with the older kids, when I was learning. It's difficult when you're not sure yourself. But I think with the younger kids, I'm much more relaxed. I don't want to shield them and I would never say you can't watch this on TV. But my biggest thing is the sexual side of it – probably my own puritanical ways, 'cause I was born in the West Indies where it's like Victorian England really. But there's a lot to be said for that. But that's how it affects me more.

What is perhaps most significant here is Joan's acknowledgement that she has *learnt* to be a parent: her sense of being more 'relaxed' is not a matter of 'slipping standards' (as it was seen, perhaps a little ironically, by Josie in Family 3), but on the contrary of growing in 'confidence'.

Perhaps one aspect of this was Joan's tendency to adopt a more 'pedagogical' approach to television, rather than simply banning particular programmes outright. Like Josie (Family 3), she appeared to maintain a running commentary during soap operas:

*Joan:* With me, I make a point, I've always had this thing, if they're watching something and it's / I find soaps good for that, maybe they're discussing abortion or some topic like that, and I don't want to indoctrinate my kids, but I give my view of it, right, so they know that what they see might not be how I feel. So I let them realise that there are different sides to everything, and question it ... 'Cause you watch these things and everything gets solved / so quickly that if, you know, if your kids aren't sharp, they'll think that's how life is ...

*Interviewer:* So do you quite often keep up a running commentary when you're watching things together?

*Joan:* I do tend to, yeah. I don't know if anybody listens.

In general, Joan felt that soaps were likely to be more influential than violent films, not least because they were concerned with experiences that were more likely to happen to her children. Yet her approach to violence was similarly pedagogical:

*Interviewer:* So why doesn't violence bother you so much then?

*Joan:* Because I'm not a violent person. I don't preach violence. And

I've always taught my kids this, that if someone hits you, you hit them back, right, but you don't go round hitting people for the sake of it. You shouldn't have to turn to violence / I know it goes on, and I want my kids to be aware of the sort of situations where you find violence. And I think that comes from idleness, not having anything to do / being lost in yourself maybe, just growing up and you don't understand things, and you'd be influenced if you see things happening on the screen and your friends are into it as well, and they're going to try to influence you. / I wouldn't blame it all on television, because it's up to you as a parent to know what your kids are doing, to try and teach them right from wrong ... I've got more influence, because it's my home, I can turn the TV off [*laughs*]. It's only gonna be a problem if I let it become a problem.

Joan clearly acknowledges that 'violence' is a social problem – and indeed, elsewhere in the interview, she argued that her local area had become much more dangerous than it was when she first arrived thirty years before. Yet she argues that the causes of violence are complex, and that television is unlikely to play a direct causal role. Here again, the argument about television is situated within broader assertions about child-rearing: television only becomes a problem if parental guidance in general is seen to be lacking.

However, Joan also suggested that violence in films might have a positive educational dimension. She argued that violence in films did partly reflect violence in society, and that children needed to know that 'it's a violent world'. She felt that her children did not take violence in American films particularly seriously, largely because 'life here and life in America is two different things'. Yet she also suggested that such films might make them more 'aware' and better prepared for a violent future, as in the case of *Goodfellas*:

*Joan:* I know that film had a lot of violence in it ... but then I'd make a joke about the amount of ketchup or whatever they'd used, so that it's not real. But it does happen, 'cause the Mafia does exist and they do kill. I don't want to worry them too much, I don't want them to be frightened. I want them to be aware of the world they're living in, you know. Things you see, especially the gangster business that will happen in America, as I always tell them, it's going to happen here – but in my heart of hearts, I don't think it will happen as badly as it does there, because we are different people here than they are. But you can see it on a smaller scale, and if they can see the situations and friendships and lifestyle that's going to bring you into that and keep away from it, that's what I can do, try and guide them – but always being aware that if you say to a kid 'don't do something', that's what they want to do. I know 'cause I was a little sod, right [*laughs*].

On one level, Joan seeks to reassure the children that the film is not real, yet she also wants to draw their attention to the ways in which it represents the causes of violence in real life. In this way, she is attempting to strike a balance between frightening her children and making sure that they are 'aware' and informed about the real world. As in the previous extract, violence is seen to arise from 'situations and friendships and lifestyle', rather than simply from the media. While the issue of imitative effects is certainly raised here, Joan appears to use the film as an opportunity for precisely the opposite kind of lesson – although again she is also aware of the dangers of an approach that will prove counterproductive. While she does not believe she has the power to 'indoctrinate' her children, she clearly does feel that she has more power than television to shape the kind of people they will become.

### Family 5

This was a white, middle-class family consisting of two parents (Nigel and Carolyn), two girls (Emily, 18, and Jenny, 12) and one boy (Jeff, 16). Currently unemployed, the father had formerly run his own small business; while the mother worked part-time. They were practising Christians. There were three TV sets in the house, one in the main living room (with a recently acquired VCR), and one each in Jenny's and Jeff's bedrooms (both monochrome).

Like most of the parents of older children, Nigel and Carolyn had attempted to regulate their children's viewing primarily in order to ensure that they did their homework. When the children were younger, they had insisted that the television would be turned off for at least an hour at 6 o'clock, and this had now become a set pattern. Jenny and Jeff had since acquired sets in their bedrooms, but these were used primarily for resolving conflicts of taste, for example over sport; and to this extent, they were described as 'a blessing'.

On the other hand, these parents did express concerns about television content that were explicitly informed by their religious convictions – although these did not appear to be shared by their children. Here again, violence was much less of an issue than sexual content: as Emily succinctly put it, 'violence is OK, but sex isn't'. For example, the parents complained about 'innuendo' in programmes like the sitcom *Birds of a Feather*; and they had prevented Jenny from watching *Born on the Fourth of July* because of a 'sex scene' – an event which still appeared to cause some resentment on her part. Nigel expressed particular concern about what he called the 'normalising' of such behaviour in society in general:

*Nigel:* By putting it out, we're slowly getting our children accustomised [*sic*] to this as being normal, and that is my biggest fear, you know. / Do you know what I mean? And by saying that it's, you know, affairs are normal and swearing's normal and to make sexual jokes and innuendoes about people is normal and funny and it's all right ... it's the normalising, it makes it normal.

One particular film that had caused some concern here was the biopic *The Doors*, which Jeff had seen, and which Nigel described as 'sick': 'the sex, the drugs and the death wish and the wanting to sleep with his mother and wanting to kill his father, and, you know, what else is there?'

A further concern here was with the representation of the occult in films such as *The Omen 2*, which the parents feared might cultivate a dangerous fascination. The children clearly regarded this as something of a joke, citing instances where the parents had banned films like *Ghostbusters* and *Ghost*:

*Emily:* It's like if you're gonna watch a programme on the occult, later you'll be worshipping Satan –

*Jeff:* – and sacrificing virgins on the gravestone, or whatever.

In fact, none of the children expressed much interest in horror films, and Emily condemned them as 'rubbish', particularly on the grounds of the special effects.

While the parents had managed to prevent their children from watching 'adult' material in the past – and still did so with Jenny – they acknowledged that they were increasingly powerless in this respect. For example, Carolyn described how Jeff had hired one of the *Child's Play* films to watch with his friends, and how she had made him turn it off; while Nigel described a similar experience with a 'filthy' video of the comedian Bernard Manning. Nevertheless, they suspected that Jeff had seen both of these at other people's houses – and, indeed, that banning such material would only make this more likely. They recognised that other parents had different standards from their own, and quoted one example where Jenny had seen 'pornographic' films at a friend's house. Yet it was for this reason that they argued that broadcasters themselves should exercise greater responsibility:

*Nigel:* What we're worried about is it becoming normal. / I keep stressing this normalised, 'cause as far as those people are concerned, they can't see anything wrong in it, you see. And it's not my job to moralise to them or to preach –

*Carolyn:* It's their home.

*Nigel:* – it's their home, they can do what they like, yeah. And it's not my job to say you shouldn't watch this, that or the other or you should do this. But the TV companies do have a responsibility in my opinion, because they're so powerful, and the government, especially the BBC, yeah, which is run by me, I own the BBC, yeah, to take care of these things with the children.

While Nigel and Carolyn seem to refuse to take the moral high ground in judging other parents, they ultimately argue for stricter central control. As in the case of *Birds of a Feather*, they argued that the broadcasters had become 'a bit slack' about the watershed: Nigel complained about the expression 'I don't give a toss' in the rural police series *Hartbeat*, while Carolyn condemned the way in which 'affairs' were featured in soap operas like *Neighbours* that were particularly popular with children.

On the other hand, they recognised that they themselves had

become more lenient with their subsequent children, partly out of a recognition that they could not totally control what they watched:

*Carolyn:* We used to be very strict about the cinemas, you know. They weren't allowed to go and see a film [if they were under the age limit]. But we've got sort of a bit more lenient, so by the time we got to Jenny, we were more, if she goes to see a '15', well, you know. Whereas Emily just wouldn't have been allowed to, or Jeff. So we've sort of eased up a bit ... I suppose it's just it's out of sort of exhaustion or laziness, I don't know what it is, or whether she's a bit more mature anyway ... You sort of grow up with them, I mean you sort of grow up with the older ones, and by the time the younger ones you see how well you know [*laughs*].

Here again, there is a sense in which the parents feel that they have changed, not simply out of 'exhaustion', but also because they too have 'grown up', and learnt from the experience of bringing up their older children. At the same time, Carolyn does acknowledge the possibility of differences between siblings, and that 'maturity' is not simply a function of age. Yet despite this, they did set the point at which the children would 'come of age' significantly later than most other parents: Nigel argued that sixteen was the 'age of consent', and the age at which children should be able to 'make their own minds up'. Nevertheless, as in the above extract, there was also a sense in which this had to be decided on the basis of individual personalities:

*Carolyn:* In a way they sort of let you know. / I can't really explain it.

*Nigel:* They set their own agenda really.

*Carolyn:* They change / they grow up and they change and you just sort of sense it, that that's the time, you know. Nigel's better at it than me, you know. He sort of pushes me to let go more ... But you sort of know when they're mature enough in a way to handle various things.

Despite this emphasis on 'knowing your children', it was clear that, in some cases, the children had become upset quite unexpectedly. For example, Carolyn had been surprised by the fact that

Jenny had had a nightmare after watching an episode of *Sherlock Holmes*. Jeff had also been disturbed by television coverage of twentieth century history:

*Nigel:* They've had a lot on the TV about the Russian Revolution and about the Holocaust and that, and the Japanese prisoner of war camps and stuff ... and he's been absolutely disgusted at that, you know, the way people could –

*Carolyn:* Yeah, he's been upset.

*Nigel:* He's been upset about that ... how people can sink to that depth, you know what I mean. But that's factual and so therefore you can't hide him from that. But / that's the thing about TV, it brings it right into your front room. It's not like a book or even a photograph or even the radio, which leaves it up to your imagination. With television it's very powerful.

While Nigel clearly sees this kind of factual information as important, he also appeared to resent the 'power' of television. Although he claimed to watch the news regularly, he argued that television tended to bring 'problems into my home' without him having any choice in the matter – for example, in programmes like *EastEnders* or in documentaries about issues like the conflict in Northern Ireland. Television, he argued, should be an 'entertainment centre', like a stereo system, which could be controlled more easily.

Broadly speaking, these parents were among the least permissive in our sample; and they were among the very few to call for stricter censorship. However, it is notable that even here the attempt to exercise rigid control over the children's viewing had been effectively abandoned well before the age of eighteen (the highest rating in video classification) – and not simply because it was seen to be a lost cause. Despite the parents' explicit religious convictions, they too acknowledged that their children would have to learn to make their own decisions, and that the attempt simply to impose their own values could well prove counter-productive.

### Family 6

This was a white working-class family, consisting of two parents (Veronica and Bill) and four boys (Liam, 13, Mike, 12, Donald, 10, and Lewis, 9). The parents had both left school at sixteen: the mother worked as a childminder, while the father was unemployed. They lived in a council flat in a suburban area. There were three television sets in the house: one in the main living room (with VCR), and one in each of the boys' bedrooms (the boys shared two bedrooms).

As in most other families with younger children, bedtimes were the main constraint on the children's viewing here. The older two were required to do 'chores' in the evening, but were allowed to watch the TV in their bedroom until about 10 pm. Rules for the younger children, both in terms of viewing times and in terms of content, were slightly tighter, although it appeared that differences here were gradually disappearing. In practice, the parents argued that none of the children were 'telly addicts', and did not seem to regard the *amount* of viewing as a particular problem. Family viewing consisted of programmes like *Quantum Leap* and the science fiction sitcom *Red Dwarf*. There was a particular enthusiasm, shared by all, for action movies like *Terminator* and *The Last Action Hero*, and for martial arts films. The parents had an extensive collection of videos, including many martial arts and horror titles – although the latter were strictly proscribed for the children. In the case of both genres, they made very clear distinctions, both in terms of what they enjoyed, and in terms of what they felt was suitable for their children – although significantly, these judgments were quite different from those of ratings system.

In the case of violence, for example, the father argued that there were crucial distinctions between fact and fiction. According to him, the children were most upset by scenes of violence on the news – 'when you get things that happen to real people, real animals, then they can relate more to them, and that's where you've got to be careful'. By contrast, while he was ambivalent about the thought of his children watching the *Child's Play* films, for example, he clearly perceived them as comparatively trivial:

*Bill:* I don't know what all the palaver's about / compared to some of the films that are out now, with the new technology that they've got to give you the visual impressions and what have you, *Child's*

*Play* is nothing.

*Veronica:* But would you still let the children watch it?

*Bill:* ... um I suppose, no, not really. It's one of them sort of things that I suppose the kids would find a little bit [scary] / But I dare say someone like Donald would probably sit there and laugh at it ... If there's a few things in it that would make you jump, then I'd think twice about letting the kids see it, or if there's lots of real mindless violence in it, then yeah. But I think *Child's Play*, the first one that I saw was very tongue-in-cheek, about a little doll walking around, coming to life and killing people in various ways. It's old hat now. Blimey, you see that on the news, people going round blasting people and what have you. And you hear about it, not so much on the visuals on the news you know, and about all the kids getting molested in real life. And I think kids nowadays, they just take it for granted that's the way of the world.

The crucial concern here is clearly not with imitative effects, but with the possibility that the children might become upset. Yet as this extract suggests, the parents perceived clear differences between the children in this respect. Donald (10) was seen to be much more able to cope with such experiences, while Lewis (9) had suffered nightmares in the past. This was confirmed when we spoke to the children: Donald expressed a positive relish for films like *Silence of the Lambs*, and some resentment at the fact that he was not allowed to watch the *Nightmare on Elm Street* series, whereas Lewis and Mike said they would be more inclined to avoid them.

At the same time, Bill makes a distinction here between 'mindless' violence and violence that is somehow justified, which recurred in their discussion of martial arts and action movies. In the case of *Robocop*, for example, it was the first scene in which the policeman was 'dismembered with a shotgun' that was seen to be unduly 'mindless' and 'graphic', whereas the rest of the film was seen as acceptable for the children to watch. Likewise, some very clear distinctions were made between the unrealistic fighting in films like *Karate Kid* and the more authentic approach of Steven Seagal and Jean-Claude Van Damme. While she claimed that Seagal was '*very* violent', Veronica clearly enjoyed these films herself, and reported that her children had bought her the videos for Christmas. All the boys attended karate classes, and it was partly for this reason that they were seen to be capable of distinguishing between them:

*Veronica:* [Seagal] is a *true* fighter. So therefore when / my children will view those films differently to a lot of other boys, because my children all do karate. Therefore my children will sit here, it's a karate film / it's not an '18', it's not a violent film, it's a karate film ... They're watching him, they know he's got so many black belts, they know he is the only white man to go to Japan and learn a certain martial art and get to the highest point he could get to. They know all that about him. Same with Van Damme, they know he was a European champion. So therefore his films, it's karate. It's not violence, it's karate.

Significantly, however, a line was still being drawn here between the younger and the older children, although this had begun to shift:

*Bill:* Now, Steven Seagal, the bigger ones we would have allowed to watch him. But to show you the difference between the two we would let the little ones watch stuff by Jackie Chan ... Because he's more entertaining. There was hardly any blood and guts in it. It was just fantastic fight sequences and that set-up in his films and it was more enjoyable and light hearted to watch, but they still got to see their martial arts.

*Interviewer:* Yeah, whereas [Seagal] is a bit more hard edged?

*Bill:* Hard edged, and a lot more violent, a few legs floating about. And that's where we would draw the line. But now the [younger] ones are catching up, we're saying right, we're grouping them together now.

While the parents implicitly acknowledge the possibility of a 'mindless' reading of this kind of violence (on the part of 'a lot of other boys'), they define their own children as an especially discerning audience, for whom the categories 'violence' and '18' no longer seem to apply. Age differences are still an issue here, in that different standards are operated for Mike and Liam as compared with Donald and Lewis; although most Jackie Chan movies are in fact classified at '18', which also implies that the ratings are seen to be redundant. Yet again, the children are seen to have 'come of age' in this respect several years ahead of the estimates embodied in the ratings system.

By contrast, the parents did appear to have stricter 'viewing rules' in other areas. Although both parents were horror fans themselves, and explicitly said that they enjoyed 'a bit of blood and gore', Veronica was adamant that her children would not be watching the *Nightmare on Elm Street* films until they were fifteen or sixteen – a ruling which Donald in particular strongly resented. Although Donald had seen *Silence of the Lambs*, he had done so at a friend's house, very much against their wishes (although Bill noted with some amazement that the friend's father was a psychiatrist); and while Donald did describe the gory parts of the film with great enthusiasm, Bill suspected that he was not 'old enough' to fully understand it.

Sex was an area that provoked similar concerns. For example, Veronica described how the children had attempted to stay up very late to watch *American Gladiators*, and had seen programmes like *The James Whale Show* and *The Good Sex Guide*, which the parents had since banned. While the children had televisions in their bedrooms, and were allowed to watch after their official bedtime, this was still subject to parental control:

*Bill:* If we're sitting here [in the living room] and we're watching something and something comes up, say, sexually related, then I'll quickly go in [the boys' bedroom] and whack it off. [*laughter*] Or stick me nose round, and if they're watching it, then it goes off.

In general, however, it was 'bad' language rather than sex itself that was seen to be the problem:

*Bill:* I don't believe that kids should be completely sheltered from sex ... The old Victorian values of 'oh no, dirty, you can't do that', that's out the window. There's nothing wrong with that. It's basically the swear words, yeah? That's the only other time I'll cut back on a video, that I won't let them watch. Because you get some of these American ones, they go well over the top on the swear words. And you get some of them where every other word is an f-word ...

> I think by telling them they can't watch something that's got lots of swear words in it, then they know that they might know the words but they'll get the gist and the message that it's wrong to say them, yeah?

Bill acknowledges that the children do know 'those words', and accepts that they would not necessarily repeat them; yet he sees his banning of this material as a way of reinforcing a more general 'message'.

Even in these areas, however, the parents argued that they should retain ultimate discretion about what their children should see. They were particularly scathing about what they saw as the inaccuracies and inconsistencies of the ratings system:

*Bill:* I think the certification that they give some of these videos are well out of date, as far as I'm concerned ... It seems like you've got a bunch of sixty-year-olds sitting on a committee, you know, thinking of the old Victorian values ...

*Veronica:* All the boys have watched films like *Dirty Dancing* / which I think was done at a '15'. I mean none of mine are fifteen / *Gremlins* is '15'. All right, admittedly we sat down and watched it first and we told them there were a couple of bits in it. And I mean now they just watch it / fine. / This film *Mrs Doubtfire*, my two little ones are so upset because they can't go and see it, because they thought it was gonna be a 'PG'. Mike and Liam have seen it and they said they couldn't understand why it wasn't a 'PG' ... They're advertising it as a family film, but families can't go and see it.

The case of *Mrs Doubtfire* was a particularly notorious one at the time, since the film had been heavily promoted to children despite the fact that it was rated as a '12'. Veronica very pointedly argued that she would allow the children to see the film when it was released on video.[13] The parents also drew attention to the way in which the merchandising of toys associated with films like *Terminator* (rated '15'), *Gremlins* (rated '15') and *Batman* (rated '12') was specifically targeted at much younger children: as Bill said, 'obviously the merchandisers know the kids watch them'.

Likewise, while they did express concern about 'bad' language, they also challenged the notion that this should determine the classification – 'a few f-words and that's it, straight away they put an "18" on it'. Even in the case of horror films, where they did feel there was a strong case for certification, the '18' rating was described as 'outdated'. On the other hand, as the above extract indicates, they did exercise control of their children's viewing to the extent of previewing videos where they were in doubt; and in cases such as *Gremlins*, *Robocop* and (some years earlier) *Jaws*, they had warned the children in advance of particularly frightening or gory parts of the film. Yet they insisted that these judgments were based on 'individual films', rather than on general criteria – with the exception of horror films, which were subject to a total ban.

In general, however, they preferred to mediate and discuss such material, rather than banning it outright. This applied particularly where the children became upset:

*Bill:* Donald, with *Dances With Wolves*, he got all upset there. 'Cause the wolf, when they were shooting at the wolf, Whitesocks, yeah?

*Veronica:* And the horse got killed, didn't it? I mean, he sat here and cried his eyes out. / And we have to talk about it afterwards and then you have to, you know, explain to them it's a *film*, the horse didn't really get killed. And he can watch it again and he'll still have the same reaction to it *again*. Yeah, we do have to do it then as well.

*Interviewer:* Do you think that works? ... Do you think it helps them?

*Veronica:* If you've got the kids who will actually tell you that a certain part upsets them, then yeah, you can talk to them and explain to them and they accept that to a certain degree. But I should imagine you've got other kids in the world that keep that to themselves and that's where the problem lies. It's that the kids won't actually come out and admit to their mum or dad or whoever and say 'I saw this film the other day and I really got upset, 'cause I saw that bit', you know. And a lot of kids don't. And I think that's probably where the problem might lie.

Despite Veronica's comment about Donald having to be reassured again on subsequent viewings, the parents had watched particular films with their children on several occasions, and had a substantial collection of tapes they had bought. As Veronica said, 'the more they see it, they can work it out for themselves – because I think children, they can listen to us, but I still think in the end they've got to work it out for themselves'. In the case of *J. F. K.*, for example, the boys had asked them a great many questions, and Liam had been encouraged to get a book about Kennedy from the library.

As this extract suggests, Veronica encourages the children to share their feelings, and perceives television to have an important role in this process. As we have seen (Chapter 5), she described how the children had cried over *The Incredible Journey*, arguing that this might counteract their 'macho tendency'. She made them watch the news coverage around the Live Aid concert for similar reasons:

*Veronica:* When the Live Aid concert was first on, I actually made the boys sit down and watch the news item. / And there was one bit in it where the child was actually dead, and it was in a bag on the floor ... I actually made the boys watch it / because I wanted them to feel well off. / I wanted them to know that there was a lot of people in the world worse off than them and I think it worked. / I think it really worked / All right, it upset them / and I think I'm saying I wanted to upset them, because I wanted them to feel.

Here again, the wish to avoid upsetting one's children is set against the need to ensure that they are informed about their place in the world. While these parents are protective, they are also reserving the right to make their own judgments, and to use their own discretion about what their children should watch. They acknowledge differences between their children, but they do not simply define these in terms of chronological age; and they are prepared to revise their approach in the light of what they learn from the children themselves. Yet again, the potential 'effects' of television are not seen in isolation, but are situated within broader experiences of child-rearing and family relationships.

## Conclusion

In different ways and to different degrees, all the parents here were concerned to regulate and control their children's viewing. As I have shown, the grounds for regulation and the strategies that parents use vary considerably; and it remains difficult to trace these variations to predictable social factors. The notion – which was repeatedly rehearsed in the debates that followed the James Bulger case – that it is working-class parents who are inevitably more 'feckless and irresponsible' in this respect is one that cannot be sustained.

In accounting for the role of television in their family lives, these parents inevitably drew on broader discourses about child development and child-rearing, which in turn reflect assumptions about the responsibilities of parents and the capacities of children. Nevertheless, these discourses do not simply amount to a fixed body of received wisdom. On the contrary, the attempt to find a balance between shielding your children from undesirable realities and preparing them for the complex demands of adult life is a dilemma that is incapable of easy resolution. This is not an issue that can be decided by the application of fixed rules or prescriptions, but one that is played out on a daily basis in the negotiations between parents and children, and between parents themselves. For all sorts of reasons, the parents here acknowledged that they were unable to exercise complete control of their children's viewing, or of their responses to what they watched; and yet many implicitly accepted that this was not something they would have wanted in any case. Many of them were willing to acknowledge that they had made mistakes, and that they had learnt from their own children. More significantly, most of them refused easy generalisations about what children of particular ages should or should not watch. They argued that individual differences between children were more important and more complex than any notion of 'maturity' based simply on age. While they took note of centralised forms of regulation, such as the watershed and the video ratings, they ultimately reserved the right to make their own decisions about what their children should and should not watch.

Yet regulation is not simply a matter of allowing or proscribing particular kinds of material. On the contrary, as I have shown, parents also played an important role in enabling their children to regulate their *own* responses to what they watched. They sought to mediate and to intervene in their viewing, not only in order to help them cope with upsetting experiences, but in an attempt to make it more pleasurable and more worthwhile. It is these more positive educational responses to children's involvement with television that are emphasised in my concluding chapter.

## Notes

1 Lazarus and Folkman (1984); Allerton (1995).
2 Wood (1993).
3 See also Buckingham (1994).
4 See Holman and Braithwaite (1982); Gunter and Svennevig (1987); Buckingham (1993a), Chapter 5.
5 For example, Messaris and Sarrett (1981), Messaris (1986, 1987). Alexander *et al.* (1984) make similar arguments about the role of siblings.
6 Buckingham (1993a), Chapter 5.
7 See Rossiter and Robertson (1975); Holman and Braithwaite (1982).
8 See Wober *et al.* (1986).
9 As noted in Chapter 1, the social class of the parents was determined by a range of indicators including occupation, level of education and residential status.
10 See also Buckingham (1993a).
11 For a critique of these arguments, see Walkerdine (1993).
12 David Morley's *Family Television* (1986) and Ann Gray's *Video Playtime* (1992), for example, barely mention children at all.
13 A cut version was eventually released as a 'PG'.

# 9

# *Conclusion*

In the year since the James Bulger trial, stories about the harmful effects of television and video have repeatedly made the headlines. In March 1994, three young men convicted of kicking a man to death in Cardiff were reported to have been inspired by the film *Juice*, about four youths growing up in Harlem. *Natural Born Killers*, Oliver Stone's satire about the media's obsession with serial killers, has been linked with a number of killings in the US and with a murder spree by two French students. Meanwhile, an American mother claimed that the MTV cartoon *Beavis and Butthead* had caused her five-year-old child to burn down the family home; and the parents of two British six-year-olds blamed the children's game show *Finder's Keepers* when their children ransacked a neighbour's house. And *Mighty Morphin Power Rangers*, the massively popular children's science fiction series, has been linked with a child's death in Norway, and with playground fighting in Britain.[1]

Such stories are obviously welcome material for journalists with column inches to fill – and indeed for daytime chat-show hosts with hours of airtime to spare. Yet they create a climate in which the regulation of viewing has become an extremely delicate political issue. At the time of writing, Quentin Tarantino's *Reservoir Dogs*, one of the box office hits of 1993, remains without a certificate for video release; while *Natural Born Killers* was only granted a certificate for cinema exhibition after a long and controversial delay. Meanwhile, *Mighty Morphin Power Rangers* has been banned in some countries,[2] and several British schools have instructed parents to prevent their children from watching it.

Whether such debates accurately represent public concern is, however, a rather more complex issue. On the one hand, surveys repeatedly find that viewers feel there is 'too much' violence on television; and a majority agree that violence on television makes children more likely to commit violent acts.[3] Yet on the other hand, when people are asked about what they *dislike* on television, violence is much less of an issue than the number of repeats; and when they are asked about the causes of violence in society, television generally comes low on the list.[4] Of course, the findings of such surveys are crucially dependent upon how and when the questions are asked. Yet the figures themselves do not necessarily support the kinds of interpretations that are often put upon them. As I have argued, a concern about 'violence' should not necessarily be equated with a concern about imitative behaviour. While parents may express the belief that *other* children copy what they see, their primary concerns in relation to their *own* children are more often to do with them becoming frightened or upset. These are quite different issues, and they should not be conflated.

The problems with such debates about the 'effects' of television have been identified at a number of points in this book. From the perspective of researchers, it often seems as though journalists are unable to tolerate any degree of ambivalence or complexity on such issues – or, at least, that they assume their readers are unable to do so. All too often, the debate is presented in terms of simplistic either/or choices. Research that appears to challenge or qualify the certainties of 'commonsense' is frequently ignored. Furthermore, what counts as proper scientific knowledge here is often extremely narrowly defined. If we cannot say that $x$ causes $y$, or that $a$ has gone down and $b$ has gone up, and if we are unable to attach numbers to such assertions, then we clearly have no right to speak. What is needed is unambiguous, objective proof; and if we refuse to provide it, then we are simply wasting everybody's time with academic pedantry.

Qualitative research of the kind reported in this book does not fit easily into such debates, not least because it is inclined to question many of the premises on which the debates are defined in the first place. This is research that is concerned to build theory, and to offer detailed accounts of individual cases, rather than to generate causal predictions. It does not easily yield 'findings', or clear statements of proven fact. On the contrary, the temptation is to conclude with the banal observation that everything is terribly complex and contradictory. In the context I have outlined, however, such a conclusion gives hostages to fortune – or alternatively serves to guarantee that one's research will be ignored. If you do not spell out the findings and implications of your work, it is likely that others will do it for you. In this brief conclusion, therefore, I want to risk summarising what the research has found; what it has left unresolved; and where it might lead in terms of policy.

## Some findings

As in all research, it is important to be aware of the dangers of generalising from a limited sample, and on the basis of a limited range of instruments and methods. Including those in the pilot study, we interviewed a total of 124 children, in some cases on two or three occasions; and we spoke to just twenty sets of parents. The interviews with the children were conducted in groups, mainly in the context of schools; and our own role in these interviews – most obviously in terms of our choice of questions – cannot be seen as neutral. As qualitative research goes, this is in fact a comparatively large sample; and the data that it has yielded have been subjected to a systematic – and, I believe, reliable – process of analysis. Nevertheless, the findings of such research are bound to be somewhat tentative. Bearing these constraints in mind, it is possible to conclude the following.

**1**  *The centralised regulation of children's viewing – in the form of video 'ratings' and the television watershed – is widely ignored.*
All the parents, and most of the children, were aware of the system of video classification and of the existence of the watershed. While many parents (and some children) consciously used such systems as a form of guidance, they were frequently seen to be inconsistent or insufficiently informative. Both parents and children claimed the

right to make their own decisions about what they should and should not watch – although they frequently came into conflict with each other. Almost all the children had seen films and videos they were not officially permitted to watch; and most had seen programmes transmitted well after the 9 pm watershed. This obviously became more common as children got older. A minority of six-year-olds had seen '15'- or '18'-rated horror films, for example; while a majority of twelve-year-olds had done so. This was more the case with working-class children, although by no means exclusively so.

**2** *Parents' attempts to restrict their children's viewing are increasingly ineffective, and are gradually abandoned, as children enter their teenage years.*

Children used a range of strategies to evade or challenge their parents' regulation of their viewing, which became increasingly effective as they achieved greater independence and mobility. Broadly speaking, children in larger families, particularly those with older siblings, were less subject to parental regulation. While parents with strong religious convictions were likely to be more protective, most parents argued that children should be able to make their own decisions about what they watched from around the age of thirteen. For their own part, children often actively claimed the right to watch things which their parents felt to be 'inappropriate' for their age.

**3** *Both parents and children express concerns about the 'effects' of television; although these are frequently displaced onto other people.*

Most parents and children challenged the view that television alone was a sufficient cause to provoke violent behaviour. While parents occasionally expressed such concerns about other people's children, their concerns in relation to their *own* children were rather different (see point 4 below). Meanwhile, children themselves tended to displace such concerns onto younger children: they argued that, while younger children might fail to perceive the difference between fiction and reality, and hence copy what they had seen, they themselves were no longer at risk.

**4** *Although some parents are concerned that younger children will copy 'play fighting' from television, their primary concerns in relation to violence are that their children will become frightened or upset.*

In their accounts of imitative behaviour, parents clearly indicated that their children were aware of the difference between real violence and play violence. In general, parents were much less concerned about violent action movies – which were widely perceived as 'unrealistic' – than about horror: although in the case of horror, they were principally concerned about their children becoming frightened or traumatised, rather than that they might copy what they had seen. Similar concerns applied to violence shown on the news or in other non-fictional programmes.

**5** *'Negative' emotional responses to television – fright, disgust, sadness and worry – are common experiences.*

All the children we interviewed were able to recall examples of such responses. Many reported how television programmes and films had given them nightmares after viewing, or had caused them longer-term anxieties, such as a fear of crime. Nevertheless, such responses were rarely seen to be lasting or very severe. While there are rare cases of children being traumatised by what they have seen on television, such cases would appear to be confined to children who already suffer from social or psychological problems.[5]

**6** *The material that provokes such 'negative' responses is diverse and sometimes unpredictable.*

Children reported 'negative' responses, not only to more predictable genres (such as horror films and melodramas), but also to a wide range of other material, including children's programmes, news and documentaries, advertisements, cartoons and many other apparently 'innocuous' programmes. Of course, such responses do not only occur in relation to television and video, but also in relation to books and real-life experiences. Many parents reported that they had been surprised by such responses, particularly among younger children, and that they had found it difficult to know how to intervene.

**7** *However, there are common themes in such material, which seem to cut across generic distinctions; and children also make distinctions within genres.*

Common themes which evoked such responses cut across boundaries between genres, and between fact and fiction. These themes were largely predictable, and included bodily violation, the supernatural, the death of animals, threats to family harmony and to children. Such themes appeared to be capable of evoking fear or distress irrespective of whether they occurred in horror films, in the news or even (in some cases) in comedies. At the same time, children were developing the ability to make distinctions *within* genres, for example between different types of horror films, or in terms of different degrees of realism in drama (see points 12–14 below).

**8** *In the case of fiction, 'negative' responses are often inextricably connected with 'positive' ones, such as excitement and enjoyment.*

A majority of children had learnt to avoid such experiences, yet a significant minority actively chose to seek them out. Most children, for example, avoided horror films on the grounds that the fear they evoked was much greater than the pleasure; yet for some, the intensity of their enjoyment had encouraged them to watch more. Similar observations apply to melodramas or 'weepies', where some viewers actively pursued the pleasures of 'having a good cry'. While there were social differences in terms of taste (particularly in relation to gender and social class), these were by no means fixed or exclusive; and what motivates particular individuals to become 'fans' of such genres is an issue that is in need of further research.

**9** *In the case of non-fiction or realist drama, 'negative' responses are often perceived to be necessary in order to learn important information.*

Here again, there were children who actively avoided material such as coverage of wars and disasters on the news. Yet while such material was often described as upsetting, it was also regarded by many as 'important to watch', in the sense that it provided necessary information about the real world. For example, 'true crime' programmes on television were seen to intensify the fear of crime; but they were also seen to encourage viewers to adopt sensible

strategies for crime prevention. Likewise, coverage of wars or disasters in distant countries often evoked feelings of pity and disgust;
yet it also led (in some cases) to more positive forms of social
action.

**10**  *In both fact and fiction, such responses appear to derive primarily
from a fear of victimisation, rather than any 'identifi-cation' with
the perpetrators of violence.*

In children's accounts of horror films, for example, there was little
sense of vicarious 'identification' with the monster or killer. As in
their accounts of true crime programmes, their central concern
here was that they might themselves become victims of such acts.
Likewise, in responding to melodramas, the central anxiety derived
from a sense of bereavement, a loss of the happy ending that might
have been. In psychoanalytic terms, such responses could be seen
as 'masochistic' rather than 'sadistic'. They depend upon a kind of
imaginative, hypothetical projection of events from the text into
real life, rather than a projection of the viewer into the text.

**11**  *Children develop a variety of 'coping strategies' that enable them to
avoid or deal with these responses.*

The children described a broad range of strategies that they used
in order to protect themselves from possible distress. These strategies included: partial or total avoidance (leaving the room, hiding
one's eyes, turning down the sound); changing the context of
viewing (watching at another time, with other people); 'psychological' strategies (distracting oneself, seeking comfort, seeking
more information); and actively reinterpreting the text (inventing
alternative endings, using one's knowledge of genre, or challeng-
ing the text's reality status). These strategies can of course be
taught or 'modelled' by parents and other more experienced viewers (see point 16 below). Nevertheless, children also learn that
there is no single strategy that appears to work in every situation.

**12**  *Questioning the 'reality status' (or modality) of the text is a crucial strategy in this respect, although its effects are not guaranteed.*

One significant means that was used by parents and by children here was to challenge the modality of the text, both in general terms (reminding oneself that 'it's only a story') and in particular (for example, by drawing attention to aspects of the production process, or by comparing events in the text with similar events in real life). Yet 'negative' responses such as fright and sadness often seemed to be based, not so much on a suspension of disbelief, but on a willingness to entertain the possibility that the events that are shown might really happen in one's own life (point 10 above). As a result, challenges on the grounds of modality may only be partially effective.

**13**  *Nevertheless, responses to fiction are quite different to those for non-fiction, as are the coping strategies that are applied in each case.*

Broadly speaking, children found it easier to distance themselves from fictional material: while some fictional material was perceived to have a plausible relationship with real life, much of it was not. By contrast, factual material could not be easily dismissed as 'unrealistic', and appeared to be much harder to cope with for this reason. While some younger children looked to forms of social action (such as collecting for charity) in response to news coverage of wars and disasters, for example, older children were more likely to perceive themselves as powerless to change such events. It was often unclear whether children fully understood the causes and the wider context of the events that concerned them.

**14**  *Films or programmes that cross the boundaries between fact and fiction are likely to generate problematic and ambivalent responses.*

Crime reconstruction programmes such as *Crimewatch* generated a complex mixture of responses, being seen as entertaining but also as potentially 'sick' and disturbing. The spoof documentary *Ghostwatch* was consistently described as extremely frightening; although some children who had been frightened also expressed the wish to watch it again. Only in this latter case, however, was it possible to identify a programme that deliberately set out to mislead viewers in this respect. Nevertheless, there may be a sense in which it is necessary for television to cross these boundaries in order for viewers to learn about them.

**15** *There is no evidence here that children are any less upset by real-life violence as a result of watching* fictional *violence.*
While it was clear that watching fictional violence could enable viewers to become habituated to more *fictional* violence, there was no evidence that this translated to their perceptions of *real-life* violence, whether mediated by television or in their own experience. The children who were most enthusiastic about horror films or violent action movies were certainly no less worried or upset by violence on the news, or by the threat of victimisation in real life, than those who actively avoided them. This could be seen to question the popular notion that television violence 'desensitises' viewers to violence in real life.[6]

**16** *Parents can play a major role in helping children to cope with such upsetting experiences, and in learning about television in general.*
While there were often conflicts between parents and children over what was seen as 'appropriate' to watch, parents also played a positive role in mediating and intervening in their children's viewing. Parents offered advice and instruction in dealing with 'negative' emotional responses, not least by drawing attention to the ways in which programmes were constructed, and by discussing the relationship between television and the real world. At the same time, parents also learnt from their children, and indeed from their own mistakes, in this respect.

## Some broader questions

This research has been carried out within a punishing time-scale, and it is perhaps inevitable that many broader issues will remain unresolved. In this section, I would like to identify four aspects which I feel are in need of further research and debate.

### 1. Beyond 'effects'?

My persistent use of inverted commas here reflects a sense in which the term 'effects' has become something of a dirty word in academic Media Studies. The notion of 'effects' has, it would seem, been irredeemably contaminated with the behaviourism and empiricism of mainstream psychology: it is seen to be fundamentally incompatible with a truly complex social theory. Furthermore, to talk about 'effects' is often seen to be giving ground to the discourse of 'moral panics', and hence to reflect a kind of irrational paranoia. So is the notion of 'effects' one that can simply be discarded?

Throughout this book, I have maintained a distinction between 'effects' and what I have termed 'responses'. In general, I have used the term 'effects' to refer to those phenomena which have been the predominant – indeed, some would say obsessive – focus of public debate: that is, imitative (and mainly violent) behaviour. Yet there are, of course, other effects which have been addressed within media research – effects which might broadly be termed 'ideological'. For example, the extensive debates about media representations of women or of ethnic minority groups are clearly premised on assumptions about their potential influence on public attitudes. For obvious reasons, the attempt to establish evidence of ideological effects has been fraught with difficulty: broadly speaking, such effects are much more long-term and much less easily observed than short-term behavioural effects, or indeed than the responses considered here. Such phenomena are undoubtedly complex, and cannot easily be explained in terms of *singular* causes. Yet it remains to be seen how one might analyse them *without* having recourse to some notion of 'effect'.

In relation to this research, interesting questions remain about the relationships between these different kinds of 'effect' – and in particular between short-term emotional responses and longer-term ideological effects. The *political* consequences of such emotional responses have been raised in passing throughout this book, particularly in Chapters 4, 5 and 6; but they clearly remain in need of further debate and investigation.

## 2. The role of texts

Audience researchers in Media Studies are now conventionally criticised for neglecting the 'power' of texts, and hence (it is alleged) for ignoring 'politics' – as though texts were somehow the only repository of 'politics'. Yet to suggest that studying audiences necessarily implies a denial of the power of texts is empty polemic. Just as textual analysis can be a useful source of hypotheses for audience research – which is how I have occasionally used it here – so the reverse can be the case.

In relation to children, the overarching question here would seem to be: how do texts teach what readers learn?[7] In the case of horror, for example, there is a sense in which viewers are explicitly taught to anticipate and to cope with the emotional shocks that lie in store. The texts teach viewers how to make sense of them, and hence define what it means to be a skilled viewer (or a 'fan') in quite specific ways. As I have suggested, a competent horror viewer may be able to operate on the level of 'meta-responses', reflexively monitoring the 'effects' of the text as it is watched. This teaching is achieved in a variety of ways – for example, through elements of narrative structure, through forms of 'identification', and through references to other texts.

In terms of 'content', the common themes identified in point 6 above are of course not specific to children. Yet the reasons why some children might be drawn to horror films, or to texts that adults might dismiss as crudely melodramatic or sentimental, need further investigation. Many would argue that, far from being a carefree and joyful period, childhood is characterised by intense anxiety and insecurity. The ways in which media texts which are popular with children articulate those anxieties – and attempt to assuage them – are clearly 'ideological'. Media texts may offer fantasies that compensate for children's own lack of power, but they often do so on adult terms. Of course, the media are only one of the many forces that serve to define what it means to be a child – and children themselves may well challenge and resist those definitions, since it is often in their interests to do so. Yet the ways in which the media 'speak to' children's concerns – and thereby help to construct them – are in need of much more systematic analysis.

*3. The meaning of 'emotion'*

I have argued throughout this book that 'emotions' cannot be separated either from 'cognition' or from the social contexts in which they are displayed. How we respond emotionally to a text depends upon what we perceive it to mean; and our perception of its meaning depends upon our emotional response. Furthermore, emotional displays are produced according to social conventions that are gradually learnt through interaction with others. Talk plays a crucial role in this process: as children develop, they learn to label and describe their emotions in language, which in turn determines how they 'feel'. It is partly through the display of emotion that we negotiate our social relationships, and define our identities in relation to other people. As I have suggested, this approach has far-reaching methodological implications. It means that we cannot afford to regard accounts of emotional responses as though they were personal confessions. On the contrary, we need to regard them as forms of social action, which are used to achieve particular social purposes.

Nevertheless, there is a risk here of reducing displays of 'emotion' to a kind of dramatic role-playing which is wholly determined by the social context. Yet the question of why people choose to adopt particular social roles – and indeed why they choose to undergo particular emotional experiences – cannot be so easily swept aside. For example, why do particular individuals choose to become horror 'fans', while others do not? This kind of question cannot easily be answered in sociological terms, as though it were simply a reflection of one's social position; although psychological explanations which are based on notions of individual pathology are scarcely more helpful. I have sought to explain this process here as a kind of balancing act, through which 'pleasures' are set against 'un-pleasures'. Yet this is to present the process almost as a matter of rational calculation; and it is to run the risk of ignoring what individuals may have *invested* in those pleasures in the first place. As I have argued, audience research in this field has generally manifested a 'cognitive bias', in which emotion is either defined in terms of generalised categories such as 'fright' or 'enjoyment', or simply neglected altogether. Yet continuing to rely on talk as a primary method of investigation may do little to displace this: it may be that more innovative methods are required in order to gain access to the subjective investments and personal histories that may be at stake.

## 4. The limits of social difference

Having argued for the importance of social context, it remains striking that social differences have played a comparatively minor role here. It has been hard to trace a consistent influence of key 'demographic variables' that might have been expected to play a role in children's responses – or indeed, in their *accounts* of those responses. There were many girls, for example, who were interested in horror and in violent action movies; and many boys who positively disliked them. Enjoying horror was partly about a 'show of strength', but there is little evidence here that this was defined mainly in terms of gender. While boys were definitely less interested in melodrama and soap opera than girls, they were not significantly less willing to admit that they had been upset or cried over what they had watched – although there was some decline with age here. While a minority of middle-class children (both girls and boys) expressed some interest in the news, it was consistently described as 'boring' by the large majority of the sample. Particularly when it comes to age, such differences of *taste* are partly a result of differences of *access*. Younger children, for example, generally go to bed earlier and are likely to be prevented from watching more 'adult' material.

In the case of parents, the key factors would appear to be the age and composition of the family and the parents' religious beliefs (which exert a significant influence on their philosophy of child-rearing). There was no evidence here that working-class parents are in general any more permissive or any less concerned to protect their children than middle-class parents. Similar arguments apply to single parents. What remains particularly striking here are the significant differences *within* families, and between siblings (frequently those of the same sex) – differences that tended to be explained in terms of 'personality'.

The difficulty here, I would suggest, is to find ways of taking account of social differences that do not reduce them to a mechanical application of given demographic categories. Indeed, one can

easily end up reinforcing differences that it might be more produc-
tive to challenge and to deconstruct. While there was a range of
ethnic groups within the sample, for example, there were no consistent differences here – and indeed, it would be hard to see what
differences one might wish to hypothesise in the first place. (Are
black boys more interested in violence, for example?) The danger
of beginning with a search for such differences is that one can end
up with a form of essentialism. Likewise, the notion that there are
'masculine' and 'feminine' genres – and that males read in one
way, and females in another – can easily slip back towards bio-
logical essentialism, or at least a gloomy form of determinism.

## Some implications for policy

One of my main intentions in writing this book has been to help
shift the agenda of public debate about children and television.
Rather than simply denying that television has negative 'effects' on
children, I have sought to redirect attention to effects that I believe
genuinely concern parents and children themselves. As I have indicated, we are currently in the midst of a series of technological
changes that will seriously undermine the attempt to exert centralised control over the circulation of moving images. Yet more
constructive alternatives to increasing censorship have yet to be
found. In my view, any such alternative will have to begin with
parents and with children themselves. It will need to respect their
ability to make their own decisions about what is appropriate, and
try to support them in doing so. It will need to be a positive *educational* strategy, rather than a negative one that is based on censorship. I have six specific, and fairly modest, suggestions here.

1  *There should be more objective information for parents (and indeed
for all viewers) about the content of programmes and videotapes,
particularly where this relates to areas of general concern.*
Of course, providing such information could well have precisely the
opposite effect, of identifying 'forbidden fruit'. But we cannot expect
viewers to make informed decisions unless we are prepared to
advise them more effectively than we do at present. Recent moves

in this direction on the part of the video retail industry are certainly welcome, and should be extended.

**2** *While some form of centralised censorship is inevitable, a great deal could be done to make the system more accountable.*

The reasons for decisions should be published or made freely available for interested parties (for example, through video shops); and it should be possible for decisions to be challenged by the public and independently reviewed. Steps could be taken to ensure that ordinary parents are involved in the decision-making process, or at least consulted – for example through establishing a representative panel of parents, and by conducting research. There is no doubt that decisions like the BBFC's granting of a '12' certificate to *Mrs Doubtfire* (a film heavily promoted to a younger audience) brings the system into disrepute among many parents. While there may be good reasons for such decisions, no purpose is served by keeping them secret from the very people on whose behalf they are made.

**3** *The age classifications on video distribution – and particularly the '18' certificate – should be reconsidered in the light of changing cultural assumptions about childhood.*

This research would suggest that the notion that childhood continues until the age of eighteen simply does not square with most parents' perceptions, let alone children's. Most parents seem to agree that by the time they reach thirteen (and in many cases before), children should be free to make their own decisions about what they watch.

**4** *The debate about 'violence' needs to take much greater account of responses to* factual *material.*

Producers of news and other non-fictional programming need to be more aware of the possibility that children may be distressed by scenes of violence and suffering that they are ill-equipped to understand. Indeed, as I have indicated, there is evidence that viewers in general understand and recall comparatively little of what they watch on the news – which would suggest that the 'mission to explain' is currently far from successful. This is to argue, not so much for self-censorship, but for a more concerted effort to explain such events in a form that is accessible and comprehensible to the majority of the population.

**5**  *Our responsibilities towards children as an audience need to be defined, not merely in terms of prevention and control, but also in terms of the* positive *provision that is made for them.*

We need to ensure that the films and television programmes that are produced explicitly for children are both diverse, and of the highest quality – while acknowledging that there are many forms of 'quality'. All too often, the characteristics of film and television for children are defined negatively, in terms of the absence of sex or violence or 'negative role models'; and as a result, they are sometimes anodyne and conservative. While the government persistently employs a rhetoric about protecting childhood, and bemoans the negative aspects of children's relationship with the media, investment in positive alternatives has been conspicuously lacking.

**6**  *Media education, both for parents and for children, should be regarded as a major priority.*

One of the most contradictory aspects of recent debates about 'video violence' has been the way in which plans to increase censorship have coincided with the government's attempt to remove media education from the National Curriculum, and to replace it with a much more traditional emphasis on preserving the 'cultural heritage'. While media education has now been partly reinstated, it remains a comparatively marginal aspect of compulsory schooling. Yet the study of the most significant means of contemporary communication should surely be a central entitlement for all children. Parents too can play an important role in discussing television with their children, and in taking their concerns and enthusiasms seriously. Like reading, television viewing should be seen as an area for educational partnership and dialogue between children, parents and teachers.

Of course, the importance of media education extends well beyond the issues addressed in this book. If it is to be effective, media education must be seen not as a prophylactic designed to protect people from things that are deemed to be 'bad' for them, nor indeed as something that is solely concerned with 'violence'. On the contrary, it should be regarded as an essential guarantee of an informed and critical audience for all media output. Today's children will be growing up in a media-saturated society that is very different from our own. If we are to equip them to cope with the new and ever-changing demands of that society, we will need to enable them to use the media in constructive and imaginative ways.

## Notes

1 This concern about the dangers of 'play fighting' is particularly apparent among teachers – and there clearly is a justified concern here about children being injured, however unintentionally. The cases listed here are derived from a useful report by the organisation Young Minds (1994).

2 Currently including Canada and New Zealand.

3 The former finding is a regular feature of the Broadcasting Standards Council's annual review. The latter finding was reported, for instance, in the MORI poll conducted for BBC2's *The Late Show* in 1994 – although it is worth noting the fact that this followed in the wake of the Bulger case.

4 Another MORI poll, conducted for the *Reader's Digest* (April 1994), found that drugs, unemployment and poor parental discipline were perceived to be the major causes of rising crime.

5 See Buckingham and Allerton (1995) for a brief review of clinical studies. Similar arguments apply to the rare cases of 'copycat' violence.

6 There is evidence from experimental research to support the notion that, as they watch more, viewers are gradually 'desensitised' to further *representations* of violence. Yet the notion that this somehow 'spills over' into their responses to *real-life* violence is only weakly supported. See Buckingham and Allerton (1995).

7 This question derives from Margaret Meek's seminal work on children's literature, specifically in Meek (1990).

# References

Alexander, A., Ryan, M. S., and Munoz, P. (1984) 'Creating a learning context: investigations on the interaction of siblings during television viewing', *Critical Studies in Mass Communication* 1, 4, 345–64

Allen, R. C. (1985) *Speaking of Soap Opera* Chapel Hill: University of North Carolina Press

Allerton, M. (1995) 'Emotions and coping: children's talk about negative emotional responses to television', *Early Child Development and Care* (in press)

Anderson, J. (1990) 'Constitutions of the audience in research and theory: implications for media literacy programs', paper presented at the International Visual Literacy Association Conference, London

Ang, I. (1985) *Watching 'Dallas': Soap Opera and the Melodramatic Imagination* London: Methuen

Averill, J. R. (1986) 'The acquisition of emotions during adulthood', in R. Harré (ed.) *The Social Construction of Emotions* Oxford: Blackwell.

Barker, M. (1989) *Comics: Ideology, Power and the Critics* Manchester University Press

—— (1992) 'Stuart Hall, *Policing the Crisis*', in M. Barker and A. Beezer (eds.) *Reading into Cultural Studies* London: Routledge

Barker, M. (ed.) (1984) *The Video Nasties* London: Pluto Press

Barlow, G. and Hill, A. (1985) *Video Violence and Children* London: Hodder and Stoughton

Barwise, P. and Ehrenberg, A. (1988) *Television and its Audience* London, Sage

Bazalgette, C. (1992) 'Key aspects of media education', in M. Alvarado and O. Boyd-Barrett (eds.) *Media Education: An Introduction* London: British Film Institute

Bazalgette, C. and Buckingham, D. (1995) 'Introduction: the invisible audience', in C. Bazalgette and D. Buckingham (eds.) *In Front of the Children* London: British Film Institute

Bazalgette, C. and Staples, T. (1995) 'Unshrinking the kids: children's cinema and the family film', in C. Bazalgette and D. Buckingham (eds.) *In Front of the Children* London: British Film Institute

Bordwell, D. (1985) *Narration in the Fiction Film* London, Methuen

Boss, P. (1986) 'Vile bodies and bad medicine', *Screen*, 27, 1, 14–25

Bourdieu, P. (1984) *Distinction: A Social Critique of the Judgment of Taste* London: Routledge Kegan Paul

Brophy, P. (1986) 'Horrorality: the textuality of contemporary horror films', Screen 27, 1, 2–13

—— (1987) 'Violence on the screen', *Cinema Papers*, 62, 18–22

Brown, B. (1984) 'Exactly what we wanted', in M. Barker (ed.) *The Video Nasties* London: Pluto Press

Brummett, B. (1985) 'Electronic literature as equipment for living: haunted house films', *Critical Studies in Mass Communication* 2, 3, 247–61

Brunsdon, C. (1990) 'Problems with quality', *Screen* 31, 1, 67–90

Brunvand, J. H. (1983) *The Vanishing Hitchhiker: American Urban Legends and Their Meanings* London: Pan

Buckingham, D. (1987) *Public Secrets: 'EastEnders' and its Audience* London: British Film Institute

—— (1992) 'Sex, lies and newsprint: young people reading the *Sun*', *English and Media Magazine* 26

—— (1993a) *Children Talking Television: The Making of Television Literacy* London: Falmer Press

—— (1993b) 'Boys' talk: television and the policing of masculinity', in D. Buckingham (ed.) *Reading Audiences: Young People and the Media* Manchester University Press

—— (1993c) 'Going critical: the limits of media literacy', Australian Journal of Education, 37, 2, 142–52

—— (1994) 'Television and the definition of childhood' in B. Mayall (ed.) *Children's Childhoods Observed and Experienced* London: Falmer Press

—— (1995) 'Doing them harm? Children's conceptions of the negative effects of television', in K. Swan and S. de Maio (eds.) *Social Learning from Broadcast Television* Cresskill, N.J.: Hampton Press

Buckingham, D. and Allerton, M. (1995) *Fear, Fright and Distress: A Review of Research on Children's Emotional Responses to Television* London: Broadcasting Standards Council

Campbell, B. (1993) *Goliath: Britain's Dangerous Places* London: Methuen

Cantor, M. (1991) 'Fright responses to mass media productions', in J. Bryant and D. Zillmann (eds.) *Responding to the Screen: Reception and Reaction Processes* Hillsdale, N.J.: Erlbaum

Cantor, M. and Sparks, G. (1984) 'Children's fear responses to mass media: testing some Piagetian predictions', *Journal of Communication*, 34, 2, 90–103

Cantril, H. (1940) *The Invasion from Mars: A Study in the Psychology of Panic* Princeton: Princeton University Press

Carroll, N. (1990) *The Philosophy of Horror: Or Paradoxes of the Heart* London: Routledge

Clover, C. (1992) *Men, Women and Chainsaws: Gender in the Modern Horror Film* London: British Film Institute

Cohen, S. (1985) *Visions of Social Control* Cambridge: Polity

Creed, B. (1986) 'Horror and the monstrous feminine: an imaginary abjection', *Screen*, 27, 1, 44–71

Cullingford, C. (1984) *Children and Television* Aldershot: Gower

Cumberbatch, G. and Howitt, D. (1989) *A Measure of Uncertainty: The Effects of the Mass Media* London: John Libbey

Doane, M. A. (1987) *The Desire to Desire: The Woman's Film of the 1940s* Bloomington: Indiana University Press

Docherty, D., Morrison, D. and Tracey, M. (1987) *The Last Picture Show: Britain's Changing Film Audience* London: British Film Institute

Dorr, A. (1983) 'No shortcuts to judging reality', in J. Bryant and D. Anderson (eds.) *Children's Understanding of Television* New York: Academic Press

Drotner, K. (1992) 'Modernity and media panics', in M. Skovmand and K. C. Schroder (eds.) *Media Cultures: Reappraising Transnational Media* London: Routledge

Edwards. D. and Potter, J. (1992) *Discursive Psychology* London: Sage

Elsaesser, T. (1987) 'Tales of sound and fury: observations on the family melodrama', in C. Gledhill (ed.) *Home is Where the Heart Is: Studies in Melodrama and the Woman's Film* London: British Film Institute

Feilitzen, C. von (1975) 'Findings of Scandinavian research on child television in the process of socialisation', *Fernsehen und Bildung*, 9, 54–84

Feshbach, S. (1972) 'Reality and fantasy in filmed violence', in J. P. Murray, E. A. Rubenstein and G. A. Comstock (eds.) *Television and Social Behavior Volume 2* Washington, D.C.: US Government Printing Office

Fiske, J. (1987) *Television Culture* London: Methuen

Foucault, M. (1980) *Power/Knowledge* (ed. C. Gordon) Brighton: Harvester

Furnham, A. (1988) *Lay Theories: Everyday Understandings of Problems in the Social Sciences* Oxford: Pergamon

Galtung, J. and Ruge, M. H. (1965) 'The structure of foreign news: the presentation of the Congo, Cuba and Cyprus crises in four foreign newspapers', *Journal of Peace Research*, 2, 64–91

Gans, H. (1974) *Popular Culture and High Culture* New York: Basic Books

Geraghty, C. (1991) *Women and Soap Opera* Cambridge: Polity

Gerbner, G., Gross, L., Morgan, M. and Signorielli, N. (1980) 'The "mainstreaming" of America: violence profile no. 11', *Journal of Communication*, 30, 3, 10–29

Gledhill, C. (1985) 'Genre', in P. Cook (ed.) *The Cinema Book* London: British Film Institute

—— (1987) 'The melodramatic field: an investigation', in C. Gledhill (ed.) *Home is Where the Heart Is: Studies in Melodrama and the Woman's Film* London: British Film Institute

Gray, A. (1992) *Video Playtime: The Gendering of a Leisure Technology* London: Routledge

Gunter, B. (1985) *Dimensions of Television Violence* Aldershot: Gower

—— (1987a) *Poor Reception: Misunderstanding and Forgetting Broadcast News* Hillsdale, N.J.: Erlbaum

—— (1987b) *Television and the Fear of Crime* London: John Libbey

—— (1991) 'Responding to news and public affairs', in J. Bryant and D. Zillmann (eds.) *Responding to the Screen: Reception and Reaction Processes* Hillsdale, N.J.: Erlbaum

Gunter, B. and Svennevig, M. (1987) *Behind and In Front of the Screen: Television's Involvement with Family Life* London: John Libbey

Hagell, A. and Newburn, T. (1994) *Young Offenders and the Media: Viewing*

*Habits and Preferences* London: Policy Studies Institute

Harré, R. (ed.) (1986) *The Social Construction of Emotions* Oxford: Blackwell

Harris, P. L. (1989) *Children and Emotion: The Development of Psychological Understanding* Oxford: Blackwell

Hawkins, R. P. (1977) 'The dimensional structure of children's perceptions of television reality', *Communication Research*, 4, 3, 299–320

Hobson, D. (1982) *'Crossroads': The Drama of a Soap Opera* London: Methuen

Hodge, B. and Tripp, D. (1986) *Children and Television: A Semiotic Approach* Cambridge: Polity

Holland, P. (1992) 'Tears or fears', paper presented at the British Film Institute Melodrama Conference, London

Holman, J. and Braithwaite, V. A. (1982) 'Parental lifestyles and children's television viewing', *Australian Journal of Psychology*, 34, 3, 375–82

Howitt, D. (1982) *The Mass Media and Social Problems* Oxford: Pergamon

Huyssens, A. (1984) 'Mapping the postmodern', *New German Critique*, 33, 5–52

Jaglom, L. M. and Gardner, H. (1981) 'The preschool television viewer as anthropologist', in H. Kelly and H. Gardner (eds.) *Viewing Children Through Television* San Francisco: Jossey-Bass

Kerr, P. (1990) 'F for fake? Friction over faction', in A. Goodwin and P. Whannell (eds.) *Understanding Television* London: Routledge

Kuhn, A. (1984) 'Women's genres', *Screen*, 25, 1, 18–29

Lazarus, R. S. and Folkman, S. (1984) *Stress, Appraisal and Coping* New York: Springer

Lewis, J. (1985) 'Decoding television news', in P. Drummond and R. Paterson (eds.) *Television in Transition* London: British Film Institute

Lewis, M. and Saarni, C. (eds.) (1985) *The Socialisation of Emotions* New York: Plenum

Liebes, T. and Katz, E. (1990) *The Export of Meaning* Oxford University Press

Lowery, S. and de Fleur, M. (1983) *Milestones in Mass Communication Research* London: Longman

Lutz, C. A. and Abu-Lughod, L. (eds.) (1990) *Language and the Politics of Emotion* Cambridge University Press.

Matthews, T. D. (1994) *Censored* London: Chatto and Windus

Medved, M. (1992) *Hollywood versus America: Popular Culture and the War on Traditional Values* New York: Harper Collins

Meek, M. (1990) *How Do Texts Teach What Readers Learn?* London: Thimble Press

Messaris, P. (1986) 'Parents, children and television', in G. Gumpert and R. Cathcart (eds.) *Inter Media: Interpersonal Communication in a Media World* New York: Oxford University Press

—— (1987) 'Mothers' comments to their children about the relationship between television and reality', in T. Lindlof (ed.) *Natural Audiences* Newbury Park: Sage

Messaris, P. and Sarrett, C. (1981) 'On the consequences of TV-related parent–child interaction', *Human Communication Research* 7, 3, 226–44

Miles, M. B. and Huberman A. M. (1984) *Qualitative Data Analysis* London: Sage

Moretti, F. (1983) 'Kindergarten', in *Signs Taken for Wonders* London: Verso

Morley, D. (1986) *Family Television: Cultural Power and Domestic Leisure* London: Comedia

Mulvey, L. (1987) 'Notes on Sirk and melodrama', in C. Gledhill (ed.) *Home is Where the Heart Is: Studies in Melodrama and the Woman's Film* London: British Film Institute

Neale, S. (1986) 'Melodrama and tears', *Screen*, 27, 6, 6–23

Newson, E. (1994) 'Video violence and the protection of children', *The Psychologist* (June), 272–4

Nordenstreng, K. (1972) 'Policy for news transmission' in D. McQuail (ed.) *Sociology of Mass Communications* Harmondsworth: Penguin

Pearson, G. (1984) 'Falling standards: a short, sharp history of moral decline', in Martin Barker (ed.) *The Video Nasties* London: Pluto

Phillips, P. and Robie, J. H. (1988) *Horror and Violence: The Deadly Duo in the Media* Lancaster, Pennsylvania: Starburst

Plato (1987) *The Republic* (trans. D. Lee) Harmondsworth: Penguin

Potter, J. and Wetherell, M. (1987) *Discourse and Social Psychology* London: Sage

Preston, M. I. (1941) 'Children's reactions to movie horrors and radio crime', *Journal of Pediatrics*, 19, 2, 147–68

Rathgeb, D. L. (1991) 'Bogeyman from the id', *Journal of Popular Film and Television*, 19, 1, 36–43

Ross, A. (1989) *No Respect: Intellectual and Popular Culture* New York: Routledge

Rossiter, T. S. and Robertson, J. R. (1975) 'Children's television viewing: an examination of parent–child consensus', *Sociometry*, 38, 2, 308–26

Sarbin, T. R. (1986) 'Emotion and act: roles and rhetoric', in R. Harré (ed.) *The Social Construction of Emotions* Oxford: Blackwell

Sarland, C. (1994a) 'Attack of the teenage horrors: theme and meaning in popular series fiction', *Signal*, 73, 48–62

—— (1994b) 'Revenge of the teenage horrors: pleasure, quality and canonicity in (and out of) popular series fiction', *Signal*, 74, 113–31

Schlesinger, P., Dobash, R. E., Dobash, R. P. and Weaver, K. C. (1992) *Women Viewing Violence* London: British Film Institute

Schlesinger, P. and Tumber, H. (1991) 'Fighting the war against crime: television, police and audience', paper presented to the International Television Studies Conference, London

Segal, L. (1987) *Is the Future Female?* London: Virago

Segal, L. and McIntosh, M. (1992) *Sex Exposed: Sexuality and the Pornography Debate* London: Virago

Seiter, E., Borchers, H., Kreutzner, G. and Warth, E. M. (1989) ' "Don't treat us like we're so stupid and naive": towards an ethnography of soap opera viewers', in E. Seiter et al. (eds.) *Remote Control: Television, Audiences and Cultural Power* London: Routledge

Shattuc, J. (1992) 'Having a good cry over *The Color Purple*: the problem of affect and imperialism in feminist theory', paper presented at the British Film Institute Melodrama Conference, London

Simons, D. and Silveira, W. R. (1994) 'Post-traumatic stress disorder in children after television programmes', *British Medical Journal* 308, 6925, 389–90

Smith, David James (1994) *The Sleep of Reason* London: Century

Sparks, G. (1986) 'Developmental differences in children's reports of fear induced by the mass media', *Child Study Journal*, 16, 55–66

—— (1991) 'The relationship between distress and delight in males' and females' reactions to frightening films', *Human Communication Research*, 17, 4, 625–37

Sparks, R. (1992) *Television and the Drama of Crime* Buckingham: Open University Press

Strauss, A. and Corbin, J. (1992) *Basics of Qualitative Research* London: Sage

Swanson, G. (1981) ' "Dallas", part 1', *Framework*, 14, 32–5

Tamborini, R. and Stiff, J. (1987) 'Predictors of horror film attendance and appeal: an analysis of the audience for frightening films', *Communication Research*, 14, 415–36

Twitchell, B. (1985) *Dreadful Pleasures: An Anatomy of Modern Horror* New York: Oxford University Press

Viviani, C. (1987) 'Who is without sin? The maternal melodrama in American film, 1930–39', in C. Gledhill (ed.) *Home is Where the Heart Is: Studies in Melodrama and the Woman's Film* London: British Film Institute

Walkerdine, V. (1993) ' "Daddy's gonna buy you a dream to cling to (and mummy's gonna love you just as much as she can)": young girls and popular television', in D. Buckingham (ed.) *Reading Audiences: Young People and the Media* Manchester University Press

Warner, C. T. (1986) 'Anger and similar delusions', in R. Harré (ed.) *The Social Construction of Emotions* Oxford: Blackwell.

Webster, D. (1989) ' "Whodunnit? America did": *Rambo* and post-Hungerford rhetoric', *Cultural Studies*, 3, 2, 173–93

Wober, J. M., Fazal, S. and Reardon, G. (1986) *Parental Control of Children's Viewing: Patterns of Discipline and Viewing Experience* London: Independent Broadcasting Authority

Wood, J. (1993) 'Repeatable pleasures: notes on young people's use of video', in D. Buckingham (ed.) *Reading Audiences: Young People and the Media* Manchester University Press

Wood, R. (1985) 'An introduction to the American horror film', in B. Nichols (ed.) *Movies and Methods, Volume 2* Berkeley: University of California Press

Young Minds (1994) *Screen Violence and Children's Mental Health*, mimeo, London: Young Minds

Zillmann, D. (1980) 'The anatomy of suspense', in P. H. Tannenbaum (ed.)

*The Entertainment Functions of Television.* Hillsdale, N.J.: Lawrence Erlbaum
—— (1991) 'Empathy: affects from bearing witness to the emotions of others',
in J. Bryant and D. Zillmann (eds.) *Responding to the Screen: Reception and Reaction Processes* Hillsdale, N.J.: Lawrence Erlbaum
Zillmann, D., Weaver, J. B., Mundorf, N. and Aust, C.F. (1986) 'Effects of an opposite-gender companion's affect to horror on distress, delight and attraction', *Journal of Personality and Social Psychology*, 51, 3, 586–94.